Fractal and Wavelet Image Compression Techniques

Tutorial Texts Series

- *Fractal and Wavelet Image Compression Techniques,* Stephen Welstead, Vol. TT40
- *Fundamentos de Electro-Óptica para Ingenieros,* Glenn D. Boreman, translated by Javier Alda, Vol. TT37
- *Infrared Design Examples,* William L. Wolfe, Vol. TT36
- *Sensor and Data Fusion Concepts and Applications, Second Edition,* L. A. Klein, Vol. TT35
- *Practical Applications of Infrared Thermal Sensing and Imaging Equipment, Second Edition,* Herbert Kaplan, Vol. TT34
- *Fundamentals of Machine Vision,* Harley R. Myler, Vol. TT33
- *Design and Mounting of Prisms and Small Mirrors in Optical Instruments,* Paul R. Yoder, Jr., Vol. TT32
- *Basic Electro-Optics for Electrical Engineers,* Glenn D. Boreman, Vol. TT31
- *Optical Engineering Fundamentals,* Bruce H. Walker, Vol. TT30
- *Introduction to Radiometry,* William L. Wolfe, Vol. TT29
- *Lithography Process Control,* Harry J. Levinson, Vol. TT28
- *An Introduction to Interpretation of Graphic Images,* Sergey Ablameyko, Vol. TT27
- *Thermal Infrared Characterization of Ground Targets and Backgrounds,* P. Jacobs, Vol. TT26
- *Introduction to Imaging Spectrometers,* William L. Wolfe, Vol. TT25
- *Introduction to Infrared System Design,* William L. Wolfe, Vol. TT24
- *Introduction to Computer-based Imaging Systems,* D. Sinha, E. R. Dougherty, Vol. TT23
- *Optical Communication Receiver Design,* Stephen B. Alexander, Vol. TT22
- *Mounting Lenses in Optical Instruments,* Paul R. Yoder, Jr., Vol. TT21
- *Optical Design Fundamentals for Infrared Systems,* Max J. Riedl, Vol. TT20
- *An Introduction to Real-Time Imaging,* Edward R. Dougherty, Phillip A. Laplante, Vol. TT19
- *Introduction to Wavefront Sensors,* Joseph M. Geary, Vol. TT18
- *Integration of Lasers and Fiber Optics into Robotic Systems,* Janusz A. Marszalec, Elzbieta A. Marszalec, Vol. TT17
- *An Introduction to Nonlinear Image Processing,* E. R. Dougherty, J. Astola, Vol. TT16
- *Introduction to Optical Testing,* Joseph M. Geary, Vol. TT15
- *Image Formation in Low-Voltage Scanning Electron Microscopy,* L. Reimer, Vol. TT12
- *Diazonaphthoquinone-based Resists,* Ralph Dammel, Vol. TT11
- *Infrared Window and Dome Materials,* Daniel C. Harris, Vol. TT10
- *An Introduction to Morphological Image Processing,* Edward R. Dougherty, Vol. TT9
- *An Introduction to Optics in Computers,* Henri H. Arsenault, Yunlong Sheng, Vol. TT8
- *Digital Image Compression Techniques,* Majid Rabbani, Paul W. Jones, Vol. TT7
- *Aberration Theory Made Simple,* Virendra N. Mahajan, Vol. TT6
- *Single-Frequency Semiconductor Lasers,* Jens Buus, Vol. TT5
- *An Introduction to Biological and Artificial Neural Networks for Pattern Recognition,* Steven K. Rogers, Matthew Kabrisky, Vol. TT4
- *Laser Beam Propagation in the Atmosphere,* Hugo Weichel, Vol. TT3
- *Infrared Fiber Optics,* Paul Klocek, George H. Sigel, Jr., Vol. TT2
- *Spectrally Selective Surfaces for Heating and Cooling Applications,* C. G. Granqvist, Vol. TT1

Fractal and Wavelet Image Compression Techniques

Stephen Welstead

Tutorial Texts in Optical Engineering
Volume TT40

Arthur R. Weeks, Jr., Series Editor
University of Central Florida

SPIE OPTICAL ENGINEERING PRESS

A Publication of SPIE—The International Society for Optical Engineering
Bellingham, Washington USA

Library of Congress Cataloging-in-Publication Data

Welstead, Stephen T., 1951–
Fractal and wavelet image compression techniques / Stephen Welstead
        p. cm. — (Tutorial texts in optical engineering; v. TT40)
    Includes bibliographical references and index.
    ISBN 0-8194-3503-1 (softcover)
    1. Image processing—Digital techniques. 2. Image compression—Mathematics. 3. Fractals.
    4. Wavelets (Mathematics). I. Title. II. Series.
TA1637.W45 1999
621.36'7—dc21   99-051601
                                                                      CIP

Published by

SPIE—The International Society for Optical Engineering
P.O. Box 10
Bellingham, Washington 98227-0010
Phone: 360/676-3290
Fax: 360/647-1445
Email: spie@spie.org
WWW: http://www.spie.org/

Printed in the United States of America.

To the memory of my parents

Introduction to the Series

The Tutorial Texts series was initiated in 1989 as a way to make the material presented in SPIE short courses available to those who couldn't attend and to provide a reference book for those who could. Typically, short course notes are developed with the thought in mind that supporting material will be presented verbally to complement the notes, which are generally written in summary form, highlight key technical topics, and are not intended as stand-alone documents. Additionally, the figures, tables, and other graphically formatted information included with the notes require further explanation given in the instructor's lecture. As stand-alone documents, short course notes do not generally serve the student or reader well.

Many of the Tutorial Texts have thus started as short course notes subsequently expanded into books. The goal of the series is to provide readers with books that cover focused technical interest areas in a tutorial fashion. What separates the books in this series from other technical monographs and textbooks is the way in which the material is presented. Keeping in mind the tutorial nature of the series, many of the topics presented in these texts are followed by detailed examples that further explain the concepts presented. Many pictures and illustrations are included with each text, and where appropriate tabular reference data are also included.

To date, the texts published in this series have encompassed a wide range of topics, from geometrical optics to optical detectors to image processing. Each proposal is evaluated to determine the relevance of the proposed topic. This initial reviewing process has been very helpful to authors in identifying, early in the writing process, the need for additional material or other changes in approach that serve to strengthen the text. Once a manuscript is completed, it is peer reviewed to ensure that chapters communicate accurately the essential ingredients of the processes and technologies under discussion.

During the past nine years, my predecessor, Donald C. O'Shea, has done an excellent job in building the Tutorial Texts series, which now numbers nearly forty books. It has expanded to include not only texts developed by short course instructors but also those written by other topic experts. It is my goal to maintain the style and quality of books in the series, and to further expand the topic areas to include emerging as well as mature subjects in optics, photonics, and imaging.

Arthur R. Weeks, Jr.
University of Central Florida

Contents

Preface   **xiii**

1. Introduction   **1**
   1.1 Images   2
   1.2 The image compression problem   3
   1.3 Information, entropy, and data modeling   4
   1.4 Scalar and vector quantization   5
   1.5 Transform methods   7
   1.6 Color images   8
   1.7 The focus of this book   9

PART I: FRACTAL IMAGE COMPRESSION

2. Iterated Function Systems   **11**
   2.1 Iterated function systems as the motivation for fractal image
          compression   11
   2.2 Metric spaces   12
      2.2.1 Basic concepts   13
      2.2.2 Compact sets and Hausdorff space   15
      2.2.3 Contraction mappings   16
   2.3 Iterated function systems   18
      2.3.1 Introduction   18
      2.3.2 The Collage Theorem   19
      2.3.3 What the Collage Theorem says   20
      2.3.4 Affine transformations   21
   2.4 Implementation of an iterated function system   22
      2.4.1 Points and transformations   22
      2.4.2 Affine coefficients   24
      2.4.3 Computing the fractal attractor image from the IFS   25
            2.4.3.1 Deterministic algorithm   25
            2.4.3.2 Random algorithm   29
   2.5 Examples   34
      2.5.1 Sierpinski triangle   34
            2.5.1.1 Fractal dimension   35
      2.5.2 Constructing an IFS from a real image   37
      2.5.3 A few more IFS examples   38

3. Fractal Encoding of Grayscale Images   **43**
   3.1 A metric space for grayscale images   43
   3.2 Partitioned iterated function systems (PIFS)   44
      3.2.1 Affine transformations on grayscale images   44
      3.2.2 Contraction mappings on grayscale images   45
      3.2.3 Contraction mapping theorem for grayscale images   45
      3.2.4 Collage Theorem for grayscale images   47
   3.3 Fractal image encoding   48

3.3.1 Domain cells	50
3.3.2 Quadtree partitioning of range cells	51
3.3.2.1 A scheme for keeping track of quadtree partitioning	53
3.3.3 Mapping domains to ranges	54
3.3.4 Encoding times	56
3.4 Image decoding	57
3.4.1 Measuring the error	58
3.5 Storing the encoded image	60
3.5.1 Range file format	60
3.5.2 Binary range file format	61
3.5.2.1 Efficient quadtree storage	62
3.5.2.2 Bit structure for storing range information	63
3.5.2.3 Transmission robustness	64
3.6 Resolution independence	65
3.7 Operator representation of fractal image encoding	66
3.7.1 "Get-block" and "put-block" operators	66
3.7.2 Operator formulation	67
3.7.3 Solution of the operator equation	68
3.7.4 Error analysis	69
4. Speeding Up Fractal Encoding	**71**
4.1 Feature extraction	71
4.1.1 Feature definitions	71
4.1.2 Encoding algorithm using feature extraction	73
4.1.3 Sample results using feature extraction	76
4.2 Domain classification	81
4.2.1 Self-organizing neural networks	82
4.2.2 Fractal image encoding using self-organizing domain classification	84
4.2.3 Sample results using self-organizing domain classifier	86
4.3 Other approaches for speeding up fractal encoding	90
PART II: WAVELET IMAGE COMPRESSION	
5. Simple Wavelets	**93**
5.1 Introduction	93
5.2 Averaging and detail	94
5.3 Scaling functions and wavelet functions	96
5.4 Multiresolution analysis	101
5.5 Normalization	104
5.6 Wavelet transform	105
5.7 Inverse wavelet transform	109
5.8 Wavelet transform in two dimensions	111
5.8.1 What a wavelet transform looks like	113
5.8.2 Simple wavelet compression scheme	116

6. Daubechies Wavelets   **119**
6.1 Weighted averages and differences   119
      6.1.1 Lowpass and highpass filtering   119
      6.1.2 Matrix representation   120
6.2 Properties and conditions on the coefficients   121
6.3 Wavelet transform   122
6.4 Scaling functions and wavelet functions   123
6.5 Daubechies wavelets   124
6.6 Simple image compression with Daubechies wavelets   126
6.7 Other wavelet systems   129

7. Wavelet Image Compression Techniques   **131**
7.1 Introduction   131
7.2 Wavelet zerotrees   133
      7.2.1 An implementation of wavelet zerotree coding   135
            7.2.1.1 Terminology: Which way is up?   135
            7.2.1.2 Handling the insignificant coefficients   137
            7.2.1.3 The zerotree encoding algorithm   141
            7.2.1.4 Bit planes   142
      7.2.2 Decoding a zerotree encoded image   143
      7.2.3 Where is the compression?   149
      7.2.4 Encoding speed   150
7.3 Hybrid fractal-wavelet coding   150
      7.3.1 Operator approach to hybrid fractal-wavelet
            coding   152
      7.3.2 Other hybrid approaches   153

8. Comparison of Fractal and Wavelet Image Compression   **155**
8.1 Rate distortion   155
8.2 Encoding speed   159
8.3 Larger images   160
8.4 Conclusions   163

Appendix A: Using the Accompanying Software   **165**
A.1 IFS System   165
      A.1.1 Points window   166
      A.1.2 Transformation window   167
      A.1.3 IFS window   169
A.2 IMG System: Fractal Image Compression   172
      A.2.1 Encode window   172
            A.2.1.1 Encode setup   174
            A.2.1.2 Running image encoding   176
      A.2.2 Self-organizing encoding window   177
            A.2.2.1 Setting up the self-organizing network   177
            A.2.2.2 Running self-organized image encoding   179
      A.2.3 Decode window   179
      A.2.4 Subtraction window   181
      A.2.5 Plot window   182

A.3 WAV System: Wavelet Image Compression 184
    A.3.1 Wavelet compression window 184
    A.3.2 Wavelet zerotree encoding 186
    A.3.3 Wavelet zerotree decoding 187
    A.3.4 Image subtraction with the WAV System 188
    A.3.5 Wavelet plotting window 188
        A.3.5.1 Setting Up the Graph Parameters 189

Appendix B: Utility Windows Library (UWL) **191**
    B.1 Windows Programming 191
        B.1.1 Multiple Document Interface (MDI) 192
        B.1.2 Dialogs 193
            B.1.2.1 Modal vs. modeless dialogs 193
            B.1.2.2 Windows Common Dialogs 194
    B.2 Utility Windows Library (UWL) 195
        B.2.1 The *twindow* class 195
        B.2.2 MDI frame window 197
        B.2.3 MDI windows 200
        B.2.4 Graph window 202
        B.2.5 *WinMain* in a UWL application 204
        B.2.6 UWL dialogs 210
        B.2.7 Building UWL 211
    B.3 Windows Programming References 212

Appendix C: Organization of the Accompanying Software Source
            Code **215**
    C.1 IFS System 215
        C.1.1 IFS classes 215
        C.1.2 IFS code files 217
        C.1.3 UTM Library 218
    C.2 IMG System 218
        C.2.1 IMG classes 218
        C.2.2 IMG code files 219
    C.3 WAV System 221
        C.3.1 WAV classes 221
        C.3.2 WAV code files 223

References 225
Index 229

Preface

This book is a tutorial text that examines the techniques behind fractal and wavelet approaches to image compression. The field of image compression has experienced an explosion of interest recently because of the growth of the Internet and other multimedia applications. While standard image and data compression methods exist and are in extensive use today, the demand for ever increasing storage requirements and transmission speed have spurred continued research for improved methods. Fractals and wavelets provide two different avenues for such research. For scientists, engineers, students and researchers interested in learning more about fractal and wavelet image compression, this book provides both an introduction to the subject matter and implementation details sufficient for beginning their own investigations into these exciting new technologies.

Prior knowledge of image compression, fractal geometry or wavelet concepts is not necessary to benefit from this book. The level of mathematical presentation is accessible to advanced undergraduate or beginning graduate students in technical fields. Mathematical concepts that would be helpful to know include the idea of convergence of a sequence, multiple integrals, linear independence and basis vectors. Experienced image processing practitioners will probably be disappointed at the minimal amount of coverage devoted to traditional techniques such as the discrete cosine transform and entropy coding. These topics are covered in depth in other books. For example, entropy coding, which can be applied to the output of any compression algorithm, including fractal and wavelet approaches, is not included in the system applications developed here. The present book focuses on the mathematical aspects of fractal and wavelet image compression.

In addition to learning the theory behind fractal and wavelet image compression, readers of this book will have access to software that will enable them to explore these ideas on their own. The software accompanying this book can be found on the web at **http://www.spie.org/bookstore/tt40/**. Details on how to use the software, and how it is constructed, are covered in the book's Appendixes A, B, and C. Three complete Windows-compatible software systems are included with the accompanying software. The IFS System allows readers to create their own fractal images using iterated function systems. The IMG System compresses images using fractal techniques, displays the decoded images, and computes the error between the original and decoded images through image subtraction. The WAV System performs similar functions on images using wavelet techniques and, in addition, displays the wavelet transform of an image. Each system uses a standard Windows interface and includes options for saving and retrieving information from files. The programs run on 32-bit Windows systems, including Windows NT, 95 and 98. Finally, to enable readers to explore beyond the boundaries of the included software, complete C/C++ source code is provided.

The source code for the accompanying software is written in a combination of C and C++. It is not necessary to know either of these languages to benefit from the ideas of this book or to run the programs included with the software. There are a few code examples listed with the text. For the most part, the computational code is written in C. When there is an obvious benefit to exploiting the object-oriented characteristics of C++, then that language is used. In either case, the computational code is kept separate from the user-interface and display code modules that access Windows. Thus, the computational source code, with perhaps minor modifications, should be portable to other platforms, such as UNIX. The user-interface code, where there is an obvious benefit to using object-oriented properties such as inheritance, is written in C++. The source code includes its own C++ application framework for developing simple Windows applications. It does not depend on Microsoft's Foundation Classes (MFC) or other third-party frameworks. The code here was developed using Borland's C++ for Windows, version 4.5. It has also been compiled with Symantec C++ 7.2 and Microsoft Visual C++ 4.0. It should be possible to re-compile the code with any C++ compiler that accesses the Windows Application Programming Interface (API) and supports development of 32-bit Windows applications from source code files.

Outline of Topics

The book begins with an overview of the image compression problem, including a brief discussion of general topics such as information and entropy, arithmetic coding, and a look at current compression approaches such as JPEG. These general topics are introduced in order to place fractal and wavelet image compression techniques in the context of the overall theory of image compression. The remainder of the book is devoted to fractal and wavelet topics and will not focus on general compression topics, such as entropy coding, which are covered in other texts.

Fractal image compression is motivated by initially looking at iterated function systems (IFS). The mathematics of IFS theory, including the contraction mapping theorem, Barnsley's collage theorem, and affine transformations, is covered here. These topics are important to understanding why fractal image compression works. Computer examples show how to use IFS techniques to synthesize fractal images resembling natural objects.

Partitioned iterated function systems extend the ideas of IFS theory to more general real-world images and enable fractal encoding and compression of those images. Once the theory behind fractal encoding has been established, the book considers practical implementation issues such as how to set up a system of domain and range subimages and the transformations between these subimages. Computer examples illustrate concepts such as quadtree partitioning of range cells and the convergence of image sequences to an attractor image.

Long encoding times have hindered the acceptance of fractal techniques for image compression. Two approaches for speeding up the encoding process have received recent attention in the literature. Feature extraction reduces the number of computations needed for domain-range comparisons. Classification of domains reduces search times for finding a good domain-range match. This book examines techniques for feature extraction and the use of neural networks for domain classification. Examples show that these techniques reduce encoding times from hours to seconds and make PC implementation viable.

The book then introduces wavelets as an alternative approach to image compression. Basic Haar wavelets illustrate the idea of wavelet decomposition as a process of averaging and detail extraction at different resolution levels. The book presents a unifying approach to the seemingly disparate multiple entry points into wavelet analysis. Image resolution leads the reader from the ideas of averaging and detail extraction on discrete sequences to scaling functions and wavelet functions. The fact that these functions form basis sets in certain vector spaces leads to the idea of multiresolution analysis. The wavelet transform can be derived from any of these entry points. Averaging and detail extraction can be represented as matrix operators, which leads to a particularly simple formulation of the wavelet transform. The essential features of these operators can be extended to more general highpass and lowpass filtering operators. This analysis leads to more complex wavelet systems, such as the Daubechies wavelets, which provide high compression of commonly occurring signal and image components. With the wavelet framework established, the book examines wavelet image compression techniques, beginning with simple wavelet coefficient quantization schemes and moving on to more complex schemes such as wavelet zerotree encoding. Code samples will illustrate key implementation steps, and computer examples will show how the techniques work. The book also discusses recent research in hybrid techniques which apply the ideas of fractal encoding to data in the wavelet transform domain. Computer examples compare the performance of fractal, wavelet, and hybrid image compression techniques.

Acknowledgments

Special thanks to Bill Pittman, without whose vision and extraordinary scientific curiosity this tutorial would never have been developed. Thanks also to Rick Hermann and SPIE Press for their encouragement during the preparation of this manuscript. Thanks to Bob Berinato for thoughtful and insightful discussion and comments on the manuscript. Finally, thanks to the reviewers, whose comments made this a better book. Any errors that remain are solely those of the author.

Stephen T. Welstead
October 1999

Fractal and Wavelet
Image Compression
Techniques

1

INTRODUCTION

Digital images are claiming an increasingly larger portion of the information world. The growth of the Internet, along with more powerful and affordable computers and continuing advances in the technology of digital cameras, scanners and printers, has led to the widespread use of digital imagery. As a result, there is renewed interest in improving algorithms for the compression of image data. Compression is important both for speed of transmission and efficiency of storage. In addition to the many commercial uses of compression technology, there is also interest among military users for applications such as the downlink of image data from a missile seeker and for archival storage of image data, such as terrain data, for defense-related simulations. The problem of image compression or, more generally, image coding, has made use of, and stimulated, many different areas of engineering and mathematics. This book focuses on two relatively new areas of mathematics that have contributed to recent research in image compression: fractals and wavelets.

Recognition of structure in data is a key aspect of efficiently representing and storing that data. Fractal encoding and wavelet transform methods take two different approaches to discovering structure in image data. Barnsley and Sloan (1988,1990) first recognized the potential of applying the theory of iterated function systems to the problem of image compression. They patented their idea in 1990 and 1991. Jacquin (1992) introduced a method of fractal encoding that utilizes a system of domain and range subimage blocks. This approach is the basis for most fractal encoders today. It has been enhanced by Fisher and a number of others (Fisher 1995; Jacobs, Boss, and Fisher 1995). This block fractal encoding method partitions an image into disjoint range subimages and defines a system of overlapping domain subimages. For each range, the encoding process searches for the best domain and affine transformation that maps that domain onto the range. Image structure is mapped onto the system of ranges, domains and transformations. Much of the recent research in fractal image compression has focused on reducing long encoding times. Feature extraction and classification of domains are two techniques that have proved to be successful. This book includes techniques and discusses recent results (Bogdan and Meadows 1992; Saupe 1994; Bani-Eqbal 1995; Hamzaoui 1995; Welstead 1997) for improving fractal image encoding performance.

Wavelet transform approaches to image compression exploit redundancies in scale. Wavelet transform data can be organized into a subtree structure that can be efficiently coded. Hybrid fractal-wavelet techniques (Davis 1998; Hebert and Soundararajan 1998) apply the domain-range transformation idea of fractal encoding to the realm of wavelet subtrees. The result is improved compression and decoded image fidelity.

This chapter provides background material on some general topics related to image coding. Following an overview of the image compression problem, we will briefly look at information theory and entropy, scalar and vector quantization, and competing compression technologies, such as those of the Joint Photographic Experts Group (JPEG). The purpose of this chapter is to place fractal and wavelet compression techniques into the overall context of image compression. Details on the alternative approaches introduced in this chapter can be found in the references.

1.1 IMAGES

From a mathematical point of view, a grayscale image can be thought of as a real-valued function f of two real variables, x and y. This image function $f(x,y)$ is typically defined on a rectangular region of the plane, and most of the images in this book are defined on square regions. Since the image doesn't "know" what region it is defined on, we typically assume that this region is the unit square $[0,1] \times [0,1]$. The grayscale values are positive real numbers. Fig. 1.1.1 shows a grayscale image and the graph of the corresponding function representation $f(x,y)$. Color images correspond to vector-valued functions on the plane. There are different ways of representing color information. Electronic image display systems, such as computer displays, represent color as red, green, and blue (RGB) values. Printing systems use cyan, magenta, and yellow for color, in addition to black (CMYK). Either way, color is represented as a three-dimensional vector. Coding algorithms that work for grayscale images can be applied to each of the components of a color image, although more efficient approaches are possible. While it might be expected that the color image coding problem is three times as hard as the corresponding problem for grayscale images, it turns out that the situation is not quite that bad. It is possible to take advantage of the properties of human perception of color to reduce the coding requirements for color images. We will revisit this topic later in this chapter.

 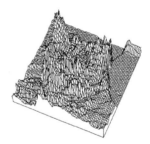

Fig. 1.1.1 A grayscale image (left) and its corresponding representation (right) as a function on the plane.

Human perception of images is an analog process, but the realm of computers is a digital world. Thus, the computer representation of a grayscale image is a two-dimensional array of nonnegative values. Each entry of the array is a pixel of the image. The pixels take on a finite number of values, which we can assign to a range of nonnegative integers. The range may be expressed in absolute terms, such as "256 gray levels", or in terms of the number of bits necessary to represent the values, as in "8 bits per pixel".

While most of the literature on image processing and compression is devoted to human perception of images, it is worth noting that for some applications, machine perception may be more important. For example, an automatic target recognition system may extract features from an image (such as edge locations or texture variations). In that case, the performance of a compression algorithm may be judged on how well it preserves feature values after compression, which may not correspond exactly with human perception of the same image.

1.2 THE IMAGE COMPRESSION PROBLEM

Fig. 1.2.1 shows an overview of the image compression process. A digital image is an array of pixel values, which we can think of as a list of numbers. The compression problem consists of two main parts: encoding and decoding. Encoding attempts to represent the original list of numbers in a different way, hopefully requiring less storage than the original list. Decoding tries to recover something like the original image from the encoded information. If the decoded image is always exactly the same as the original image, then the encoding-decoding algorithm is said to be a *lossless* algorithm. If the decoded image differs from the original image, then the algorithm is a *lossy* algorithm. The fractal and wavelet methods covered in this book are lossy algorithms, as are most compression algorithms.

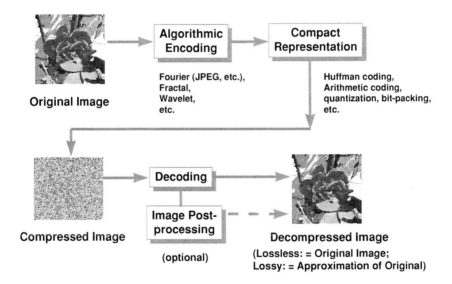

Fig. 1.2.1 Overview of the image compression process.

There are two ways that you can try to compress a set of data represented by a list of numbers. You can try to make the list shorter, that is, consist of fewer numbers, or you can try to make the numbers themselves shorter, that is, use fewer bits on average to represent each number. Either approach will result in fewer total bits required to represent the list. Complete compression schemes do both.

Fig. 1.2.1 refers to the first of these approaches as algorithmic encoding. This class of algorithms includes Fourier transform and discrete cosine transform (DCT) methods, which are the basis for most JPEG compression methods. It also includes wavelet transform and fractal methods, the subjects of this book. With transform methods, the idea is to transform the image data to a different domain where it is easy to identify data that may safely be deleted. This enables the discarding of an appreciable amount of data content with little loss of image quality. In the case of the Fourier transform, this is usually high-frequency data. For wavelet transforms, it is high-detail data. Fractal methods attempt to directly represent image information in a compact way.

The output of algorithmic encoding can be further compressed through compact representation of the encoded numbers. Quantization can result in both fewer numbers in the list and fewer bits per number. Digital images by definition have already undergone some type of quantization before the encoding stage. Entropy coding methods, such as Huffman coding and arithmetic coding, examine the distribution of values to arrive at an efficient bit representation for each value. Values that occur frequently in the list are assigned a smaller number of bits, while rarely occurring values are assigned longer bit strings.

Decoding attempts to restore the original image from the encoded data. For transform methods, the decoding step applies the inverse transform. Additional post-processing may accompany the decoding step to improve the quality of the decoded image, for example to remove blocking artifacts that may result from the compression algorithm.

1.3 INFORMATION, ENTROPY, AND DATA MODELING

Let A be some event that occurs with probability $P(A)$. Then the *information* associated with A is defined to be:

$$i(A) = \log_x \frac{1}{P(A)} = -\log_x P(A). \tag{1.3.1}$$

Note that this implies that when $P(A)$ is small, $i(A)$ is large, while $P(A) = 1$ implies $i(A) = 0$. Small probability events carry a lot of information while virtually certain events carry very little information. If you are told that it is going to snow in Alaska this winter, you have not been given much information. However, if you are told that Florida is going to be covered in snow, then you might want to start looking at orange juice futures.

In information theory literature, the phenomenon that generates the random events A_j is called the *source*. Suppose we have a set of independent events A_j occurring with probabilities $P(A_j)$. The *entropy* of the source associated with these events is the average information:

$$H = \sum P(A_j) i(A_j). \tag{1.3.2}$$

For our purposes here, we are interested in images as sources. Suppose that $A_j, j = 1,...,n$, represents a sequence of pixel values from an image, and let x, the basis of the log function in (1.3.1), equal 2. Then the entropy associated with the image is a measure of the average number of bits needed to code the pixel values.

In general, it is not possible to know the true entropy associated with a source, because we don't know the true values of $P(A_j)$ in (1.3.2). The best we can do is to estimate the values for $P(A_j)$ and use (1.3.2) to arrive at an estimate for the apparent entropy of the source.

Recognizing structure in data can reduce the apparent entropy. Consider the following example, from Sayood (1996). We start with the sequence

$$1\ 2\ 1\ 2\ 3\ 3\ 3\ 3\ 1\ 2\ 3\ 3\ 3\ 3\ 1\ 2\ 3\ 3\ 1\ 2.$$

If we ignore structure and consider the numbers one at a time, we see that there are three symbols, 1, 2, and 3, that occur with the following probabilities:

$$P(1) = 5/20 = 0.25;\ P(2) = 5/20 = 0.25;\ P(3) = 10/20 = 0.5.$$

The apparent entropy is:

$$-(0.25\ \log_2(1/4) + 0.25\ \log_2(1/4) + 0.5\ \log_2(1/2)) = 1.5 \text{ bits per symbol.}$$

However, if we consider the numbers in the sequence two at a time, we discover structure: 12 and 33 always occur together, and the entire sequence consists of just these two symbols. Moreover,

$$P(12) = 5/10 = 0.5,$$
$$P(33) = 5/10 = 0.5,$$

and the apparent entropy is now

$$-(0.5\ \log_2(1/2) + 0.5\ \log_2(1/2)) = 1 \text{ bit per symbol.}$$

In the first case, it would take $(1.5)(20) = 30$ bits to encode the sequence, while the second case requires only 10 bits. The process of associating a structure with a data sequence is called *data modeling*. Fractal encoding methods provide a data model for an image that can reduce apparent entropy and lead to compression. Transform methods, such as wavelets, provide structure in the transform domain, which also reduces apparent entropy and leads to compression.

Entropy is the basis for Huffman coding and arithmetic coding. Given any sequence of data values, such as the output of a fractal or wavelet compression scheme, one can always apply an entropy coding technique, such as Huffman or arithmetic coding, to the sequence to achieve further compression. These techniques examine the distribution of data values, and assign low bit rates to frequently occurring values, and high bit rates to less frequently occurring values. We will not explore entropy coding techniques any further in this book. Details can be found in the references, such as Sayood (1996).

1.4 SCALAR AND VECTOR QUANTIZATION

Quantization is another way of reducing the amount of stored information. Scalar quantization reduces the precision of scalar quantities to some fixed number of levels. For example, 16- or 32-bit numbers may be reduced to 8 bits. In this case, there are 256 levels in the quantization. Quantization may be uniform or non-uniform. Uniform quantization spaces the quantization levels evenly across the range of numeric values. Not surprisingly, this type of quantization works best when the values to be quantized are uniformly distributed.

If the values are not uniformly distributed, it may be advantageous to concentrate more quantization levels in the region of highest density of numeric values. *Decimation* is one example of non-uniform quantization. Decimation consists of setting some portion of the numeric values equal to zero. The portion may be determined as some percentage of the total number of values, or it may be determined using a threshold test. For example, one approach to wavelet image compression is to set some percentage, say 90%, of the transformed wavelet coefficient values equal to zero. The "quantization" of the remaining values merely consists of retaining those values. The number of levels is reduced to 0 plus the number of different values of the 10% remaining coefficients (remarkably, as we will see in later chapters, a quite good decoded image can be recovered from just this 10% of the original coefficients).

Vector quantization represents arrays of values with a single quantized number. Color images provide a good motivation for the use of vector quantization. The pixels in a color image typically consist of a triplet of values. In an RGB system, this triplet consists of red, green and blue values. For true reproduction of the color image, the entire (R,G,B) vector must be stored. A 24-bit color image devotes 8 bits to each of the three values per pixel. In this case, any value in the three-dimensional RGB space can be used for a given pixel. However, a good approximation to the original image can be obtained by restricting the pixel values to some finite list of RGB vectors. Such a scheme is called a *color map*, or, in Windows programming, a *palette*. For example, the color map, or palette, may consist of 256 values, so that the index into this list requires only 8 bits for storage. In this case, once the color map is known, each pixel can be represented with 8 bits, rather than the original 24.

Obviously, the choice of color map affects the quality of the approximated image. In vector quantization in general, the choice of the best such list, known as a *codebook* in general vector quantization applications, is nontrivial. One approach is to use adaptive clustering of the data. In this approach, the means of the clusters become the codebook entries. Note that in vector quantization, the codebook must be known to the decoder, and it is usually data dependent. This usually means that the codebook must be stored along with the encoded data, which reduces the effective compression. Fig. 1.4.1 shows an example of the vector quantization process, as it might be applied to a color RGB image.

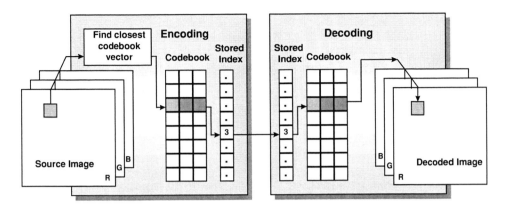

Fig. 1.4.1 Vector quantization, as it might be applied to a color RGB image. The red (R), green (G) and blue (B) pixel values form vectors of length 3. Encoding finds the closest entry in a table of vectors known as the codebook. Only the index of the table entry is stored. Decoding converts this index back to a vector. Note that the decoder needs to know the codebook table. Finding the optimum codebook for a given image is nontrivial.

1.5 TRANSFORM METHODS

JPEG is the most widely accepted standard for image compression. JPEG users can choose either a lossless version or one of several lossy options. The lossy versions provide better compression rates. Compression ratio and restored image quality can be controlled (though not precisely specified) through parameter selection. The basis for the lossy versions of JPEG is the discrete cosine transform, which is a variation of the Fourier transform. Quantization is applied to the transform coefficients to achieve compression. Sayood (1996) discusses the JPEG method, and Lu (1997) provides a detailed example. Barnsley and Hurd (1993) also have a detailed discussion of JPEG with sample source code. Complete source code is available on the Internet.

Lossless JPEG applies linear predictive coding. Linear prediction makes use of relationships among neighboring pixels to achieve compression. It is an example of seeking inherent structure in the image, and hence reducing the apparent entropy.

JPEG has a video cousin, MPEG (Moving Picture Experts Group). Video compression can take advantage of considerable frame-to-frame redundancy to achieve much greater compression ratios than is possible for still pictures.

> ### *Why consider new image compression approaches when perfectly good standards (JPEG, MPEG) exist?*
>
> The establishment of JPEG and MPEG as standards does not mean the end of a need for research in image and video compression. Rather than stifle new research, standards have increased the number of applications using image and video data and have thereby helped uncover challenging new problems: robust transmission, digital image and video libraries, content-based retrieval, and digital watermarking are a few examples. Our understanding of the fundamental structure of image and video sources is limited. There is little reason to believe that today's standards are optimal for these sources. Fractal methods, in particular, take a whole new look at how to model fundamental image structure. Continuing research is needed to improve our understanding and to improve the performance of compression methods. In fact, the JPEG Standards Committee has recognized that the original JPEG standard, developed more than 10 years ago, needs to be updated to meet the expanding requirements of today's digital imaging consumer. The committee is actively developing a new JPEG 2000 standard, which uses wavelet technology in place of the DCT compression methods of the original JPEG standard. See (Chen 1998) for a further discussion on the role of standards in image compression.

1.6 COLOR IMAGES

As we have already seen, digital color image pixels consist of three values, representing red, green, and blue values in the RGB system used for most displays (print systems use cyan, magenta, and yellow for color, in addition to black (CMYK)). At first glance, it might appear that compression of color images is three times as hard as grayscale image compression. However, due to human perception of color, it is possible to transform RGB values in a way that allows greater compression. The RGB values are transformed to YIQ values, where Y is *luminance*, I is *hue*, and Q is *saturation* (the notation I and Q is a holdover from the *in-phase* (I) and *quadrature* (Q) terminology of signal processing). It turns out that the I and Q channels can be greatly compressed with little perceived degradation. Thus, the overall compression of color images is greater than what is possible for grayscale images, typically 2 to 2.7 times greater (Fisher 1995). The transformation from RGB to YIQ, and vice versa, is linear. The matrices representing the transformation and its inverse are shown below:

$$\begin{bmatrix} Y \\ I \\ Q \end{bmatrix} = \begin{bmatrix} 0.299 & 0.587 & 0.114 \\ 0.596 & -0.274 & -0.322 \\ 0.211 & -0.523 & 0.312 \end{bmatrix} \begin{bmatrix} R \\ G \\ B \end{bmatrix}$$

$$\begin{bmatrix} R \\ G \\ B \end{bmatrix} = \begin{bmatrix} 1.000 & 0.956 & 0.621 \\ 1.000 & -0.273 & -0.647 \\ 1.000 & -1.104 & 1.701 \end{bmatrix} \begin{bmatrix} Y \\ I \\ Q \end{bmatrix}$$

Color television transmission in North America uses the YIQ representation.

Fisher (1995) and Lu (1997) discuss compression of color images in more detail. The examples in this book will focus on compression of grayscale images.

1.7 THE FOCUS OF THIS BOOK

The remainder of this book focuses on the algorithmic aspects of fractal image compression and wavelet image compression. We will investigate the mathematics behind these methods in order to understand how they work. We will look at how to implement these methods on a computer, showing samples of source code. Examples using the book's accompanying software will illustrate the methods and their implementation. The examples will be applied only to grayscale images, since the algorithms do not change when applied to color images (though the implementation details do change). While complete image compression systems would employ entropy coding and decoded image post-processing to improve results, the systems developed in this book are tutorial in nature and thus will focus only on the implementations of the fractal and wavelet compression algorithms. For this reason, performance results presented here should be used only to compare the relative performance of these algorithms to each other, and not, for example, to the research-level implementations of other image compression practitioners. The references contain more information on the details of compact representation, such as entropy coding and bit-packing, image post-processing, color image compression, video compression, as well as other compression topics and approaches.

Part I

FRACTAL IMAGE COMPRESSION

2

ITERATED FUNCTION SYSTEMS

In the early 1980's, Michael Barnsley introduced the idea of synthesizing a predetermined image as the attractor of a chaotic process. Other researchers had previously shown that chaotic systems were capable of producing fascinating images known as *strange attractors*. Barnsley, however, was the first to take a step toward solving the inverse problem: Given a specified image, can one come up with a chaotic system that has the given image as its strange attractor? Barnsley used a particular system of mappings which he called an *iterated function system (IFS)*. IFS's are, at best, only a crude form of image compression. It should be stressed that IFS's in their original form, and as they are presented in this chapter, are not the basis of current approaches to fractal image compression (a misconception held by some of the detractors of fractal image compression). However, IFS's were the inspiration for fractal approaches to image compression. And while IFS's are not viable themselves as complete image compression systems, an understanding of IFS theory is essential to understanding how fractal image compression works. In this chapter, we will develop the mathematical background of IFS theory and see how to implement such a system on a computer.

2.1 ITERATED FUNCTION SYSTEMS AS THE MOTIVATION FOR FRACTAL IMAGE COMPRESSION

The quintessential example of a fractal image generated by an IFS is a fern, such as that shown in Fig. 2.1.1. (a). The IFS used to generate this image consists of four transformations. These transformations map the entire image onto the four subimage regions shown in Fig. 2.1.1 (b). Each transformation has a fixed form that can be specified with six real-valued coefficients. Thus, all of the information needed to produce the image in (a) is contained in 24 floating point numbers.

These 24 coefficients represent a code for the image (a). This code is particularly compact and requires much less storage than a pixel version of the image (a). This is the motivation for fractal approaches to image compression: IFS's provide an image code that represents a compression ratio of hundreds- or thousands-to-one.

Simple IFS's such as the one that produced Fig. 2.1.1 (a) do not work for arbitrary images. First of all, the image in Fig. 2.1.1 (a) is a binary image, that is, its pixel values are limited to 0 or 1. More general grayscale images require a more sophisticated system that the next chapter will develop. Also, simple IFS's apply only to images that are *self-similar*, that is, images that are made up of subimages that are copies of the entire image. Notice that each leaf of the fern is actually a copy of the entire fern. This is not true of arbitrary images. In general, we can only hope to find subimages that are copies of other subimages, which is what the system developed in the next chapter will do. In the remainder of this chapter, we will develop the mathematics needed to determine the coefficients for a simple IFS, and we will see how such an IFS can produce an image such as Fig. 2.1.1 (a).

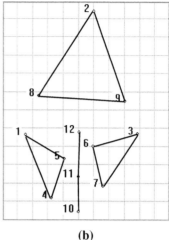

(a)   (b)

Fig. 2.1.1 (a) A fern image created with an IFS. This IFS consists of the 4 transformations mapping the entire image onto the 4 subimage regions shown in (b). All of the information needed to reproduce the image shown in (a) can be stored using just 24 floating point values.

What is a fractal?

The term *fractal* was first introduced by Benoit Mandelbrot (1983). Fractals are more easily described than defined. The key property that characterizes fractals is *self-similarity*. That is, fractals show the same amount of detail regardless of the scale at which they are viewed. Most objects lose detail when one zooms in for a closer view. Because the scale is arbitrary, infinity is lurking behind the scene here. True fractals are always the result of some type of process involving infinity, such as an iterative process. A second property that characterizes fractals is non-integer dimension. While the very concept of non-integer dimension may seem counter-intuitive, it is possible to take the idea of ordinary Euclidean dimension that we are used to (that is, the dimension that assigns the number 1 to lines, 2 to filled-in rectangles on a flat sheet of paper, and 3 to the world in which we live) and extend it to a definition for which non-integer values make sense. The name *fractal*, in fact, comes from the fractional values that the dimension of fractal objects can assume. See (Mandelbrot 1983) for more details.

2.2 METRIC SPACES

Mathematicians like to extend concrete concepts into the abstract. The concept of measuring distance between real-world objects is certainly well defined. But how do we measure the distance between two images? What properties of the concept of distance do we want to preserve when extending its definition to more abstract objects such as images? Sometimes the abstract frees us from looking at the world in conventional ways and allows us to consider new approaches to solving problems. In this section, we'll extend the idea of distance to the more abstract notion of *metric*. We will also view objects in more abstract terms as points in space. This will allow us to consider images as points in a special type of space known as a *metric space* and to measure distance between images. We can then tap into the machinery of classical metric space mathematics to develop an algorithm for generating custom-made fractal images.

2.2.1 Basic concepts

In the Euclidean plane $\mathbf{R}^2$, the usual definition of the distance $d_2(x,y)$ between two points $x = (x_1,x_2)$ and $y = (y_1,y_2)$ is:

$$d_2(x,y) = ((x_1-y_1)^2 + (x_2 - y_2)^2)^{1/2}. \tag{2.2.1}$$

This is not the only way to measure distance in $\mathbf{R}^2$. Another distance function is:

$$d_1(x,y) = |x_1 - y_1| + |x_2 - y_2|. \tag{2.2.2}$$

These two distance functions do not yield the same answer for the distance between two points. For example, $d_2((0,0),(1,1)) = \sqrt{2}$, while $d_1((0,0),(1,1)) = 2$. However, they both satisfy the essence of being measures of distance. What is this essence? That is, what properties should a "sensible" distance function satisfy? Here is what mathematicians have deemed the essential properties of a distance function:

1. It shouldn't matter whether distance is measured from x to y or from y to x. That is, we should have:

$$d(x,y) = d(y,x).$$

2. The distance from a point to itself ought to be 0:

$$d(x,x) = 0.$$

3. It shouldn't be possible to find a shorter distance between two points by jumping off to some intermediate point (in other words, the shortest distance between two points is a straight line – whatever that is!):

$$d(x,y) \le d(x,z) + d(z,y).$$

This is also known as the triangle inequality.

4. Finally the distance measure itself ought to be real-valued, finite, and positive when applied to any two distinct points x and y:

$$0 < d(x,y) < \infty.$$

A distance function satisfying properties (1) - (4) above is called a *metric*. A set of points **X** together with a metric d defined on **X** is called a *metric space*, and is denoted (**X**,d).

We will be working with images as sets of points in the plane $\mathbf{R}^2$. One might wonder why we are bothering with abstract metric space concepts when we are dealing with such a concrete space as $\mathbf{R}^2$. Actually, we are interested in defining a metric space whose *points* are in fact images. When we make this leap, we will have available to us all of the machinery of metric space theory to guide us through a space where intuition is not always reliable.

We need some basic definitions that apply to a general metric space (**X**,d). A sequence of points $\{x_n\}$ is said to *converge* to a point $x \in \mathbf{X}$ if, by choosing n large enough, we can get x_n arbitrarily close to x. In precise mathematical terms, this is stated as follows: Given any $\varepsilon > 0$, there is an $N > 0$ such that $d(x_n,x) < \varepsilon$ whenever $n \geq N$. The point x is called the *limit* of the sequence $\{x_n\}$, and we denote this convergence by:

$$x_n \rightarrow x.$$

A sequence $\{x_n\}$ is called a *Cauchy sequence* if points x_n and x_m get arbitrarily close to one another as m and n get large. Once again, there is a precise mathematical definition: Given $\varepsilon > 0$, there is an $N > 0$ such that $d(x_m,x_n) < \varepsilon$ for all $m,n > N$. Convergent sequences are Cauchy sequences, however the converse is not necessarily true. That is, it is possible to define a space S and a Cauchy sequence $\{x_n\}$ in S such that S does not contain the limit of the sequence $\{x_n\}$. Consider the following somewhat contrived example. Suppose S is the set of points in $\mathbf{R}^2$ that are less than distance 1 (Euclidean distance) from the origin, excluding the origin itself:

$$S = \{(x,y) \in \mathbf{R}^2 : 0 < d_2((x,y),(0,0)) < 1\}.$$

Now consider the sequence of points $\{(1/n,1/n)\}$, $n > 1$, in S. This is a Cauchy sequence in S, yet it does not converge to a point in S. Similarly, $\{((n-1)/n,0)\}$, $n > 1$, is also a Cauchy sequence in S that does not converge to a point in S.

A metric space in which each Cauchy sequence does converge to a point in the space is called a *complete* metric space. $(\mathbf{R}^2,d_2)$ is a complete metric space. The space (S,d_2), where S is the set defined above, is not a complete metric space.

While the sequences defined above do not converge to points in S, they do have limits in the larger space $\mathbf{R}^2$: $(1/n,1/n) \rightarrow (0,0) \in \mathbf{R}^2$ and $((n-1)/n,0) \rightarrow (1,0) \in \mathbf{R}^2$. The points (0,0) and (1,0) are called *limit points* of the set S. A point x is called a *limit point* of a set S if there is a sequence of points $\{x_n\}$ in $S \setminus \{x\}$ such that $x_n \rightarrow x$. Here, $S \setminus \{x\}$ is defined as the set of all points in S excluding x. A set A in a metric space (**X**,d) is *closed* if it contains all of its limit points. The set S defined above is not closed. However, the following set is:

$$\overline{S} = \{(x,y) \in \mathbf{R}^2 : d_2((x,y),(0,0)) \leq 1\}.$$

A set A together with its limit points is called the *closure* of A, denoted $\overline{A}$. In the above example, $\overline{S}$ is the closure of S.

One final definition for this section: A set B in $(\mathbf{X},d)$ is *bounded* if there is a point $x_0 \in \mathbf{X}$ and a finite value R, $0 < R < \infty$, such that for every $x \in B$ we have

$$d(x_0,x) < R.$$

The sets S and $\overline{S}$ defined above are both bounded, as are all of the image sets we will consider in this chapter.

2.2.2 Compact sets and Hausdorff space

The mathematical notion of an "image" in this chapter is somewhat different from the grayscale images considered in later chapters. A binary image such as the fern in Fig. 2.1.1 (a) can be considered as a special case of a grayscale image, that is, as a two-dimensional matrix of grayscale values, where each pixel is either black or white. However, in this chapter, when we refer to a binary image, mathematically we are referring only to the set of points in $\mathbf{R}^2$ represented by the black pixels. That is, the "image" is a set of points contained within a bounded subset of $(\mathbf{R}^2,d_2)$. Rather than working with these images directly as sets, we will take advantage of the concept of abstract metric space to define a space in which these images themselves are *points*. This will allow us to apply a well-known result from classical metric space theory to derive an algorithm for producing fractal images. We will define a metric to measure the distance between these image sets, and the sets themselves will be points in a metric space.

Binary images are closed and bounded subsets of $(\mathbf{R}^2,d_2)$. To place these images as points in a more abstract metric space, we need to generalize the idea of "closed and bounded". A set C in a metric space $(\mathbf{X},d)$ is *compact* if every infinite sequence in C has a convergent subsequence with a limit in C. $(\mathbf{R}^2,d_2)$ is not compact since, for example, the sequence $\{(n,0)\}_{0..\infty}$ does not have a convergent subsequence. Note that the definition of a compact set implies that it must contain its limit points and, hence, be closed. The set S defined in section 2.2.1 therefore is not compact since it is not closed. In Euclidean space, such as $(\mathbf{R}^2,d_2)$, the compact sets are exactly the sets that are closed and bounded, a nontrivial fact known as the Bolzano-Weierstrass theorem.

Let $(\mathbf{X},d)$ be a complete metric space, and define $H(\mathbf{X})$ to be the space consisting of the compact subsets of $\mathbf{X}$. That is, each point in $H(\mathbf{X})$ is a compact subset of $\mathbf{X}$. Define the distance between a point $x \in \mathbf{X}$ and $B \in H(\mathbf{X})$ as the shortest distance between x and any point $y \in B$:

$$d(x,B) = \min \{d(x,y): y \in B\}.$$

Note that this minimum exists and is finite because B is compact, and hence closed and bounded. Now we can define the distance between two compact sets A and B as:

$$d(A,B) = \max \{d(x,B): x \in A\}.$$

The compactness of A ensures that this maximum exists and is finite. But does $d(A,B)$ define a metric? Consider the situation shown in Fig. 2.2.1.

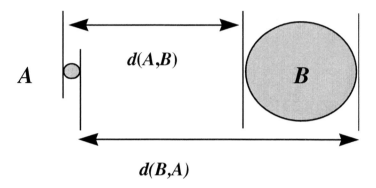

Fig. 2.2.1 $d(A,B) \neq d(B,A)$ in general.

It is clear from Fig. 2.2.1 that $d(A,B) \neq d(B,A)$ in general (in fact, these quantities are rarely equal). We can fix this by defining a new distance measure $h(A,B)$ by:

$$h(A,B) = \max \{d(A,B),d(B,A)\}.$$

Now $h(A,B) = h(B,A)$ and h is a metric on $H(\mathbf{X})$. The metric h is called the *Hausdorff metric* and the metric space $(H(\mathbf{X}),h)$ is called a *Hausdorff metric space*. Barnsley (1993) calls $(H(\mathbf{X}),h)$ "the space where fractals live". It is the space where we will develop the machinery to generate a certain type of fractal using iterated function systems. The space $(H(\mathbf{X}),h)$ is a complete metric space (Barnsley 1993). When the underlying space is $\mathbf{R}^2$ (as it will be for the binary images considered in this chapter), the notation $H(\mathbf{R}^2)$ will be shortened to H.

2.2.3 Contraction mappings

Transformations assign points in one space to points in another (possibly the same) space according to some pre-defined rule. For example, the function

$$f(x,y) = (0.5x + 0.3y + 2, 0.2x - 0.5y + 1)$$

is a transformation that sends one point in $\mathbf{R}^2$ to another point in $\mathbf{R}^2$. Transformations are also called *mappings*, and we write $f: \mathbf{X}_1 \to \mathbf{X}_2$ to denote a transformation from one space $\mathbf{X}_1$ to a second space $\mathbf{X}_2$.

A transformation $f:\mathbf{X} \to \mathbf{X}$ on a metric space $(\mathbf{X},d)$ is called a *contraction mapping* if there is a constant s, $0 \leq s < 1$, such that

$$d(f(x_1),f(x_2)) \leq s\, d(x_1,x_2)$$

for all $x_1, x_2 \in \mathbf{X}$. The constant s is called the *contractivity factor* for f. Fig. 2.2.2 shows an example of a contraction mapping on $(\mathbf{R}^2, d_2)$ acting on a set of points in $\mathbf{R}^2$.

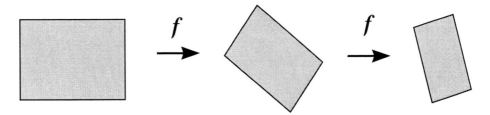

Fig. 2.2.2 A contraction mapping f acting on a set of points in $\mathbf{R}^2$.

Fig. 2.2.2 depicts a transformation that is applied more than once. That is, once $f(x)$ is computed for a point x, the value $f(f(x))$ is computed by applying f to the result. You can continue this process to compute $f(f(f(x)))$ and so on. The transformations obtained by applying f over and over again in this way are called *iterates* of f. The nth iterate of f is denoted $f^{\circ n}$, that is, $f^{\circ n}(x) = f(f(\dots f(x)\dots))$, where f is applied n times.

Note that $f(x), f^{\circ 2}(x), f^{\circ 3}(x), \dots$ forms a sequence in $\mathbf{X}$. Suppose f is a contraction mapping with contractivity factor s. Note that

$$d(f^{\circ n}(x), f^{\circ(n+k)}(x)) \le s\, d(f^{\circ(n-1)}(x), f^{\circ(n+k-1)}(x))$$

$$\le s^n d(x, f^{\circ k}(x)).$$

Note also that

$$d(x, f^{\circ k}(x)) \le d(x, f(x)) + d(f(x), f^{\circ 2}(x)) + \dots + d(f^{\circ(k-1)}(x), f^{\circ k}(x))$$

$$\le (1 + s + s^2 + \dots + s^{k-1})d(x, f(x))$$

$$\le \frac{1}{1-s}d(x, f(x)),$$

where the final inequality follows from the series expansion of $(1-s)^{-1}$ which is valid here because $0 \le s < 1$. So, for example, if $n < m$, we have

$$d(f^{\circ n}(x), f^{\circ m}(x)) \le \frac{s^n}{1-s}d(x, f(x)).$$

Since $s < 1$, the expression on the right approaches 0 as $n, m \to \infty$. In other words, the sequence $\{f^{\circ n}(x)\}$ is a Cauchy sequence in $(\mathbf{X}, d)$. Since $(\mathbf{X}, d)$ is a complete metric space, this sequence converges to a limit $x_f \in \mathbf{X}$, that is,

$$\lim_{n \to \infty} f^{\circ n}(x) = x_f.$$

This point x_f has a special property. What happens if we apply f to x_f?

$$d(x_f, f(x_f)) \le d(x_f, f^{\circ n}(x)) + d(f^{\circ n}(x), f(x_f))$$
$$\le d(x_f, f^{\circ n}(x)) + s\, d(f^{\circ(n-1)}(x), x_f).$$

Since $f^{\circ n}(x) \to x_f$, the two terms on the right converge to 0, and so the term on the left must be 0. In other words,

$$f(x_f) = x_f.$$

We say that x_f is a *fixed point* of f. How many fixed points can a contraction mapping have? Suppose y_f is another fixed point of f, so that $f(y_f) = y_f$. Then:

$$d(x_f, y_f) = d(f(x_f), f(y_f)) \le s\, d(x_f, y_f).$$

Since $s < 1$, the above inequality implies $d(x_f, y_f) = 0$, that is, $x_f = y_f$. So a contraction mapping f on $(\mathbf{X}, d)$ has one and only one fixed point in $\mathbf{X}$. Note that since there is only one fixed point, it follows that $\{f^{\circ n}(x)\}$ converges to this fixed point regardless of the starting point x. These results are summarized in the following theorem:

The Contraction Mapping Theorem*: Let $f : \mathbf{X} \to \mathbf{X}$ be a contraction mapping on a complete metric space $(\mathbf{X}, d)$. Then f possesses exactly one fixed point $x_f \in \mathbf{X}$, and for any $x \in \mathbf{X}$, the sequence $\{f^{\circ n}(x) : n = 1, 2, \ldots\}$ converges to x_f, that is,*

$$\lim_{n \to \infty} f^{\circ n}(x) = x_f, \text{ for all } x \in \mathbf{X}.$$

The Contraction Mapping Theorem is a cornerstone of classical functional analysis. Many existence proofs use the technique of showing that a certain mapping is a contraction and hence possesses a unique fixed point. This theorem is the basis for all fractal image compression approaches.

2.3 ITERATED FUNCTION SYSTEMS

The above discussion mentions the fact that we will consider fractal images as points in the Hausdorff space $(H(\mathbf{X}), h)$. In this section we will define a special type of contraction mapping that acts on images, that is, on points in $(H(\mathbf{X}), h)$.

2.3.1 Introduction

Let $\{w_1, w_2, \ldots, w_N\}$ be a finite collection of contraction mappings on $(\mathbf{X}, d)$, with contractivity factors $s_1, s_2, \ldots, s_N$, $0 \le s_n < 1$. Define a mapping W that acts on compact sets of points of $\mathbf{X}$ (that is, on $H(\mathbf{X})$) by

$$W(B) = w_1(B) \cup w_2(B) \cup \ldots \cup w_N(B)$$

$$= \bigcup_{n=1}^{N} w_n(B) \text{ for each } B \in H(\mathbf{X}) \text{ (that is, } B \subset \mathbf{X}).$$

Then W maps $H(\mathbf{X})$ to $H(\mathbf{X})$ and W is a contraction mapping on $(H(\mathbf{X}),h)$ with contractivity factor s given by $s = \max \{s_1, s_2, \ldots, s_N\}$. That is,

$$h(W(B), W(C)) \le s\, h(B,C) \text{ for } B,C \in H(\mathbf{X}).$$

An *iterated function system* (IFS) consists of a complete metric space $(\mathbf{X},d)$ together with a finite set of contraction mappings $w_n \colon \mathbf{X} \to \mathbf{X}$ with contractivity factors s_n. The contractivity factor of the IFS is given by $s = \max \{s_1, s_2, \ldots, s_N\}$. The notation for an IFS is $\{\mathbf{X}, w_n \colon n = 1,2,\ldots,N\}$. If the underlying metric space is apparent, such as $\mathbf{R}^2$ in the case of images, we will shorten this notation to $\{w_n\}$.

There are a number of details we have glossed over here, including the fact that $W(B)$ is in fact a point in $H(\mathbf{X})$ when $B \in H(\mathbf{X})$ (that is, that $W(B)$ is compact when B is compact) and that W is in fact a contraction mapping. The interested reader is referred to Barnsley (1993) for a more complete discussion.

2.3.2 The Collage Theorem

The Contraction Mapping Theorem (CMT) can be applied to mappings on $(H(\mathbf{X}),h)$, and, in particular, to IFS's. The image that is the unique fixed point of the IFS (guaranteed by the CMT) in $H(\mathbf{X})$ is called the *attractor* of the IFS. Barnsley (1993) has derived a special form of the CMT applied to IFS's on $(H(\mathbf{X}),h)$ called the *Collage Theorem*. Remember that a "point" in $H(\mathbf{X})$ is actually a compact set of points in $\mathbf{R}^2$ that represents a binary image.

Collage Theorem*: Suppose we have a point L in $H(\mathbf{X})$. Let $\varepsilon > 0$ be given. Choose an IFS $\{\mathbf{X}, w_n \colon n = 1,2,\ldots,N\}$ with contractivity factor s, $0 < s < 1$, so that*

$$h\left(L, \bigcup_{n=1}^{N} w_n(L)\right) \le \varepsilon$$

then

$$h(L, A) \le (1-s)^{-1} h\left(L, \bigcup_{n=1}^{N} w_n(L)\right) \le \frac{\varepsilon}{(1-s)}$$

where A is the attractor of the IFS.

To see that this result follows from the CMT, consider a contraction mapping f on a complete metric space $(\mathbf{X}, d)$. Let x_f be the fixed point of f. Suppose $x \in \mathbf{X}$ is such that $d(x, f(x)) < \varepsilon$ for some $\varepsilon > 0$. Then

$$d(x, x_f) = d(x, f(x_f))$$
$$\leq d(x, f(x)) + d(f(x), f(x_f))$$
$$\leq d(x, f(x)) + s\, d(x, x_f).$$

It follows that

$$d(x, x_f) \leq \frac{d(x, f(x))}{(1-s)}$$
$$\leq \frac{\varepsilon}{(1-s)}.$$

from which the Collage Theorem follows.

2.3.3 What the Collage Theorem says

Suppose we have a binary image $L \subset \mathbf{R}^2$ and suppose we can determine contraction mappings w_n so that

$$\bigcup_{n=1}^{N} w_n(L)$$

covers L without missing too much and without too much overlap. We can think of each $w_n(L)$ as a smaller copy of L. Then the Collage Theorem says that the attractor A of the IFS $\{w_n\}$ is close to L in the Hausdorff metric h. The "collage" is the collection of subimages $w_n(L)$.

Because the attractor A is the result of infinitely many iterations of the IFS, it is fractal in nature. The Collage Theorem gives us a way of representing images as fractals. Fig. 2.3.1 shows an example of this. The image in Fig. 2.3.1 (a) shows a leaf image (this is a tracing of an actual maple leaf). You can cover the leaf with four subimages, as shown. This leads to an IFS with four transformations w_1, w_2, w_3, w_4. Fig. 2.3.1 (b) shows the attractor of this IFS. Note the fractal nature of this attractor set. In the following sections, we will see how to determine the transformations w_n and how to generate the attractor.

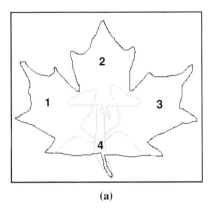 

(a)   (b)

Fig. 2.3.1 Collage Theorem example. (a) The original image and 4 subimages; (b) the attractor image.

2.3.4 Affine transformations

We need candidate transformations for contraction mappings in order to implement a practical application of the Collage Theorem for generating fractals. The transformations used by Barnsley for his IFS's are the so-called *affine transformations*. An affine transformation $T:\mathbf{R}^2 \to \mathbf{R}^2$ is a transformation of the form

$$T\begin{pmatrix} x \\ y \end{pmatrix} = \begin{pmatrix} a & b \\ c & d \end{pmatrix}\begin{pmatrix} x \\ y \end{pmatrix} + \begin{pmatrix} e \\ f \end{pmatrix}, \qquad (2.3.1)$$

where $a,b,c,d,e,f \in \mathbf{R}$. Affine transformations can accomplish rotation, translation, and contraction. Define

$$A = \begin{pmatrix} a & b \\ c & d \end{pmatrix}$$

as the matrix part of T. If S is a set of points in $\mathbf{R}^2$, then the area of the transformed set of points $T(S)$ is $|\det A|$ times the area of S, where $|\det A|$ is the absolute value of the determinant of A. Thus, T is a spatial contraction, and hence a contraction on $H(\mathbf{X})$, whenever $|\det A| < 1$. The six unknown constants (a,b,c,d,e,f) that define the transformation can be determined by specifying the action of the transformation on three points (see section 2.4.2 below). Fig. 2.3.2 shows the action of an affine transformation on a set of points in $\mathbf{R}^2$.

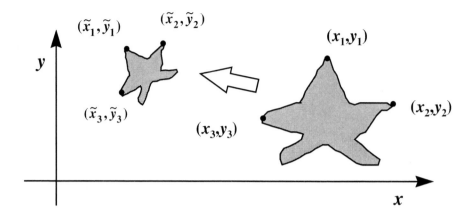

Fig. 2.3.2 An affine transformation acting on a set of points in $\mathbf{R}^2$.
This transformation maps the points $(x_i, y_i) \rightarrow (\tilde{x}_i, \tilde{y}_i)$ as shown.

Affine transformations are used in IFS systems because they are easy to specify and it is easy to compute their coefficients. However, any contractive mappings could be used to satisfy the Collage Theorem and produce IFS attractor images.

2.4 IMPLEMENTATION OF AN ITERATED FUNCTION SYSTEM

Suppose you wanted to implement a system for producing fractal images with IFS's. What would the key components of such a system be? First, you need to have in mind an image that you want to reproduce with an IFS. So, it would be helpful if your system could import existing images in some specified graphics format. Next, you'll need a way to specify points on a two-dimensional grid. You then define affine transformations by specifying three points as domain points and three points as range points. Your system would then automatically generate the affine coefficients by solving the appropriate linear equations. Finally, your system would then iterate the IFS and display the results graphically to depict the fractal attractor image. The following sections discuss some of these steps in more detail. The appendix discusses how to run the IFS software used to produce the examples shown here and also discusses the organization of the source code.

2.4.1 Points and transformations

Fig. 2.4.1 shows an example of an X-Y grid for plotting the points and transformations that define an IFS. This figure also shows the sketch of a leaf (also shown in Fig. 2.3.1 (a)) that has been imported to aid in positioning the points and transformations. The first step in producing an IFS image is to recognize at least some approximate self-similarity in the original image. In the case of the leaf image, it is not too hard to spot that the three "lobes" that make up the leaf each appear similar to the leaf itself. This gives us three candidate transformations for the IFS. Recall, however, that the Collage Theorem stipulates that the collage of subimages must come close to covering the original image. These three transformations leave a gap in covering the image. So we add a fourth transformation that covers the stem area of the leaf.

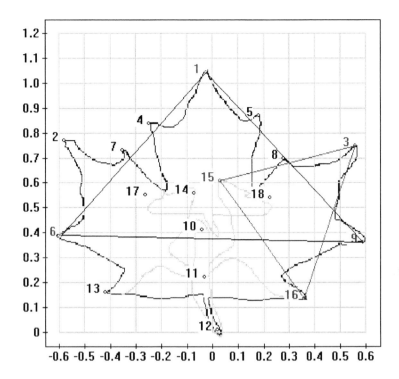

Fig. 2.4.1 X-Y grid showing imported leaf sketch with 18 points identified and one of the four transformations for the leaf IFS. This transformation maps points 1, 6, and 9 onto the points 3, 15, and 16.

Once you have an idea of what the transformations are going to be, the next step is to identify the points that will define the transformations. These points usually are associated with prominent features that identify the main image and the collage subimages. For example, the points labeled 1, 2 and 3 in Fig. 2.4.1 identify the tips of the three main lobes of the leaf, while the points 4 - 9 identify the corresponding points on each lobe. Points 10 - 12 identify the stem. Finally, the accompanying software allows you to select a color to associate with a transformation.

Trial and error is often a part of IFS image creation. The original intent with this leaf collage was to map the points 1,2,3 to the points 1,4,5 for the top lobe, 2,6,7 for the left, 3,8,9 for the right, and 11,10,12 for the stem. Fig. 2.4.2 shows the result of this choice of transformations. This choice failed to produce good coverage and, as a result, failed to produce a good IFS attractor image, as you can see from Fig. 2.4.2.

To remedy this situation, we'll use the points 1, 6, and 9 to represent the overall leaf. We now need corresponding points for the smaller lobes. These are the points 13 through 18 in Fig. 2.4.1. Note that some of these points are in the interior of the leaf, and so their exact location must be estimated. The light interior lines sketched in Fig. 2.4.1 show where smaller copies of the leaf might lie, in order to facilitate the location of the points.

Once again, trial and error is involved in deciding the exact locations. The attractor image shown in Fig. 2.3.1 (b) is the result of using the transformations {1,6,9}→{1,17,18}, {1,6,9}→{2,13,14}, {1,6,9}→{3,15,16}, and {1,6,9}→{11,12,10}.

Fig. 2.4.2 IFS attractor image formed by using the transformations {1,2,3}→{1,4,5}, {1,2,3}→{2,6,7}, {1,2,3}→{3,8,9}, {1,2,3}→{11,10,12} (numbers refer to points in Fig. 2.4.1). In this case, these transformations do not produce a good attractor image representation of the leaf. Compare with Fig. 2.3.1 (b), which was produced using the transformations {1,6,9}→{1,17,18}, {1,6,9}→{2,13,14}, {1,6,9}→{3,15,16}, and {1,6,9}→{11,12,10}.

2.4.2 Affine coefficients

Once you have determined the points and transformations for the IFS, the next step is to compute the affine coefficients. Equation (2.3.1) gives an expression for the affine transformation with coefficients $a,b,c,d,e,$ and f. Specifying the action of this transformation on three sets of points $(x_i, y_i) \rightarrow (\tilde{x}_i, \tilde{y}_i)$ leads to the following equations:

$$\tilde{x}_i = ax_i + by_i + e$$
$$\tilde{y}_i = cx_i + dy_i + f \tag{2.4.1}$$

for $i = 1, 2, 3$. Note that (2.4.1) actually decomposes into two sets of three equations. One set of equations determines the unknown coefficients a, b, and e in terms of $\tilde{x}_1, \tilde{x}_2,$ and $\tilde{x}_3$, while the other determines c, d, and f in terms of $\tilde{y}_1, \tilde{y}_2,$ and $\tilde{y}_3$. Solving each of these sets of three equations reduces to inverting the same 3×3 matrix:

$$\begin{pmatrix} x_1 & y_1 & 1 \\ x_2 & y_2 & 1 \\ x_3 & y_3 & 1 \end{pmatrix}.$$

The code in the accompanying software inverts this matrix to solve for the affine transformation coefficients.

2.4.3 Computing the fractal attractor image from the IFS

There are two algorithms for computing the fractal attractor image from the IFS. One is a straightforward application of the contraction mapping theorem, while the other is an application of the so-called "Chaos Game".

2.4.3.1 Deterministic algorithm

The deterministic algorithm for computing IFS attractor images directly applies the contraction mapping theorem to any starting image $B \in H(\mathbf{X})$. The algorithm computes a sequence of images A_n by repeatedly applying the IFS mapping $W = \{w_1, w_2, \ldots, w_N\}$:

$$A_n = W^{\circ n}(B). \tag{2.4.2}$$

Recall that the mapping W applied to the set B is defined as

$$W(B) = w_1(B) \cup w_2(B) \cup \ldots \cup w_N(B).$$

If we set $A_0 = B$, then (2.4.2) can be formulated as an iterative process:

$$A_n = W(A_{n-1}). \tag{2.4.3}$$

By the contraction mapping theorem, A_n converges to A, the attractor of the IFS.

Listing 2.4.1 shows how this iterative process is implemented in the C code in the accompanying software. (This is a partial code listing. Refer to the source code with the accompanying software for complete variable, structure and function definitions.) Two arrays, `old_image` and `new_image`, are set up to hold the binary images that result from the iterations. The array `old_image` corresponds to A_{n-1} in (2.4.3) and `new_image` corresponds to A_n. Each of these arrays consists of 1's and 0's, with a 1 indicating a pixel of the binary image. Each of these arrays has been dynamically allocated to match the display window size: `nrows` × `ncols`. In order to operate on this image with the IFS, we need to translate from the image array to the X-Y plane. This plane is nothing more than the X-Y grid shown in Fig. 2.4.1.

Fig. 2.4.3 shows how the iterative process works. Each nonzero element of the `old_image` array is mapped to a point (x, y) in the X-Y plane. Each affine transformation of the IFS then operates on this point. The number of transformation functions is denoted `no_of_fns` in the code. `coeff_list` is a list of pointers each of which points to a structure `coeff_struct`, which contains the affine coefficients. The new point (xnew,ynew) is plotted in the display window using the function `xy_to_window_color`, using the color that was chosen when that transformation was constructed. The point (xnew,ynew) is then mapped back into the `new_image` array. To complete the iteration, the array `new_image` is copied into `old_image`, new_image is reset to zero, and the next iteration begins. Iterations end when the user activates termininating_proc, which captures mouse clicks or the "escape" key.

Listing 2.4.1 Code sample implementing the deterministic IFS algorithm. On each iteration, the IFS is applied to the array `old_image` (which consists of 1's and 0's) to set the values in the array `new_image`. The array `new_image` is then plotted to the window, using the color stored with the IFS transformation. To complete one iteration, the values from `new_image` are moved to `old_image`, and `new_image` is reset back to 0.

```
iter = 0;
do {
        // If clear_scr flag is set, clear the window between
        // iterations. The structures gr_setup and gr contain
        // window graphics parameters.
        if (clear_scr)
            draw_border(gr_setup,gr,CLEAR_WINDOW);
        iter++;
        for (i=1;i<=nrows;i++)
            for (j=1;j<=ncols;j++)
            if (old_image[i][j]) {
                // Map the old image array to the virtual X-Y
                // plane:
                // Map 1 to x_min and ncols to x_max:
                x =  ((float)(j-1)/(float)(ncols-1))*x_range +
                    gr_setup->x_min;
                // Map nrows to y_min and 1 to y_max:
                y =  ((float)(nrows - i)/
                    (float)(nrows-1))*y_range +
                    gr_setup->y_min;
                // Loop through all the transformations
                // (no_of_fns) in the IFS:
                for (k = 1;k<=no_of_fns;k++) {
                    ifs = *(coeff_struct *)(coeff_list->at(k));
                    xnew = ifs.a*x + ifs.b*y + ifs.e;
                    ynew = ifs.c*x + ifs.d*y + ifs.f;
                    if (fabs(xnew) + fabs(ynew) > IFS_TOO_BIG) {
                        message_puts (MB_EXCLAIM,"IFSPROC",
                        "This system diverges!\r\n"
                        "Check to see that all
                         transformations\r\n"
                        "are contractions.");
                        goto exit_proc;
                        } // end if
                // Map the virtual X-Y plane back to the new
                // image array:
                // Map x_min to 1 and x_max to ncols:
                col = ((xnew - gr_setup->x_min)/x_range)*
                            (ncols-1) + 1;
                // Map y_min to nrows and y_max to 1:
                row = nrows -((ynew - gr_setup->y_min)
                        /y_range)*(nrows-1);
                new_image[row][col] = 1;
                // Plot the X-Y point in the window in color:
                xy_to_window_color (gr,xnew,ynew,
```

```
                    rgb_ifs_color (ifs));
            } // end k
    } // end if, i, j
    // Move new_image to old_image, and reset new_image:
    for (i=1;i<=nrows;i++)
        for (j=1;j<=ncols;j++) {
            old_image[i][j] = new_image[i][j];
            new_image[i][j] = 0;
            }
} while (!terminating_proc());
```

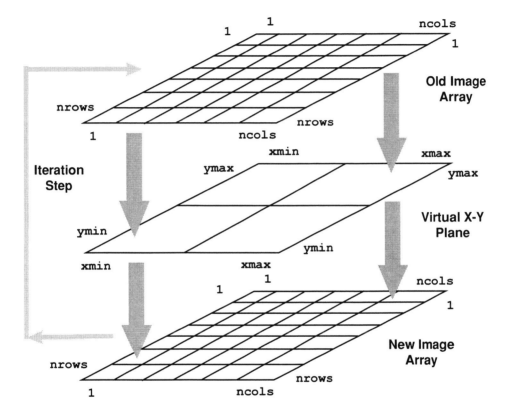

Fig. 2.4.3 Conceptualization of the relationship between the image arrays in the code and the virtual X-Y plane where the IFS operates. The image arrays consist of 1's and 0's, with a 1 indicating a point in the binary image. Each nonzero element of the "old image" is mapped onto the X-Y plane. The IFS operates on this point, producing, in general, N new points. These new points are then mapped back into the "new image" array. At the conclusion of each iteration, the "new image" array is loaded into the "old image" array, in preparation for the next iteration.

Fig. 2.4.4 shows the result of using the deterministic algorithm to compute the attractor image associated with a fern IFS consisting of 4 affine transformations. The figures (a) - (d) show the image A_n of equation (2.4.3) after, respectively, 2, 3, 10 and 30 iterations.

Fig. 2.4.5 shows the same IFS using a circle as the starting image. As we would expect from the contraction mapping theorem, the attractor image is the same in both cases.

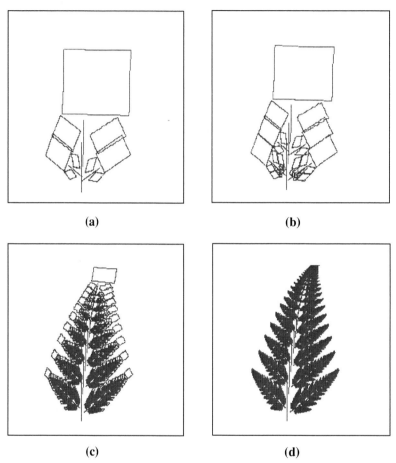

(a)   (b)

(c)   (d)

Fig. 2.4.4 The deterministic algorithm applied to a fern IFS with 4 affine transformations. The starting image in this case was a rectangle. These figures show the image A_n of equation (2.4.3) after: (a) 2 iterations; (b) 3 iterations; (c) 10 iterations; (d) 30 iterations.

From a pedagogical point of view, the deterministic algorithm is useful because it allows one to see the effect of the IFS transformations at each iteration. You can see the contraction mapping theorem in action and gain an understanding of how it works in the context of the IFS transformations acting on an image. However, from the practical point of view of producing high quality IFS attractor images, this is not the most efficient algorithm. The next section examines an alternative algorithm that is faster, easier to implement, and produces higher quality images.

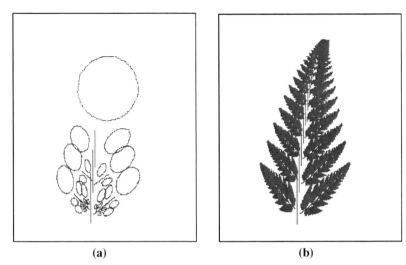

(a)   (b)

Fig. 2.4.5 Same IFS as in Fig. 2.4.4, but using a circle as the starting image. These figures show A_n after: (a) 3 iterations; (b) 30 iterations.

2.4.3.2 Random algorithm

While the deterministic algorithm provides a straightforward connection to the contraction mapping theorem, making it easy to see how this algorithm works, in practice this algorithm is too slow and is not the usual choice for displaying IFS attractor images. Instead, a random algorithm based on the "Chaos Game" is the preferred choice (see (Peitgen and Saupe 1988, Chapter 5) for a discussion of how to play the "Chaos Game").

The random algorithm assigns a probability p_i to each affine transformation w_i in the IFS. These probabilities determine how densely each part of the attractor image is covered in points. Recall from the Collage Theorem that the affine transformations are chosen according to how well they cover the desired image with smaller copies of the image itself. Thus, in some sense, each affine transformation controls a part of the image. If we want the attractor image uniformly covered by randomly generated points, that is, if we don't want one part of the image denser than others, then the probability associated with each transformation should be proportional to the area of the part of the image controlled by that transformation. That is what the code in Listing 2.4.2 does.

Recall that the area of the part of the image controlled by an affine transformation is proportional to the determinant of the matrix part of the transformation. The code in Listing 2.4.2 computes this determinant for each of the IFS transformations. The determinants are summed, and each value divided by the sum to get a true probability between 0 and 1 for each transformation. This also ensures that the probabilities sum to 1. You can modify this code to experiment with non-uniform distributions for different parts of the attractor image.

Once the probabilities p_i have been assigned to the IFS transformations w_i, $i = 1,...,N$, the random algorithm begins by picking an arbitrary point $x_0 = (x_0, y_0) \in \mathbf{R}^2$. The algorithm then computes x_1 by randomly selecting the integer $i(0)$ from the set $\{1,\ldots,N\}$ with probability $p_{i(0)}$, and applying the transformation $w_{i(0)}$ to x_0:

$$x_1 = w_{i(0)}(x_0).$$

In this way, the algorithm computes a sequence

$$x_0, x_1, x_2, \ldots$$

where

$$x_n = w_{i(n)}(x_{n-1}), \, n = 1,2,\ldots$$

where, at each step, $i(n) \in \{1,\ldots,N\}$ is chosen with probability $p_{i(n)}$. Note that

$$x_n \in A_n = W^{\circ n}(A_0) \tag{2.4.4}$$

for some starting set A_0. It doesn't really matter what set A_0 is, since the contraction mapping theorem guarantees that the iterations will converge for any starting set. All we know about A_0 is that x_0 belongs to it. The sequence of points $\{x_n\}$ forms what is called the *orbit*, or *trajectory*, of a dynamical system. The computer implementation of the random algorithm, shown in Listing 2.4.3, plots this orbit. Note that the first 10 or so points (this number is arbitrary) are "buried" (not plotted).

The random algorithm produces higher quality IFS attractor images much more quickly than the deterministic algorithm. This is due to the fact that not only does this algorithm do less work per iteration than the deterministic algorithm, but the work it does produces higher quality output. The deterministic algorithm plots the entire set A_n at each iteration n. Consider the images shown in Figs. 2.4.4 (d) and 2.4.5 (b). All of the points in these images represent the set A_{30}, that is, the set produced after 30 iterations (with different starting images). The random algorithm, on the other hand, plots only the single point x_n at iteration n, and so it can literally do thousands of iterations in the time it takes the deterministic algorithm to do one iteration. But there is an added bonus as well. The point x_n belongs to the set A_n, as indicated by equation (2.4.4). So, for example, if n is 30,000, then x_n belongs to $A_{30,000}$. The significance of this is that $A_{30,000}$ is much closer to the true attractor of the IFS than A_{30} is. Collectively, the points $\ldots, x_{n-1}, x_n, x_{n+1},\ldots$ produce an image closer to the true IFS attractor. Fig. 2.4.6 shows the result of running the random algorithm on the same fern IFS that produced the images in Figs. 2.4.4 -2.4.5. This image was produced using over 31,000 iterations, which took only a few seconds on a Pentium-class personal computer.

Fig. 2.4.6 The fern IFS attractor rendered with the random algorithm, using over 31,000 iterations. This is the same IFS used to produce the images in Figs. 2.4.4-2.4.5.

Listing 2.4.2 Code sample to compute probabilities associated with IFS for the random algorithm. Each probability is proportional to the determinant of the matrix part of the affine transformation. This determinant, in turn, is proportional to the area controlled by that transformation. You can modify this code to experiment with non-uniform distributions for different parts of the attractor image.

```
int compute_ifs_probabilities (object_list *coeff_list) {
    int i,no_of_fns = coeff_list->get_count();
    float *pr = NULL,*det_a = NULL;
        // allocated 1..no_of_fns
    float sum = 0.0,pr_sum = 0.0;
    coeff_struct ifs;

    if (!(det_a = allocate_f_vector (1,no_of_fns)))
        return 0;
    if (!(pr = allocate_f_vector (1,no_of_fns))) {
        free_f_vector (det_a,1);
        return 0;
    }

    for (i=1;i<=no_of_fns;i++) {
            ifs = *(coeff_struct *)(coeff_list->at(i));
            det_a [i] = fabs (ifs.a*ifs.d - ifs.b*ifs.c);
            sum += det_a[i];
            } /* i */
```

```
    for (i=1;i<=no_of_fns;i++) {
           pr[i] = det_a[i] / sum;
           if (pr[i] < 0.01) pr[i] = 0.01;
           pr_sum += pr[i];
           }
    free_f_vector (det_a,1);
    /*adjust pr values to get true probabilities */
    for (i=1;i<=no_of_fns;i++) {
           pr[i] /= pr_sum;
           ((coeff_struct *)(coeff_list->at(i)))->
           prob = pr[i];
       }

    free_f_vector (pr,1);
    return 1;
    }
```

Listing 2.4.3 Code sample implementing the random IFS algorithm. This algorithm is simpler to implement and faster than the deterministic algorithm, and it produces higher quality images.

```
void ifs_random_image_graph (graph_setup_rec *gr_setup,
    graph_window_struct *gr,object_list *coeff_list,
    term_proc terminating_proc) {

    int i,k;
    int no_of_fns = coeff_list->get_count();
    int *p = NULL,*pi = NULL;  /* allocated 1..no_of_fns  */
    coeff_struct ifs;

    int int_sum = 0;
    float x,y,xnew,ynew;
    unsigned long iter;

    if (!(p = allocate_int_vector (1,no_of_fns))) return;
    if (!(pi = allocate_int_vector (1,no_of_fns)))
           goto exit_proc;

    if (!compute_ifs_probabilities (coeff_list)) {
       free_int_vector (p,1);
       free_int_vector (pi,1);
       return;
       }

    for (i=1;i<=no_of_fns;i++)
           pi[i] =
       (int)(((coeff_struct *)(coeff_list->at(i)))->
           prob*MAX_INT);

    for (i=1;i<=no_of_fns;i++) {
           p[i] = int_sum + pi[i];
           int_sum += pi[i];
```

```
                     } /* i */
      p[no_of_fns] = MAX_INT;

      free_int_vector (pi,1);
      x = 0;
      y = 0;
      /* bury first 10 iterations */
      for (i=1;i<=10;i++) {
              k = pick_random_nbr (p,no_of_fns);
              ifs = *(coeff_struct *)(coeff_list->at(k));
              xnew = ifs.a*x + ifs.b*y + ifs.e;
              ynew = ifs.c*x + ifs.d*y + ifs.f;
              x = xnew;
              y = ynew;
              }   /* i */

      if (!graph_setup (gr)) /* free arrays before returning*/
         goto exit_proc;
      draw_border(gr_setup,gr,1);
      set_graph_max_min (gr_setup,gr);

      iter = 0;
      do {
              k = pick_random_nbr (p,no_of_fns);
              ifs = *(coeff_struct *)(coeff_list->at(k));
              xnew = ifs.a*x + ifs.b*y + ifs.e;
              ynew = ifs.c*x + ifs.d*y + ifs.f;

              if (fabs(xnew) + fabs(ynew) > IFS_TOO_BIG) {
                  message_puts (MB_EXCLAIM,"IFSPROC",
                  "This system diverges!\r\n"
                  "Check to see that all transformations\r\n"
                  "are contractions.");
                  goto exit_proc;
              }
              /* Plot the X-Y point in the window in color: */
              xy_to_window_color (gr,xnew,ynew,
                  rgb_ifs_color (ifs));
              x = xnew;
              y = ynew;
              iter++;
              graph_iter (gr_setup,gr,iter);
              } while (!terminating_proc());

exit_proc:
        release_dc (gr);
        free_int_vector (p,1);
        return;
        }  /* end proc */
```

2.5 EXAMPLES

We close this chapter with some examples of iterated function systems and their associated attractor images. All of the images in this section were produced using the random algorithm.

2.5.1 Sierpinski triangle

The Sierpinski triangle (also called the Sierpinski arrowhead or gasket) is one of the earliest known examples of a fractal. There are several ways of constructing a Sierpinski triangle, one of which is shown in Fig. 2.5.1. We start with a solid triangle, as shown on the left. Step 1 of the construction removes an inverted triangle from the center, as shown in the center figure. Step 2 removes 3 inverted triangles from the remaining 3 triangles, as shown in the rightmost figure. This process continues, at step n removing 3^{n-1} inverted triangles from the centers of 3^{n-1} remaining triangles. What remains (and something does remain!) is the Sierpinski triangle.

Fig. 2.5.1 The Sierpinski triangle can be constructed by starting with a triangle (left) and removing an inverted triangle from its center (center), then removing inverted triangles from the centers of the three remaining triangles (right), and continuing this process indefinitely.

The Sierpinski triangle is also easy to construct as the attractor of an IFS. Fig. 2.5.2 shows the IFS transformations and the attractor image. There are 3 transformations in the IFS: $\{1,4,3\} \rightarrow \{9,10,12\}$, $\{1,4,3\} \rightarrow \{5,4,7\}$, $\{1,4,3\} \rightarrow \{6,7,3\}$. It is easy to compute the actual affine coefficients in this case also. The transformations are:

$$T_1\begin{pmatrix} x \\ y \end{pmatrix} = \begin{pmatrix} 0.5 & 0 \\ 0 & 0.5 \end{pmatrix}\begin{pmatrix} x \\ y \end{pmatrix} + \begin{pmatrix} 0 \\ 0.5 \end{pmatrix}$$

$$T_2\begin{pmatrix} x \\ y \end{pmatrix} = \begin{pmatrix} 0.5 & 0 \\ 0 & 0.5 \end{pmatrix}\begin{pmatrix} x \\ y \end{pmatrix} + \begin{pmatrix} -0.25 \\ 0 \end{pmatrix}$$

$$T_3\begin{pmatrix} x \\ y \end{pmatrix} = \begin{pmatrix} 0.5 & 0 \\ 0 & 0.5 \end{pmatrix}\begin{pmatrix} x \\ y \end{pmatrix} + \begin{pmatrix} 0.25 \\ 0 \end{pmatrix}$$

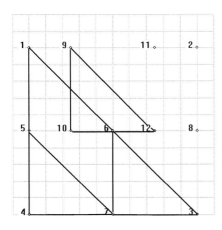 

Fig. 2.5.2 The transformations for the Sierpinski triangle IFS (left) and the attractor image (right). The three transformations are: {1,4,3}→{9,10,12}, {1,4,3}→{5,4,7}, {1,4,3}→{6,7,3}.

The Sierpinski triangle provides a good example of the two hallmarks of a fractal: self-similarity and non-integer dimension. The self-similarity is evident from the construction. To see why it makes sense to assign a non-integer dimension to this object, consider the following.

2.5.1.1 Fractal dimension

What do we mean by "dimension"? Intuitively, we know that a line has dimension 1, a solid square has dimension 2, and a solid cube has dimension 3. Is there a way to compute these numbers? Consider the situation shown in Fig. 2.5.3. Suppose we wish to cover a square S of side length 1 with smaller square blocks. It takes 1 block of side length 1 to cover the original square, $2^2 = 4$ blocks of side length 1/2, $3^2 = 9$ blocks of side length 1/3, and so on. Let $N_S(1/n)$ denote the number of blocks of side length $1/n$ required to cover the square. It is easy to see that

$$N_S(1/n) = n^2.$$

The dimension of the square, which we know to be 2, lurks as the exponent on the right side of this equation. We can extract the dimension as:

$$d = 2 = \ln(N_S(1/n))/\ln(n). \tag{2.5.1}$$

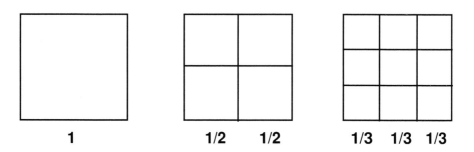

Fig. 2.5.3 A square of side length 1 requires 1 block of side length 1 to cover, $2^2 = 4$ blocks of side length 1/2, and $3^2 = 9$ blocks of side length 1/3.

Note that the left side of (2.5.1) is independent of $n > 1$, so the right side must be also. In particular, for a set A, we can define its dimension d_A to be:

$$d_A \equiv \lim_{n \to \infty} \frac{\ln(N_A(1/n))}{\ln(n)}, \qquad (2.5.2)$$

where $N_A(1/n)$ is the number of blocks of side length $1/n$ needed to cover the set A.

We can apply this definition to the Sierpinski triangle S. As Fig. 2.5.4 shows, 3 blocks of side length 1/2 are needed to cover S (assuming without loss of generality a side length of 1 for S), and $9 = 3^2$ blocks of side length $1/4 = 1/2^2$ are needed. In general,

$$N_S(1/2^n) = 3^n,$$

where $N_S(1/2^n)$ is the number of blocks of side length $1/2^n$ needed to cover S. Thus the dimension d_S of S is:

$$d_S = \lim_{n \to \infty} \frac{\ln(3^n)}{\ln(2^n)} = \frac{\ln(3)}{\ln(2)}.$$

That is, the dimension of S not only is not an integer, but is an irrational number, approximately equal to 1.58. Clearly S is a fractal object.

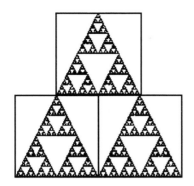 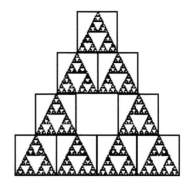

Fig. 2.5.4 The Sierpinski triangle S of side length 1 requires 3 blocks of side length 1/2 to cover, and $9 = 3^2$ blocks of side length $1/4 = 1/2^2$ to cover. The dimension of S is $\ln(3)/\ln(2) = 1.58....$

2.5.2 Constructing an IFS from a real image

While the fractal fern, such as that shown in Fig. 2.1.1 (a), is reminiscent of a real fern, it is unlike any fern actually occurring in nature. For one thing, it has infinitely many leaves, and each leaf has infinite detail. Fig. 2.5.5 (a) is a digital photograph of a real plant (though not a fern), with finitely many leaves. We can construct an IFS attractor image that approximates this image, but it will require more transformations than the fern. It is interesting to note that there is apparently an inverse relationship between image complexity and complexity of the transformations. Is there a connection between this observation and the fact that ferns were one of the earliest plants to evolve?

To obtain an IFS attractor representation of the plant in Fig. 2.5.5 (a), we'll need a transformation for each leaf. This image is a good candidate for an IFS representation because each leaf resembles the entire plant in miniature. Fig. 2.5.5 (b) shows the plant image imported into the grid layout in the accompanying software. The plant has 11 leaves, and we'll need one transformation for each of these. Each leaf is identified by three points, for a total of 33 points needed for the leaf transformations. In addition, there are three transformations that define segments of the curving stem. These require 7 additional points (two of these are used twice), for a grand total of 40 points and 14 transformations. Fig. 2.5.5 (b) shows the point labels and one of the leaf transformations (note that the points 1,2,3 identify the entire plant). Fig. 2.5.6 shows the resulting IFS attractor image. This exercise can be viewed as a crude form of image compression. However, as mentioned at the beginning of this chapter, while IFS techniques may have been the motivation for fractal image compression, the mechanisms by which fractal image compression is now practiced bear little resemblance to the process we just went through here. The next chapter will explore more practical methods for implementing fractal techniques for image compression.

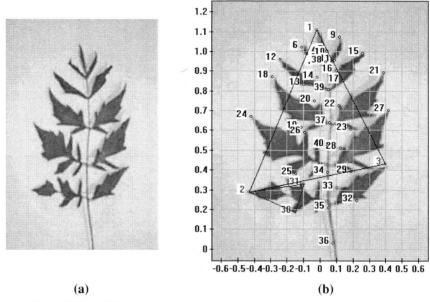

(a)   (b)

Fig. 2.5.5 (a) Digital photograph of a leaf. (b) Points and one IFS transformation superimposed on the image.

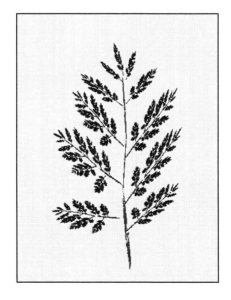

Fig. 2.5.6 The IFS attractor image, constructed with 40 points and 14 transformations. This is a crude example of compression of the image in Fig. 2.5.5 (a).

2.5.3 A few more IFS examples

We close this chapter with a look at a few more examples of IFS images, shown in Figs. 2.5.7 through 2.5.10.

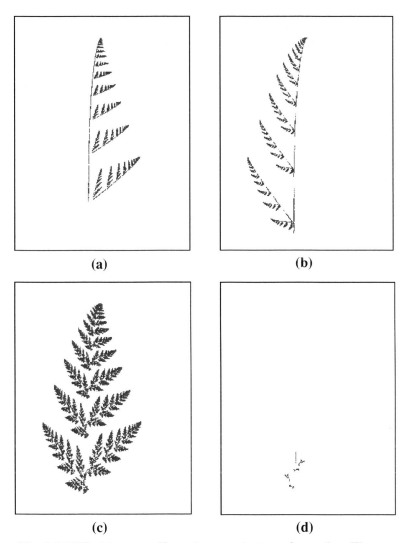

(a)   (b)

(c)   (d)

Fig. 2.5.7 What happens if you leave out a transformation. Figures (a) - (d) show what happens if you leave out one of the four transformations used to construct the fern IFS attractor shown in Fig. 2.1.1 (a). Each of the figures shown here was constructed using just three of the four transformations. Can you guess which transformation was left out of which figure?

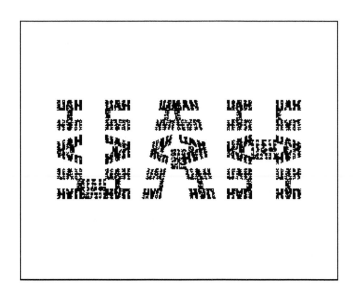

Fig. 2.5.8 "Block UAH" (for University of Alabama in Huntsville!)
IFS. This IFS was constructed using 9 transformations and 25
points. One of the transformations is shown in Fig. 2.5.9. Can you
find the others?

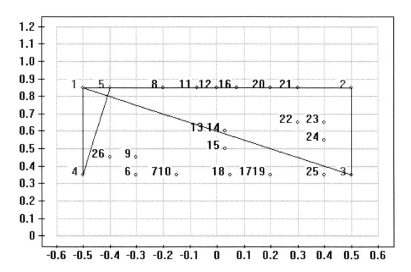

Fig. 2.5.9 One of the transformations used to construct the "Block
UAH" IFS shown in Fig. 2.5.8. This transformation maps the points
1,2,3 to 4,1,5. Note that the ordering of the points affects the
orientation of the subimage.

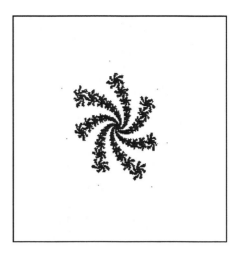

Fig. 2.5.10 A spiral IFS. This IFS was created with just 9 points and two transformations. Can you find them? This is another example of very simple transformations leading to a complex attractor image.

3

FRACTAL ENCODING OF GRAYSCALE IMAGES

An image such as the fractal fern of the previous chapter can be reproduced with a relatively simple iterated function system (IFS) because this type of image has the property of global self-similarity. That is, the entire image is made up of smaller copies of itself, or parts of itself. If one zooms in on this type of image, it will display the same level of detail, regardless of the resolution scale. Also, this type of image is a binary image, that is, each of its pixels can be represented with either a 1 or a 0. Real-world images do not exhibit the type of global self-similarity present in the IFS images of the previous chapter. Moreover, real-world images are not binary, but rather each pixel belongs to a range of values (grayscale) or a vector of values (color). If we are going to represent such an image as the attractor of an iterated system, then clearly we need a more general system than the IFS's of the previous chapter. This chapter examines the development and implementation of such a system that can be used for the fractal encoding of general grayscale images.

3.1 A METRIC SPACE FOR GRAYSCALE IMAGES

As mentioned in Chapter 1, we can consider grayscale images as real-valued functions $f(x,y)$ defined on the unit square $\mathbf{I}^2 = \mathbf{I} \times \mathbf{I}$. That is,

$$f: \mathbf{I}^2 \to \{1,2,\ldots,N\} \subset \mathbf{R},$$

where N is the number of grayscale levels. We can define a metric $d_2(\ ,\ )$ on these functions as:

$$d_2(f,g) = \left(\int_{\mathbf{I}^2} |f(x,y) - g(x,y)|^2 \, dxdy \right)^{1/2}. \tag{3.1.1}$$

Define $\mathbf{F}$ as the space of real-valued square-integrable functions on $\mathbf{I}^2$ with this metric. Then $\mathbf{F}$ is complete and the contraction mapping theorem holds.

In practice, the images we will work with are digital images. An $n \times m$ digital image is a matrix of values $[f_{i,j}]$, $i = 1,\ldots,n$, $j = 1,\ldots,m$, where $f_{i,j} = f(x_i,y_j)$. That is, a digital image is a matrix of sampled values of $f(x,y)$, taken at sample points (x_i,y_j). In this case, the metric is called the *rms* (root mean square) metric:

$$d_{rms}(f,g) = \left(\sum_{i=1}^{n} \sum_{j=1}^{m} |f(x_i,y_j) - g(x_i,y_j)|^2 \right)^{1/2}. \tag{3.1.2}$$

3.2 PARTITIONED ITERATED FUNCTION SYSTEMS (PIFS)

Fractal image compression uses a special type of IFS called a *partitioned iterated function system* (PIFS). A PIFS consists of a complete metric space $\mathbf{X}$, a collection of sub-domains $D_i \subset \mathbf{X}$, $i = 1,\dots,n$, and a collection of contractive mappings $\widetilde{w}_i : D_i \to \mathbf{X}$, $i = 1,\dots,n$. (Fig. 3.2.1)

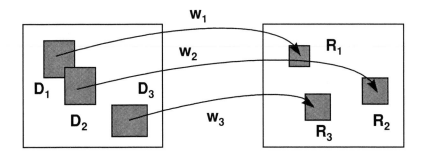

Fig. 3.2.1 A partitioned iterated function system.

3.2.1 Affine transformations on grayscale images

Let $\widetilde{w}_i(x, y)$ be an affine transformation on $\mathbf{I}^2 \to \mathbf{I}^2$, that is,

$$\widetilde{w}_i(x, y) = \mathbf{A}_i \begin{pmatrix} x \\ y \end{pmatrix} + \mathbf{b}_i \qquad (3.2.1)$$

for some 2×2 matrix $\mathbf{A}_i$ and 2×1 vector $\mathbf{b}_i$. Let $D_i \subset \mathbf{I}^2$ be some subdomain of the unit square $\mathbf{I}^2$, and let R_i be the range of $\widetilde{w}_i$ operating on D_i, that is, $\widetilde{w}_i(D_i) = R_i$ (see Fig. 3.2.2). We can now define $w_i : \mathbf{F} \to \mathbf{F}$ operating on images $f(x,y)$ by

$$w_i(f)(x,y) = s_i f(\widetilde{w}_i^{-1}(x,y)) + o_i \qquad (3.2.2)$$

provided $\widetilde{w}_i$ is invertible and $(x,y) \in R_i$. The constant s_i expands or contracts the range of values of f, and so, in the context of grayscale images, it controls *contrast*. Similarly, the constant o_i raises or lowers the grayscale values, and so controls *brightness*. The transformation $\widetilde{w}_i$ is called the *spatial* part of w_i.

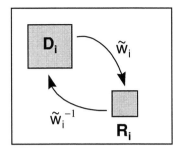

Fig. 3.2.2 Spatial affine transformation and its inverse.

Transformations of the form (3.2.2) are the basic affine transformations on grayscale images that we will use in fractal image encoding.

3.2.2 Contraction mappings on grayscale images

When is $w_i: \mathbf{F} \to \mathbf{F}$ a contraction? We need

$$d_2(w_i(f), w_i(g)) \le s\, d_2(f,g)$$

for some s, $0 < s < 1$, where d_2 is the metric given by (3.1.1). Using the formula for change of variables in a multiple integral, we have

$$d_2^2(w_i(f), w_i(g)) = \int_{w_i(D_i)} \left| w_i(f)(x,y) - w_i(g)(x,y) \right|^2 dx\,dy$$

$$= |s_i|^2 \left| \det \mathbf{A}_i \right| \int_{D_i} \left| f(x,y) - g(x,y) \right|^2 dx\,dy$$

$$\le |s_i|^2 \left| \det \mathbf{A}_i \right| d_2^2(f,g),$$

where $\mathbf{A}_i$ is the matrix part of w_i, $\det \mathbf{A}_i$ is the determinant of $\mathbf{A}_i$, and s_i is the contrast factor. In order for w_i to be a contraction, it suffices to have

$$|s_i| \sqrt{\left| \det \mathbf{A}_i \right|} \; < \; 1. \tag{3.2.3}$$

In particular, the contrast factor s_i can be greater than 1 in magnitude, provided the spatial part of w_i is a contraction with a sufficiently small contractivity factor so that (3.2.3) holds.

3.2.3 Contraction mapping theorem for grayscale images

Partition the unit square $\mathbf{I}^2$ into a collection of range cells $\{R_i\}$ that *tile* $\mathbf{I}^2$:

$$\mathbf{I}^2 = \bigcup R_i \, ,$$

$$R_i \cap R_j = \varnothing \, .$$

Let $\{\widetilde{w}_i\}$ be a PIFS such that

$$\widetilde{w}_i : D_i \to R_i$$

for some collection of domains $D_i \subset \mathbf{I}^2$ (the D_i's may overlap, and need not cover $\mathbf{I}^2$). Fig. 3.2.3 shows this configuration.

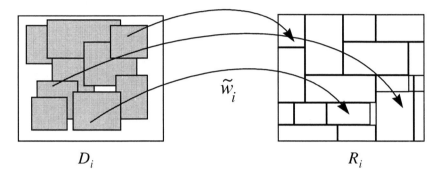

Fig. 3.2.3 Transformation $\widetilde{w}_i$ maps domain D_i to range R_i. The domains may overlap, while the ranges tile the unit square.

For each $\widetilde{w}_i$, define a corresponding contractive w_i on the image space $\mathbf{F}$:

$$w_i(f)(x,y) = s_i f(\widetilde{w}_i^{-1}(x,y)) + o_i,$$

choosing s_i so that w_i is contractive. Now define $W: \mathbf{F} \to \mathbf{F}$ by

$$W(f)(x,y) = w_i(f)(x,y) \text{ for } (x,y) \in R_i.$$

Since the ranges R_i tile $\mathbf{I}^2$, W is defined for all (x,y) in $\mathbf{I}^2$, so $W(f)$ is an image. Since each w_i is a contraction, W is a contraction on $\mathbf{F}$. Therefore, by the Contraction Mapping Theorem, W has a unique fixed point $f_W \in \mathbf{F}$ satisfying

$$W(f_W) = f_W.$$

Iteratively applying W to any starting image f_0 will recover the fixed point f_W :

$$W^{\circ n}(f_0) \to f_W \, , \text{ as } n \to \infty,$$

where $W^{\circ n}(f_0)$ is $W(W(\ldots W(f_0)))$ (n times). Fig. 3.2.4 shows the result of applying a contractive mapping W to two different starting images. The mapping W used in this figure was obtained through the fractal image encoding techniques described below.

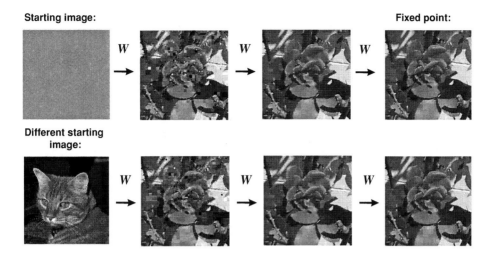

Fig. 3.2.4 The Contraction Mapping Theorem applied to grayscale images. In this example, *W* is a contractive mapping applied iteratively to two different images. Regardless of the starting image, the iterations converge to the same fixed point image.

The Contraction Mapping Theorem is the basis for all fractal image encoding techniques: Given a grayscale image f, try to find a contraction mapping W such that f_W, the fixed point of W, is close to f. W then contains all of the information needed to recover f_W. If you can store W in less space than is needed to store f, then you have achieved image compression.

3.2.4 Collage Theorem for grayscale images

As was the case for IFS's and binary images, there is a Collage Theorem for PIFS's and grayscale images. Given a grayscale image f, suppose we can find a contractive transformation W such that

$$d_2(f, W(f)) \leq \varepsilon.$$

Then

$$d_2(f, f_W) \leq \frac{\varepsilon}{1-s}, \qquad (3.2.4)$$

where s is the contractivity factor of W, and f_W is its fixed point. This means we can start with any image g and iterate W on g to get an image that is close to f:

$$W^{\circ n}(g) \to f_W \approx f.$$

While the Contraction Mapping Theorem provides the justification for fractal image encoding, the Collage Theorem actually gives us a substantial clue as to how to implement the process. Rather than having to worry about what an infinite number of iterations applied to a given image looks like, we only need to find a W such that *one application* of W, namely the image $W(f)$, is close to the desired image f. Note that W must be contractive, with contractivity factor s significantly less than 1, otherwise the bound on the right side of the inequality (3.2.4) will not be meaningful.

The Collage Theorem brings us one step closer to a procedure for fractal image encoding. Given a grayscale image f, try to find a contractive W such that $W(f)$, hence f_W, is close to f. Decoding consists of iterating W on any starting image g to recover f_W.

3.3 FRACTAL IMAGE ENCODING

As Fig. 3.3.1 shows, fractal image encoding attempts to find a set of contractive transformations that map (possibly overlapping) domain cells onto a set of range cells that tile the image. The range cells may be of uniform size, but more commonly some type of adaptive variable sizing is used. The range cells shown on the right in this figure are the result of a quadtree partitioning scheme.

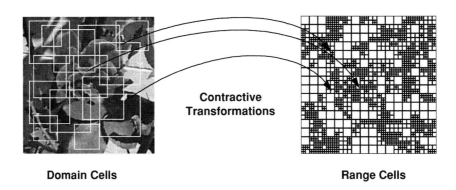

Contractive Transformations

Domain Cells   **Range Cells**

Fig. 3.3.1 Fractal image encoding attempts to find a set of contractive transformations that map (possibly overlapping) domain cells onto a set of range cells that tile the image.

The basic algorithm for fractal image encoding proceeds as follows:

   1. Partition the image f into non-overlapping range cells $\{R_i\}$. In the examples we will look at here, the range cells R_i are rectangles, however, other shapes such as triangles, may also be used. The R_i may be of equal size, but more commonly some type of adaptive variable sizing is used. This allows a concentration of small range cells in parts of the image that contain detail. One common type of adaptive partitioning scheme which we will examine below is *quadtree partitioning*, as described in Fisher (1995).

   2. Cover the image with a sequence of possibly overlapping domain cells. The domains occur in a variety of sizes, and there typically may be hundreds or thousands of domain cells. The next section discusses a scheme for constructing the set of domain cells.

3. For each range cell, find the domain and corresponding transformation that best cover the range cell. The transformations are typically affine transformations of the form (3.2.2). Adjust the transformation parameters, such as contrast and brightness, for best fit.

4. If the fit is not good enough, subdivide the range cell into smaller range cells. Continue this process until either the fit is within tolerance, or the range subdivision has reached some preset limit.

Fig. 3.3.2 shows a block diagram of the fractal encoding process, as it is implemented in the accompanying software. Note that there is an option to search for best domain. If this option is selected, the search will continue even if a domain-range match is found within the error tolerance. If this option is not selected, the domain search ends as soon as a match within tolerance is found. Not selecting this option results in faster encoding, with a small cost in decoded image quality.

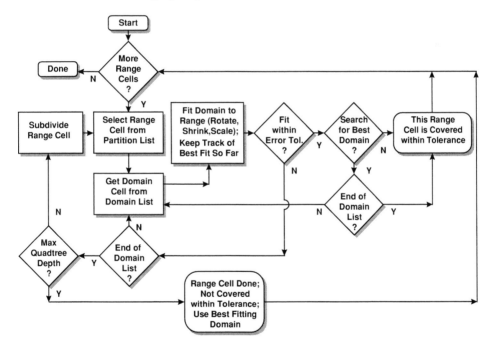

Fig. 3.3.2 Flow diagram showing the main steps in fractal image encoding, as implemented in the accompanying software.

When fitting a domain cell to a range cell, the accompanying software implements the spatial part of the affine transformation, denoted $\widetilde{w}_i$ in (3.2.2), with the operations of translation, rotation, and shrinking. Shrinking reduces the size of the domain cell to the size of the range cell. This operation is accomplished with a simple averaging across rows and columns.

The details of fractal image encoding vary with different implementations. Some range partitioning schemes, as mentioned, use non-rectangular cells, with the most common alternative choice being triangles. This can help alleviate some of the blocking artifacts present in decoded images originating from rectangular range cells. Non-affine transformations have also been investigated (Popescu, Dimca, and Yan 1997). The spatial part of the grayscale affine transformation, namely $\widetilde{w}_i$ given by (3.2.1), provides spatial contraction if $|\det \mathbf{A}_i| < 1$. We will limit the choices for $\widetilde{w}_i$ to spatial contractions with rigid translation and one of eight basic rotations and reflections, as described in Fisher (1995).

Step #3 is the most computationally intensive. For each range cell R_i, the algorithm attempts to find the domain D_i, the spatial transformation $\widetilde{w}_i$, the contrast s_i and brightness o_i such that $w_i(f)$ is close to the image f on R_i. That is, we want to find w_i such that the quantity

$$\int_{R_i} \left| w_i(f)(x,y) - f(x,y) \right|^2 dxdy \qquad (3.3.1)$$

is small. For a digitized image, the integral in (3.3.1) represents a summation over pixels. If the quantity (3.3.1) is not less than some preset tolerance after the best w_i has been found, then the adaptive range cell scheme subdivides the range into smaller range cells, and the search for an optimal transformation is repeated on these smaller ranges. This process continues until the quantity (3.3.1) can be brought within tolerance or until the maximum preset range cell subdivision has been reached.

One of the main problems with fractal image encoding is that the large numbers of domains and ranges lead to long encoding times. Recent research has focused on this difficulty, and we will investigate in the next chapter some ways of alleviating this problem.

The "code" for a fractal-encoded image is a list consisting of information for each range cell, including the location of the range cell, the domain (usually identified by an index) that maps onto that range cell, and parameters that describe the transformation mapping the domain onto the range. Thus, the compression ratio depends on the number of range cells as well as the efficiency of information storage for each range cell. A large number of range cells may provide good decoded image quality, but this comes at the expense of compression ratio.

3.3.1 Domain cells

For each range cell, we want to find a domain cell that efficiently maps onto that range cell. In order for the mapping to be a contraction, the domain should be bigger than the range. Good compression depends on the ability to find a good domain-range match without having to subdivide the range. Too much range subdivision leads to too many ranges, which hurts the compression ratio (and in fact can lead to "image expansion" rather than compression if one is not careful!). Ideally one would like a continuum of domain sizes and positions within the image to choose from for each range. Unfortunately, the computational cost of searching through so many possibilities is prohibitive. The process of setting up a system of domains is a balancing act between providing a large enough domain set for good range match possibilities and keeping the domain set small enough so that searches can be performed in a reasonable amount of time.

The accompanying software uses a system of five parameters to describe the domain system. Once these five parameters are specified, a single index unambiguously determines the location of each domain cell. The parameters are stored as part of the coding header information, and a domain index is stored with each range cell in the coded image. The five parameters are: domain rows ρ, domain columns γ, domain levels λ, horizontal overlap Δ_h and vertical overlap Δ_v. Together these parameters determine how many domains there are, how many different sizes of domains there are, and how much overlap is allowed. Parameters ρ and γ specify how many of the largest level of domain cells are in one row and column of domain blocks. So, for example, if the image size is 256×256 and ρ and γ each equal 8, then the largest domain blocks are 64×64 ($256/8 = 64$). The domain block size is halved with each increase of the domain levels parameter λ. If the largest domains ($\lambda = 1$) are 64×64, then at level $\lambda = 2$, the domain size is 32×32. Note that the number of domains quadruples at each new level. Finally, Δ_h and Δ_v control the amount of overlap. These parameters take on values between 0.0 and 1.0, with 1.0 indicating no overlap, 0.5 half overlap, and 0.0 complete overlap. The smaller these values, the more domains (in fact, 0.0 would result in infinitely many domains, but the software forces a minimum of one pixel non-overlap). Table 3.3.1 shows the number of domains that result from various choices of the domain parameters.

Domain Rows (ρ)	8	8	8	8	8	8
Domain Columns (γ)	8	8	8	8	8	8
Domain Levels (λ)	1	2	2	3	3	3
Horizontal Overlap (Δ_h)	1.0	1.0	0.5	0.5	0.25	0.1
Vertical Overlap (Δ_v)	1.0	1.0	0.5	0.5	0.25	0.1
Total Number of Domains	**64**	**320**	**1186**	**5155**	**20,187**	**125,707**

Table 3.3.1 Sample values of the domain parameters, and the resulting numbers of domains.

For example, when $\rho = 8$, $\gamma = 8$, and $\lambda = 2$, then, with no overlap, there are 64 (i.e., $8 \cdot 8$) level 1 domains of size 64×64, and 256 (i.e., $16 \cdot 16$) level 2 domains of size 32×32, for a total of 320 domains.

3.3.2 Quadtree partitioning of range cells

One way to partition the image into range cells is a method called *quadtree partitioning* (Fisher 1995). This method starts with a coarse partition, such as a subdivision of the entire image into 4 rectangles (see Fig. 3.3.3). For each range cell, the algorithm tries to find the domain and corresponding contractive transformation that best cover the range cell. In order to produce contractive transformations, range cells larger than the largest domain cells are subdivided into smaller range cells. Contrast and brightness are adjusted for the best fit through a least-squares process. If the fit is within a preset error threshold, then that range cell is considered to be covered, and the algorithm moves on to the next range cell. If the fit is not within threshold, the algorithm checks to see if the maximum quadtree depth has been reached. If it has, processing stops for that range cell, and the range cell is considered covered with the best domain and transformation available. If maximum quadtree depth has not been reached, then the algorithm subdivides that cell into 4 smaller range cells, and the search for optimal domains and transformations begins anew with these 4 new range cells. Processing is complete when all range cells have been covered, either by finding a domain-transformation fit within the error tolerance, or by reaching the maximum quadtree depth.

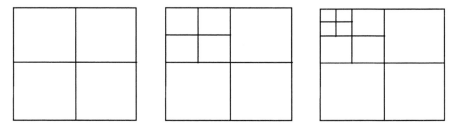

Fig. 3.3.3 Quadtree partitioning starts with a coarse partition (left). If a good domain-range match cannot be found for a particular range cell, that cell is subdivided into 4 smaller cells (center). The subdivision process continues until either a good match is found or the maximum quadtree depth is reached.

Note that using a smaller error threshold leads to more range cells, and using a larger quadtree depth also leads to more range cells. Fig. 3.3.4 shows the effect of using tighter error tolerances and larger quadtree depths. In either case, more range cells means poorer compression (and sometimes no compression at all), but usually better decoded image quality.

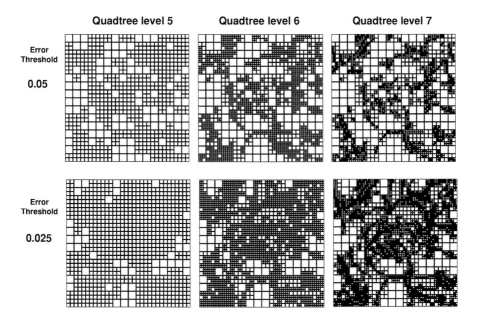

Quadtree level 5   Quadtree level 6   Quadtree level 7

Error
Threshold

0.05

Error
Threshold

0.025

Fig. 3.3.4 Increasing the quadtree level and/or decreasing the error threshold leads to more range cells in the quadtree partition.

3.3.2.1 A scheme for keeping track of quadtree partitioning

To implement a quadtree partitioning algorithm, you'll need a way of keeping track of the range cells that result from the partitioning. The accompanying software uses the following list manipulation scheme to assign a unique quadtree index to each range cell. To see how this works, consider a simple example with a maximum quadtree depth of three. We start with a list of four vectors, each with length equal to the maximum quadtree depth, in this case 3. The first component of the first vector is assigned the value 1, the first component of the second vector is assigned 2, and so on. The initial list then consists of these four vectors:

$$1,0,0$$
$$2,0,0$$
$$3,0,0$$
$$4,0,0.$$

This list corresponds to the initial, or quadtree level 1, partitioning shown on the far left of Fig. 3.3.3. By convention, the 4 list entries are assigned to the 4 range cell blocks in clockwise order, starting with the upper left. When the algorithm calls for a range cell subdivision, the list entry corresponding to that range cell is replaced with 4 new list entries. The components up to that quadtree level remain unchanged, while the component corresponding to that quadtree level is assigned the values $1, \ldots, 4$ in the four new list entries. So, for example, the list corresponding to the level 2 partitioning shown in the center of Fig. 3.3.3 would be:

$$1,1,0$$
$$1,2,0$$
$$1,3,0$$
$$1,4,0$$
$$2,0,0$$
$$3,0,0$$
$$4,0,0.$$

Following the same scheme, Fig. 3.3.5 shows a particular level 3 partitioning and resulting index list. For example, the shaded cell has index 3,2,4.

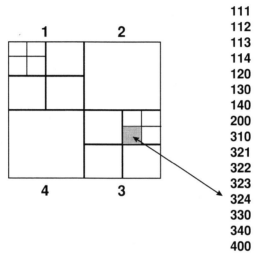

111
112
113
114
120
130
140
200
310
321
322
323
324
330
340
400

Fig. 3.3.5 A quadtree partitioning (level 3) and corresponding index list. The shaded box corresponds to quadtree index 3,2,4.

It is not difficult to imagine how quickly the quadtree index list can grow with increasing quadtree levels and tight error tolerances.

3.3.3 Mapping domains to ranges

The dominant computational step in fractal image encoding is the domain-range comparison. For each range cell, the algorithm compares transformed versions of all the domain cells (or, at least all of the domain cells in a given class, as described in the next chapter) to that range cell. The transformations are affine transformations, of the form described in section 3.2.1, with the spatial part of the transformation limited to rigid translation, a contractive size-matching, and one of eight orientations. The orientations consist of four 90° rotations, and a reflection followed by four 90° rotations. In a recent paper, Saupe (1996) claims that the use of these eight orientations is not necessary and that equally good results can be obtained by using a larger domain pool without applying rotations. The accompanying software allows you to explore this possibility, since the number of orientations is user-selectable to a value of 1 to 8, with 1 corresponding to the identity transformation.

Domain-range comparison, as implemented in the accompanying software, is a three-step process, as shown in Fig. 3.3.6. First, one of the eight (or fewer) basic rotation/reflection orientations is applied to the selected domain. Next, the rotated domain is shrunk to match the size of the range. Note that, in practice, the range must be smaller than the domain in order for the overall mapping to be a contraction. Finally, optimal contrast and brightness parameters are computed using a least-squares fitting.

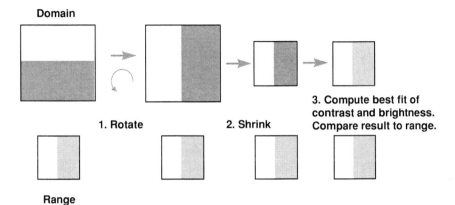

Domain

1. Rotate   2. Shrink   3. Compute best fit of contrast and brightness. Compare result to range.

Range

Fig. 3.3.6 Comparing domain and range cells. First, one of eight basic rotation/reflection orientations is applied. Next the rotated domain is shrunk to the size of the range. Finally, the contrast and brightness parameters are adjusted through a least-squares fitting to obtain optimal values. The result is compared on a pixel-by-pixel basis to the range cell to determine the quality of the fit.

To find the optimum contrast s and brightness o, we want to find the values for s and o that minimize:

$$\sum_i \sum_j (s\, d_{ij} + o - r_{ij})^2.$$

Here, $\{d_{ij}\}$ and $\{r_{ij}\}$ are, respectively, the domain and range pixel values. These pixels reside in rectangular arrays with M rows and N columns (the domain size has already been shrunk to match the range at this point).

The solution is

$$s = \alpha / \beta$$

$$o = \bar{r} - \left(\frac{\alpha}{\beta}\right)\bar{d},$$

where

$$\alpha = \sum_i \sum_j (d_{ij} - \overline{d})(r_{ij} - \overline{r})$$

$$\beta = \sum_i \sum_j (d_{ij} - \overline{d})^2$$

$$\overline{d} = \frac{1}{NM} \sum_i \sum_j d_{ij}$$

$$\overline{r} = \frac{1}{NM} \sum_i \sum_j r_{ij} \ .$$

3.3.4 Encoding times

One of the drawbacks of fractal image compression is long encoding times. Encoding times of over two days on a workstation have been reported for cases where the number of domains exceeds 100,000. Table 3.3.2 shows three examples of encoding times, using the code in the accompanying software on a 200 MHz Pentium PC. The image used here is the "Rose" image shown in Fig. 3.2.4. Note that in the second and third examples, the number of domains is larger, leading to a longer encoding time. The larger number of domains does improve the compression, as represented by the smaller number of range cells. The decoded image error is comparable in all three cases, which is to be expected since the error tolerance was the same in each case.

In the third example, the option "Search for Best Domain?" is set to "Yes". Recall that when this option is off, domain-range matching stops as soon as a match is found within the error tolerance. When this option is on, as in the third example, all domains are compared to each range cell, regardless of whether a match within tolerance occurs. The best domain-range match is kept. Not surprisingly, encoding takes much longer when this option is on. In the third example here, encoding takes over three times as long as example 2, which has identical encoding settings, except for this option. The number of range cells is the same as for example 2 (916 range cells), so there is no improvement in compression. There is a slight improvement in pixel error. Fisher (1995) notes that having this option off can lead to a bias of choosing domains that occur early in the domain index list. However, the cost in encoding time in having this option on does not appear to be justified in terms of improved compression performance. In the remaining examples in this book, this option will be turned off.

The next chapter will develop methods that will reduce these encoding times down to seconds.

Quadtree Depth	6	6	6
Error Threshold	0.05	0.05	0.05
Domain Rows	8	8	8
Domain Columns	8	8	8
Domain Levels	2	2	2
Horizontal Overlap	1.0	0.5	0.5
Vertical Overlap	1.0	0.5	0.5
Number of Domains	320	1186	1186
Number of Orientations	8	8	8
Search for Best Domain	No	No	Yes
Final No. of Range Cells	1048	916	916
Average Pixel Error	3.844%	3.839%	2.982%
PSNR	24.17 dB	24.32 dB	26.061 dB
Total Encoding Time	15 Min. 59 Sec.	42 Min. 32 Sec.	2 Hrs. 19 Min. 31 Sec.

Table 3.3.2 Encoding times on a 200 MHz Pentium PC. The methods discussed in the next chapter will significantly improve these times. See Sect. 3.4.1 for a definition of the error measures.

3.4 IMAGE DECODING

The image is decoded by iteratively applying the transformation W to an arbitrary starting image g, where

$$W(g)(x,y) = w_i(g)(x,y) \text{ for } (x,y) \in R_i.$$

If the transformations $\{w_i\}$ have been correctly chosen, the iterate $W^{\circ n}(g)$ will be close to the original image f for some reasonable value of n. Note that, according to the contraction mapping theorem, the iterates will converge regardless of the starting image. Typical decoding schemes use a starting image that is uniformly gray, but, as Fig. 3.4.1 shows, other images provide equally good performance.

To implement the iterative decoding scheme in a computer program, you must set up two image arrays, for example, called `old_image` and `new_image`. The contractive mapping W is defined as a separate transformation on each range cell. Each range cell has a transformation and domain cell associated with it. The contents of that range cell are computed by applying the transformation to the domain cell. The pixel values for the domain cell are obtained from the `old_image` array. The resulting range cell pixel values are stored in `new_image`. One iteration is complete when all of the range cells have been processed. It is important to keep `old_image` and `new_image` separate during the iteration process, otherwise you are not implementing the contractive mapping W properly. To begin the next iteration, replace `old_image` with `new_image`. Note that it is not necessary to physically move the contents of `new_image` into `old_image`. This can be accomplished much more efficiently by simply reassigning pointer values, as can be seen in the source code for the accompanying software.

Starting Image   **Iteration #1**   **Iteration #2**

Iteration #3   **Iteration #4**   **Iteration #5**

Fig. 3.4.1 An example of decoding a fractal encoded image. Any starting image may be used. The error in this example after 5 iterations was 2.2332% average error per pixel.

3.4.1 Measuring the error

Error measurement is an important aspect of determining the effectiveness of an image compression scheme. Obviously, we want to know how far off the decoded image is from the original image. Because perception of image quality is subjective, the question of how to measure this difference is not an easy one to answer. The software accompanying this book uses two simple measures: average pixel error and peak signal-to-noise ratio (PSNR). Average pixel error is computed as:

$$\frac{1}{N_{\text{Rows}}N_{\text{Cols}}} \sum_{i=1}^{N_{\text{Rows}}} \sum_{j=1}^{N_{\text{Cols}}} \left| f_{i,j} - d_{i,j} \right|.$$

PSNR is a standard measure in the image compression world, and is computed as:

$$rms = \sqrt{\frac{1}{N_{\text{Rows}} N_{\text{Cols}}} \sum_{i=1}^{N_{\text{Rows}}} \sum_{j=1}^{N_{\text{Cols}}} \left| f_{i,j} - d_{i,j} \right|^2}$$

$$\text{PSNR} = 20 \log_{10} \left(\frac{M_{\text{Graylevel}}}{rms} \right).$$

In the above, N_{Rows} and N_{Cols} are the number of rows and columns, respectively, $M_{\text{Graylevel}}$ is the maximum gray level value (255 for the examples in this book), $f_{i,j}$ is the pixel value of the original image at row i, column j, and $d_{i,j}$ is the decoded image pixel value. The quantity rms is the root mean square error. Note that PSNR will "blow up" if it ever encounters a lossless compression algorithm.

The accompanying software computes and displays the error image obtained by subtracting the decoded image from the original image, as shown in Fig. 3.4.2. The software also computes average pixel error and PSNR, as discussed above.

Fig. 3.4.2 The original "Rose" image (left), decoded image (right), and error image (center). The encoding in this case used a maximum quadtree depth of 6, an error threshold of 0.05, and 320 domain cells. Decoding was stopped after 4 iterations. The error image is actually the reverse of true error: it is computed by subtracting the error from the number of gray levels (256 in this case). The average pixel error is 3.168% (PSNR 24.898 dB).

Error measure is an area of active research in image compression. Human perception of error does not always coincide with absolute measures of error. Block artifacts, such as those visible in the image on the right in Fig. 3.4.2, are quite noticeable to human observers, yet do not contribute a great deal to either average pixel error or lower PSNR. In this case, error measures that take into account gradient differences as well as absolute differences might be more appropriate. In applications where a machine is the final consumer of the decoded image, such as automatic target recognition systems in the military, the characteristics of the recognition algorithm should be taken into account when measuring decoded image error.

3.5 STORING THE ENCODED IMAGE

Once the image has been encoded, you will want to save the encoded information in a file. The accompanying software has two formats for doing this. There is a text range file format ("*.rng") that lists the range cell information in a format that you can read with a text editor. This format enables you to see how the algorithm has encoded the image. Of course, since this is an ASCII text format, it is not very compact, and usually represents image expansion, rather than compression. The software also provides a binary range file format ("*.fbr") that stores the range cell information in a compact binary format. The next sections discuss these formats. Please note that neither of these formats are standard in the image compression community. There are no standard fractal compression formats, although Iterated Systems, Inc., has their proprietary fractal image format (fif).

3.5.1 Range file format

The range file format ("*.rng") provides a text version of the encoded image. To decode an image, you need to know how the image has been partitioned into range cells, and you need to know the domain and transformation associated with each range cell. Fig. 3.5.1 shows the partial contents of a sample range file. The sole purpose of this text version of the range file is so that you can see what the encoding algorithm has produced. The header contains information on the domain rows, columns, levels, and horizontal and vertical overlap increments, as discussed in section 3.3.1 above. From this, the system of domain cells can be deduced so that, given a single domain index, it is possible to determine the size and location of the corresponding domain cell. Lines starting with a double slash ('//') are comment lines for informational purposes only. These lines contain information about how the encoding was done, but these are not items needed by the decoder. For example, the error threshold impacts how many range cells are produced in the quadtree partition, but the decoder does not need to know the value of the error threshold.

The decoder does need to know the quadtree depth and the number of range cells ("Rects" in Fig. 3.5.1), which are the final items in the header information. The remainder of the file contains a list of range cell data, one line for each range cell. For each range cell, the file lists the quadtree indexes (integer 1 through 4 for each of the quadtree levels), the domain index, transformation index (0-7), an integer brightness level, and a real-valued contrast value.

Sample range file information:

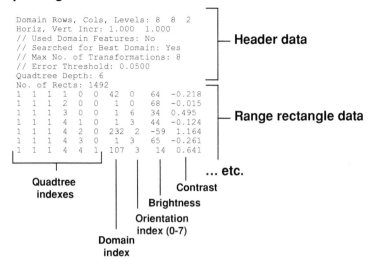

```
Domain Rows, Cols, Levels: 8  8  2
Horiz, Vert Incr: 1.000  1.000
// Used Domain Features: No
// Searched for Best Domain: Yes
// Max No. of Transformations: 8
// Error Threshold: 0.0500
Quadtree Depth: 6
No. of Rects: 1492
1  1  1  1  0  0   42  0    64  -0.218
1  1  1  2  0  0    1  0    68  -0.015
1  1  1  3  0  0    1  6    34   0.495
1  1  1  4  1  0    1  3    44  -0.124
1  1  1  4  2  0  232  2   -59   1.164
1  1  1  4  3  0    1  3    65  -0.261
1  1  1  4  4  1  107  3    14   0.641
```

Header data

Range rectangle data

... etc.

Quadtree indexes

Contrast

Brightness

Orientation index (0-7)

Domain index

Fig. 3.5.1 Sample range file information.

3.5.2 Binary range file format

To actually store a compressed version of the image, it is necessary to store the information in a binary format. Examining a line of data in the range file format shown in Fig. 3.5.1 reveals that the quadtree indexes take up over half of the numeric entries in a line. Even though each index takes on only the values 1 through 4, and so requires only 2 bits for storage, this is still a lot of data to store for each range cell. Fortunately, there is a scheme that takes advantage of the tree structure of the quadtree data. This tree structure requires only one bit per overall quadtree position, and can be stored separately as part of the header information. Each range cell then requires only domain index, orientation index (*Max. No. of Transformations* in the header information actually refers to the number of orientations), brightness and contrast. Fig. 3.5.2 shows the organization of data in the binary range file. The following sections discuss the specifics in more detail.

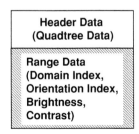

Fig. 3.5.2 Organization of data in the binary range file. The quadtree information can be stored compactly as part of the header block.

3.5.2.1 Efficient quadtree storage

While the quadtree index list is a convenient mechanism for manipulating range cell information during the partitioning process, the list itself is not an efficient way of storing this information. The list can be compactly stored as binary tree structure. A few simple observations about the quadtree index list will suggest how to construct this tree:

1. The maximum number of range cells at quadtree level n is 4^n.
2. If there is one non-zero index at a particular level, then all 4 indexes must be present (e.g., if 111 is present in the list, then 112, 113 and 114 must also be present).
3. A '0' at a level means all corresponding indexes at higher levels are also '0'.

This suggests the use of a binary tree structure with 4^n bits at level n. A '1' indicates that this cell is subdivided. A '0' indicates that there is no subdivision at this level (and hence no subdivision at any higher levels). Note that the tree needs only $N - 1$ levels for a maximum quadtree depth of N, since by definition there is no further subdivision at level N. So, for example, the 3-level partition shown in Fig. 3.3.5 could be represented with the following 2-level binary tree:

Level 1:   1   0   1   0

Level 2:   1 0 0 0   0 0 0 0   0 1 0 0   0 0 0 0

Thus all of the quadtree information in the partition of Fig. 3.3.5 can be stored in 20 bits. The information can actually be stored in fewer bits if one observes that the second and fourth blocks in level 2 consist of all 0's and are actually superfluous, since their values can be predicted by the presence of 0's in the preceding level. This scheme requires more complex decoding logic. The accompanying software does not eliminate superfluous 0's in the storage of quadtree information.

Listing 3.5.1 shows the relatively compact code that converts a range index list to a quadtree "level array" of 1's and 0's of the type shown above. It takes longer to explain what the code does than to write the actual lines of code. The variable `level_array` is an array of pointers to a structure of the type `tbyte_array`. Each `tbyte_array` is an array of four integers, each called "`bit`". The number of levels is one less than the quadtree depth. In the example above, there are two levels. The first level has one `tbyte_array`, and the second has four. In general, there will be 4^{n-1} `tbyte_array`'s at level n. The expression

```
level_array[j-1][level_index].bit[bit_index]
```

accesses the individual "bits" in the level array. The first index ($j-1$, where j is the quadtree depth) is the level. The above example has two levels, corresponding to indexes 0 and 1. The second index (`level_index`) tells which `tbyte_array` to access at that particular level. In the above example, at level 0, `level_index` can have only the value 0, while at level 1, it takes on the values 0 and 2. The final index (`bit_index`) tells which "bit" to access in `tbyte_array`. Note that each non-zero value in the array actually gets set multiple times.

Listing 3.5.1 Code sample for converting range index list to quadtree "level array".

```
typedef struct {
    short index[MAX_QUADTREE_DEPTH+1];
    unsigned int domain,transf;
    int brightness;
    float contrast;
    } range_struct;

typedef struct {
    int bit[4];
    } tbyte_array;
typedef tbyte_array *pbyte_array;
pbyte_array level_array[MAX_QUADTREE_DEPTH];
int i,j,no_of_levels = quadtree_depth - 1,
    level_index,bit_index;
int power_4[MAX_QUADTREE_DEPTH];
power_4[0] = 1;

for (i=0;i<no_of_levels;i++) {
    level_array[i] = (pbyte_array)calloc((size_t)
        power_4[i],sizeof(tbyte_array));
    power_4[i+1] = power_4[i]*4;
    }  // end i

for (i=1;i<=range_list->get_count();i++) {
    range = (range_struct *)(range_list->at(i));
    level_index = 0;
    for (j=1;j<quadtree_depth;j++)
        if (range->index[j+1] > 0) {
            bit_index = range->index[j]-1;
            level_array[j-1][level_index].
                bit[bit_index] = 1;
            level_index = level_index*4 + bit_index;
            }  // end j
    } // end i
```

3.5.2.2 Bit structure for storing range information

Listing 3.5.2 shows the bit structure for storing the information required for each range cell. The total number of bits should be a multiple of 8 so that each range cell can be stored with an integral number of bytes. The allocation in the code in Listing 3.5.2 reflects a total budget of 4 bytes per range cell. It is a trial and error process to determine the optimal allocation of bits across the four quantities (domain index, transformation index, brightness level and contrast factor). For example, allocating 8 bits for brightness and 11 bits for contrast resulted in 4.789% average error per pixel for a particular encoding of the "Lena" image, while an allocation of 9 bits for brightness and 10 bits for contrast resulted in 4.355% error. The number of bits allocated for domain index determines the maximum number of domains. In this case, the 10 bits allocated means the maximum number of domains is 1024. This is not a lot by traditional fractal encoding practices (some implementations allow hundreds of thousands of domains). However, it is a good compromise between speed and accuracy. A large number of domains is the single biggest factor in long encoding times. Note that eliminating the orientation transformations, as Saupe suggests (Saupe 1996), would free up 3 bits that could be allocated to the domain bits, thus increasing the allowable number of domains. Fisher (1995) recommends using the quantized brightness and contrast values during encoding, rather than encoding with optimal values and then quantizing.

Listing 3.5.2 Bit structure for storing range cell information.

```
#define DOMAIN_BITS 10
#define MAX_NO_OF_DOMAINS 1024 /* 2**DOMAIN_BITS */
#define TRANSF_BITS   3
/* Trial and error deciding how many bits to allot for
   brightness and contrast.  These choices seem OK for
   a 19-bit (total for both) budget.  */
#define BRIGHTNESS_BITS 9
#define BRIGHTNESS_LEVELS 512   /* 2**BRIGHTNESS_BITS */
#define CONTRAST_BITS 10
#define CONTRAST_LEVELS 1024  /* 2**CONTRAST_BITS */

typedef struct {
    unsigned domain:DOMAIN_BITS,
          transf:TRANSF_BITS,
          brightness:BRIGHTNESS_BITS,
          contrast:CONTRAST_BITS;
    } trange_bit_struct;
```

3.5.2.3 Transmission robustness

Quantization of the range cell parameters, such as what occurs due to the bit allocation discussed above, introduces a small amount of error into the decoded image. A related issue in applications that require sending compressed images across communications channels is how robust the image coding is with respect to errors introduced during transmission. This is of particular interest in military applications, which may have challenging transmission environments.

As noted in Fig. 3.5.2 above, the quadtree partition can be stored quite compactly as part of the header information. The quadtree partitioning alone usually contains enough information to make the image recognizable. It is not hard, for example, to tell the difference between "Lena" and a "cat" image merely by looking at the quadtree partition.

Any corruption of the header data would likely lead to large errors in the decoded image. However, the size of the header data is small, so it may be possible to protect this data through some type of redundancy scheme. Fig. 3.5.3 shows the effect of corrupting domain index and transformation index information. The horizontal axis is the percentage of randomly selected corrupted indexes. The vertical axis is the resulting error in the decoded image. The image in this case is "Lena" (256 × 256, 256 gray levels), compressed to a 6:1 ratio. Fig. 3.5.3 indicates that the coding is more sensitive to errors in domain index than transformation index. However, the error increases only linearly. For applications such as target recognition (rather than human perception), the degradation in image quality may be tolerable. The lack of sensitivity to corruption in the transformation index is perhaps further corroboration of Saupe's claim (Saupe 1996) that these transformations can be eliminated from the encoding process.

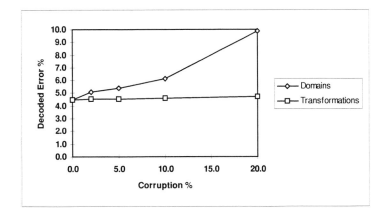

Fig. 3.5.3 Transmission corruption versus decoded error. The corruption percent represents corruption of a percentage of domain indexes and transformation indexes. The graph indicates decoded error is sensitive to errors in the domain indexes, although the error only increases linearly.

3.6 RESOLUTION INDEPENDENCE

One of the unique features of fractal image compression is that the decoding is resolution independent. Note that nowhere in the range file do we include information about the original image size. The reason for this is that such information is not needed. The decoding can proceed at any image size, regardless of the size of the image that was used for encoding. This property has led to exaggerated claims for compression performance. For example, suppose a $256 \times 256 \times 256$ grayscale image is encoded with 4000 range cells. Assuming each range cell requires 4 bytes of storage, the encoding requires approximately 16K bytes of storage. This represents an approximate compression ratio of 4:1 when compared with the 64K bytes for the original image. Now suppose the encoded image is decoded at a size of 1024×1024. One could say that this represents a compression ratio of 256:1, since a $1024 \times 1024 \times 256$ grayscale image normally requires 1024K bytes of storage. Compression ratios reported in this book do not use this device. All ratios reported here are computed by comparing with the size of the original image used for encoding.

Another claim made for the decoding of fractal encoded images is that decoding at a larger image size inserts detail into the image. This detail is artificial, in the sense that it does not originate from the image that was encoded, however it is contextually consistent. Figure 3.6.1 shows an example of "fractal zoom" versus ordinary zoom. The detail in the fractal zoom is somewhat finer. Additional examples are given in Fisher (1995) and Barnsley and Hurd (1993). However, Polidori and Dugelay (1995) claim that images obtained by zooming fractal encoded images are not better than oversampled images produced using classical interpolators.

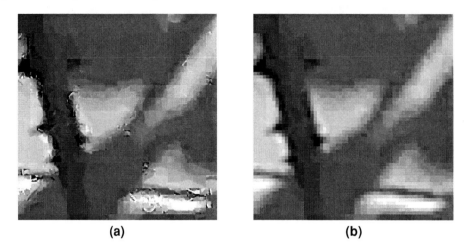

(a)   **(b)**

Fig. 3.6.1 Example of "fractal zoom" (a) versus ordinary zoom (b). The image in (a) is a segment of the "Rose" image, fractal encoded at 256×256 and decoded at 1024×1024. The image in (b) is the same image, also fractal encoded at 256×256, but decoded at 256×256, then blown up to 400% of its original size, using ordinary pixel zoom.

3.7 OPERATOR REPRESENTATION OF FRACTAL IMAGE ENCODING

We close this chapter with a discussion of an operator formulation of fractal encoding introduced by G. Davis. This formulation will be used later when we relate wavelet and fractal approaches and investigate hybrid methods of encoding. The operator formulation and the solution of the resulting operator equation provide a compact representation of the fractal encoding and decoding processes. We will use the notation and terminology of Davis. Further details can be found in Davis (1995; 1996; 1998).

3.7.1 "Get-block" and "put-block" operators

Let $\mathfrak{I}^m$ denote the space of $m \times m$ digital grayscale images, that is, each element of $\mathfrak{I}^m$ is an $m \times m$ matrix of grayscale values. We define the "get-block" operator $B_{n,m}^k : \mathfrak{I}^N \to \mathfrak{I}^k$, where $k \leq N$, as the operator that extracts the $k \times k$ block with lower corner at n,m from the original $N \times N$ image, as shown in Fig. 3.7.1.

The "put-block" operator $\left(B_{n,m}^k \right)^* : \mathfrak{I}^k \to \mathfrak{I}^N$ inserts a $k \times k$ image block into an $N \times N$ zero image, at the location with lower left corner at n,m. Fig. 3.7.2 shows the action of the put-block operator.

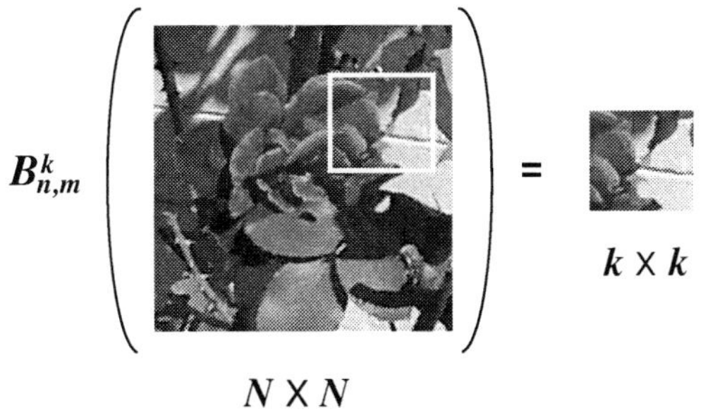

Fig. 3.7.1 The "get-block" operator $B_{n,m}^k$ extracts a $k \times k$ image block from an $N \times N$ image.

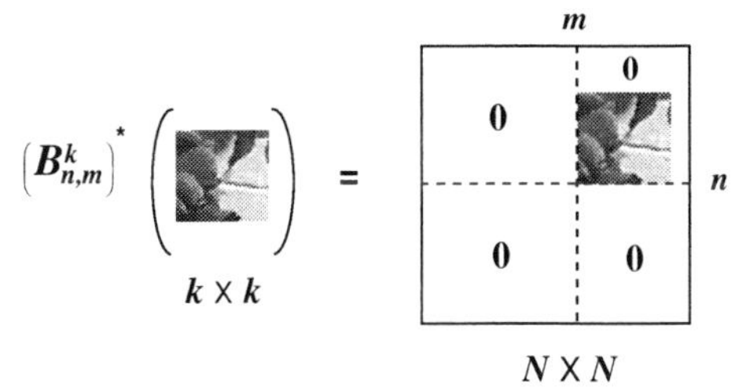

Fig. 3.7.2 The "put-block" operator $\left(B_{n,m}^k\right)^*$ inserts $k \times k$ image block into an $N \times N$ image consisting of all zeros.

3.7.2 Operator formulation

Let $F \in \mathfrak{I}^N$ be an $N \times N$ image, and let $\{R_1,\ldots,R_M\}$ be a collection of range cell images that partition F (for example, these may be the result of a quadtree partition). Each R_i has dimension $r_i \times r_i$ with lower corner located at n_i, m_i in F. Let F_i be the $N \times N$ image with all zeros except for range cell R_i, that is,

$$F_i \equiv \left(B_{n_i,m_i}^{r_i}\right)^* (R_i).$$

Then

$$
\begin{aligned}
F &= \sum_{i=1}^{M} F_i \\
&= \sum_{i=1}^{M} \left(B_{n_i,m_i}^{r_i}\right)^* (R_i).
\end{aligned}
\tag{3.7.1}
$$

What's going on in equation (3.7.1) is nothing more than what is depicted in Fig. 3.7.3.

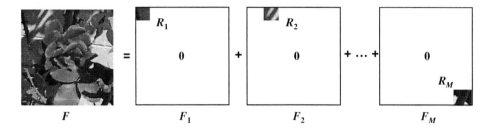

Fig. 3.7.3 The image F can be represented as the summation of the images $F_1,...,F_M$.

If the range cells R_i are the result of fractal image encoding of the image F, then for each range cell R_i there is a domain cell D_i and an affine transformation T_i such that

$$R_i \approx T_i(D_i)$$
$$= A_i(D_i) + C_i \,. \tag{3.7.2}$$

Denote the dimension of D_i by d_i, and denote the lower left coordinates of D_i by k_i, l_i. In equation (3.7.2), $A_i : \mathfrak{S}^{d_i} \to \mathfrak{S}^{r_i}$ is the operator that shrinks (assuming $d_i > r_i$), translates $(k_i, l_i) \to (n_i, m_i)$, and applies a contrast factor s_i, while C_i is a constant $r_i \times r_i$ matrix that represents the brightness offset. We can write D_i as:

$$D_i = B_{k_i, l_i}^{d_i}(F) \,.$$

Thus, (3.7.1) can be rewritten as the following approximation:

$$F \approx \sum_{i=1}^{M} \left(B_{n_i, m_i}^{r_i} \right)^* \left\{ A_i \left(B_{k_i, l_i}^{d_i}(F) \right) + C_i \right\}$$

$$= \underbrace{\sum_{i=1}^{M} \left(B_{n_i, m_i}^{r_i} \right)^* \left\{ A_i \left(B_{k_i, l_i}^{d_i}(F) \right) \right\}}_{G(F)} + \underbrace{\sum_{i=1}^{M} \left(B_{n_i, m_i}^{r_i} \right)^* (C_i)}_{H}$$

or

$$F \approx G(F) + H \,,$$

where $G : \mathfrak{S}^N \to \mathfrak{S}^N$ is an operator, and H is a known constant image in $\mathfrak{S}^N$.

3.7.3 Solution of the operator equation

The solution of the operator equation

$$X = G(X) + H \tag{3.7.3}$$

is given by:

$$X = (I - G)^{-1}(H)$$

$$= \left(\sum_{n=0}^{\infty} G^n \right)(H)$$

provided $\|G\| < 1$ in some appropriate norm $\| \circ \|$. Here, G^n is the composition of G with itself n times (for example, $G^2(H) = G(G(H))$).

This solution can be obtained iteratively. Start with any image $X^{(0)} \in \mathfrak{I}^N$, then compute $X^{(n)}$ from:

$$X^{(1)} = G\left(X^{(0)}\right) + H$$

$$X^{(2)} = G\left(X^{(1)}\right) + H = G^2\left(X^{(0)}\right) + G(H) + H$$

$$X^{(n)} = G\left(X^{(n-1)}\right) + H$$

$$= G^n\left(X^{(0)}\right) + \sum_{j=0}^{n-1} G^j(H)$$

$$\rightarrow (I - G)^{-1}(H) \quad \text{as } n \rightarrow \infty, \text{ provided } \|G\| < 1.$$

Note that this iterative process is exactly the fractal decoding process.

3.7.4 Error analysis

In general, the original image to be coded, F, is not an exact solution of the operator equation (3.7.3), but rather, F satisfies

$$F = G(F) + H + \varepsilon$$

for some error image $\varepsilon \in \mathfrak{I}^N$. Let $\tilde{F}$ be the true solution of (3.7.3). Then

$$F - \tilde{F} = G(F) + H + \varepsilon - G\left(\tilde{F}\right) - H$$

$$= G\left(F - \tilde{F}\right) + \varepsilon.$$

This implies

$$\left\| F - \tilde{F} \right\| \leq \|G\| \left\| F - \tilde{F} \right\| + \|\varepsilon\|$$

from which we get:

$$\left\| F - \tilde{F} \right\| \leq \frac{\|\varepsilon\|}{1 - \|G\|}.$$

This is exactly the Collage Theorem bound.

4

SPEEDING UP FRACTAL ENCODING

Fractal encoding is computationally intensive because of the large number of domains that must be searched for each range cell and because of the computations that must be performed for each domain-range comparison. Early implementations of fractal encoding were notorious for the amount of computation time required, typically taking many hours, and sometimes days, on the most powerful UNIX workstations. This time requirement hindered the acceptance of fractal image compression as a practical method. Attempts to improve encoding speed have focused on two areas. Classification of domains can significantly speed up encoding performance by reducing the number of domains that must be searched. Most fractal image compression implementations incorporate some type of domain classification. A second approach is to reduce the number of computations required to compare domains and ranges. This can be accomplished through feature extraction. The fastest approaches combine feature extraction with domain classification search strategies.

This chapter looks at the approach first introduced in Welstead (1997), which combines feature extraction with a domain classification and search strategy based on a self-organizing neural network.

4.1 FEATURE EXTRACTION

The comparison of range cells to candidate domain cells, illustrated in Fig. 3.3.5 in the previous chapter, demands significant computational resources. The computations include the pixel-by-pixel operations of rotating and shrinking, as well as least-squares fitting to determine optimal contrast and brightness factors. These operations must be done for every candidate domain cell until a good match is found. One way to improve the basic fractal image coding process is to extract a small number of features that characterize the domain and range cells. The comparison of domains and ranges is then based on these features rather than on individual pixels, thus reducing the complexity of the problem. Features may come from Fourier spectrum analysis (McGregor, et al., 1994), wavelet analysis (Hebert and Soundararajan 1998), or from measures of image tone and texture (Welstead 1997). This section defines five features that measure image texture and contrast distribution. Examples will show that feature extraction by itself provides a significant speedup in the encoding process.

4.1.1 Feature definitions

Five different measures of image variation are used here as features. These particular features were chosen as representative measures of image variation. However, no attempt has been made to optimize the choice of specific features or their number. The optimal selection of features remains an open question. The specific features used here are:

(i) *standard deviation*, σ:

$$\sigma = \sqrt{\frac{1}{n_r n_c} \sum_{i=1}^{n_r} \sum_{j=1}^{n_c} (p_{i,j} - \mu)^2} \, ,$$

where μ is the mean, or average, pixel value over the $n_r \times n_c$ rectangular image segment, and $p_{i,j}$ is the pixel value at row i, column j;

(ii) *skewness*, which sums the cubes of the differences between pixel values and the cell mean, normalized by the cube of σ:

$$\text{skewness} = \frac{1}{n_r n_c} \sum_{i=1}^{n_r} \sum_{j=1}^{n_c} \frac{(p_{i,j} - \mu)^3}{\sigma^3} \, ;$$

(iii) *neighbor contrast*, which measures the average difference between adjacent pixel values;

(iv) *beta*, which measures how much the pixel values change in relation to the value at the center of the cell;

(v) *maximum gradient*, which is the maximum of *horizontal gradient*, which measures change in pixel values across the cell, and *vertical gradient*, which measures change in pixel values from top to bottom. Maximum gradient is set equal to whichever of these two gradients is the largest in magnitude (i.e., has the largest absolute value).

Because eight different orientation transformations, consisting of 90° rotations and reflection, are applied to the domain cells, there is no need (nor is it desirable) to use features that are essentially equivalent under these transformations. For example, horizontal gradient is just vertical gradient rotated through 90°. That is why maximum gradient, rather than either horizontal or vertical gradient, is used as a feature.

The source code with the accompanying software has specific definitions for all of the features (i) - (v). Mean is not used as a feature, since contrast and brightness directly influence the pixel value, and these are varied during the domain-range cell matching process. For example, an image segment that has a constant value of 25 for all of its pixels can be matched exactly with another image segment that has constant value of 230 merely by adjusting the brightness factor to 205. The mean values of these image segments are quite different, but for the purposes of our domain-range matching via affine transformations that allow brightness adjustments, they are better characterized by the fact that their standard deviations (and in fact all of the above features) are zero.

How do these feature values compare for different types of images? Fig. 4.1.1 shows some representative test images. Table 4.1.1 shows the values of the features computed for the sample images shown in this figure. Note that all of the feature values are 0 for image 1, which is a constant image. The horizontal variation of image 2 provides a positive horizontal gradient, but zero vertical gradient. Image 3 is just a 90° rotation of image 2, and so has positive vertical gradient, but zero horizontal gradient. Under the domain transformations, these would be equivalent images, and so we would want these images to have equal feature vectors. This is the case provided we use maximum gradient. There would be significant distance between these images in feature space if horizontal and vertical gradient were separate features. Images 4 and 5 have the largest beta response, and the beta value has opposite sign for these two images. Images 6 and 7 have more pixel-to-pixel variation, and so neighbor contrast is high for these images. Image 7 has the largest absolute skewness, which happens to be negative in this case, which means outlying pixel values tend to be below the mean (i.e., darker).

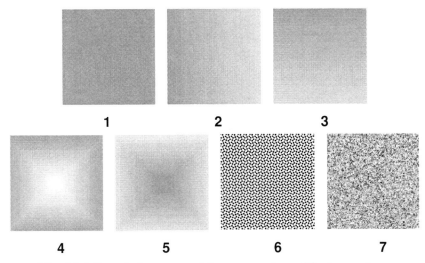

Fig. 4.1.1 Sample images used for comparison of feature values.

Image (Fig. 4.1.1):	1	2	3	4	5	6	7
Standard Dev.	0.00	17.4629	17.4624	22.5348	17.5781	**121.0294**	50.0018
Skewness	0.00	-0.0505	-0.0505	0.5376	-0.4955	-0.5164	**-0.6826**
Nbr. Contrast	0.00	0.4409	0.4409	1.3843	1.1396	**186.4964**	104.0830
Beta	0.00	-0.0002	-0.0002	**0.0534**	**-0.0413**	0.0001	-0.0016
Horz. Gradient	0.00	**0.4710**	0.0000	-0.0493	-0.0274	0.0000	-0.0009
Vert. Gradient	0.00	0.0000	**0.4710**	0.0339	-0.0500	0.0000	0.0114
Max. Gradient	0.00	**0.4710**	**0.4710**	-0.0493	-0.0500	0.0000	0.0114

Table 4.1.1 Feature values for sample images.

The feature vector must be normalized when comparing distance in feature space, otherwise the larger feature values would dominate the comparison. The next section includes a discussion of this normalization step.

4.1.2 Encoding algorithm using feature extraction

Feature extraction alone, without domain classification, can provide a significant speedup in the encoding process. The steps to implement an encoding algorithm using feature extraction are as follows:

> **1.** Compute and store feature values for all of the domain cells. Keep track of the maximum and minimum values for each feature across all of the domain cells. These values will be used for normalization.

Normalize the feature values for all of the domains. A feature value f is normalized to a value n_f between 0 and 1 according to the following:

$$n_f = (f - f_{\min})/(f_{\max} - f_{\min}), \qquad (4.1.1)$$

where $f_{\min}$ is the minimum value for this feature over all domain cells, $f_{\max}$ is the maximum value over all domain cells, and n_f is the normalized value.

2. Implement quadtree partitioning as before. However, when doing the domain-range comparison, compute the feature vector for the range cell, and normalize the feature values according to (4.1.1). Note that it is possible that the normalized values for the range cell may be outside the range $(0,1)$, since the maximum and minimum were computed over domain cells only. However, the values should not be far outside this range if a sufficiently large domain pool was used. Compute the distance between the range feature vector and each domain feature vector, according to:

$$d = \sum_{j=1}^{N_f} \left| f_r[j] - f_d[j] \right|,$$

where $f_r[j]$ is the jth feature value for the range cell, $f_d[j]$ is the jth feature value for the domain cell, and N_f is the number of features (e.g., $N_f = 5$ in this case).

3. Keep track of the best, i.e., smallest, distance value, $d_{\min}$, computed so far for this range cell. If d is less than $d_{\min}$, then compare d to f_{tol}, the feature tolerance value. If $d < f_{\text{tol}}$, then do a pixel-by-pixel domain-range comparison as in normal fractal encoding (i.e., rotate the domain, shrink to the range size, compute optimal contrast and brightness). If the pixel-by-pixel comparison is less than the error tolerance, then this range cell is covered. If not, continue checking domains. Subdivide range cell as necessary, as before.

Fig. 4.1.2 shows the flow diagram for fractal image encoding with feature extraction.

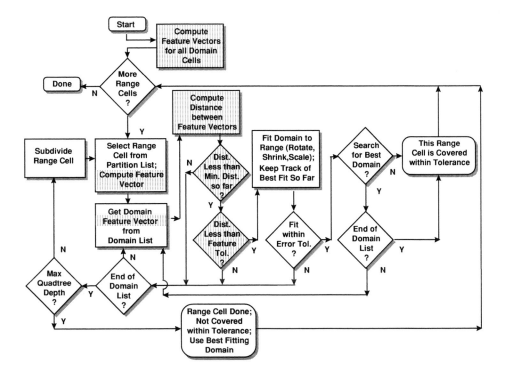

Fig. 4.1.2 Flow diagram showing the main steps in fractal image encoding with feature extraction, as implemented in the accompanying software. The shaded boxes show the steps involved with feature extraction that are additions to the basic fractal encoding algorithm shown in Fig. 3.3.2.

The checks that compare the feature distance against minimum distance computed so far, and against feature tolerance, act as gatekeepers, allowing through only those domain cells that pass both tests. These tests greatly cut down the number of domain cells for which the time consuming pixel-by-pixel domain-range comparison is performed.

The value to which f_{tol} is set impacts total encoding time and compression performance. Fig. 4.1.3 shows a graph of encoding time (on a 200 MHz Pentium PC) and number of range cells as a function of feature tolerance values. The image used here was the "Rose" image, with a quadtree depth of 6, an error tolerance of 0.05, 1186 domains (horizontal and vertical overlap set to 0.5), and the "Search for Best Domain" option turned off. This graph indicates that the minimum encoding time occurs for a value of f_{tol} near 0.05, where the total encoding time is 24 seconds. Normal fractal encoding for this example, without using feature extraction, is 2552 seconds, over one hundred times as long.

Somewhat better compression occurs, however, when f_{tol} is near 0.25, as indicated by the lower number of range cells. For values of f_{tol} larger than 0.05, more domain cells make it through to the pixel-by-pixel comparison step. This increases encoding times, but helps compression since more domains are available for comparison. The maximum possible distance between our normalized length-5 feature vectors is 5. As f_{tol} approaches this value, the encoding times level off, since f_{tol} no longer has any effect. Note also that the encoding time increases somewhat for very small values of the tolerance due to an increased number of range cells. The large number of range cells results from an insufficient number of domains surviving the tolerance check, leading to poor domain-range matches. Finally, note that the maximum encoding time (159 seconds) in Fig. 4.1.3 is much less than the normal fractal encoding time (2552 seconds), indicating that the minimum distance check is also responsible for cutting down on a large number of domain-range comparisons.

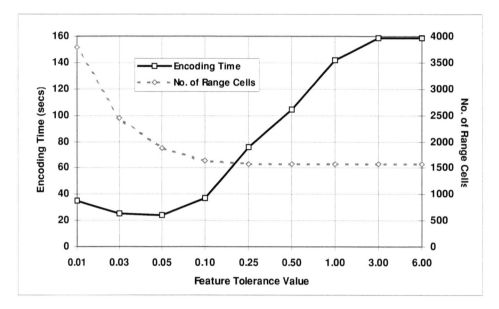

Fig. 4.1.3 Encoding time (in seconds) and number of range cells as a function of the feature tolerance value. This example used 1186 domain cells, with a maximum quadtree depth of 6 and an error tolerance of 0.05. Note that when the tolerance value approaches 3, the encoding time levels off, since this value is close to the maximum feature distance value (5). Also, the encoding time increases somewhat for very small values of the tolerance due to an increased number of range cells. Normal fractal encoding without feature extraction required 2552 seconds in this example.

4.1.3 Sample results using feature extraction

Figs. 4.1.4 - 4.1.7 show sample results comparing the feature extraction encoding approach (referred to as "FE" henceforth for convenience) with the baseline fractal compression method ("baseline") for various numbers of domains. The parameters used to produce the numbers of domains shown are those shown in Table 3.3.1. The image used is the 256×256 "Rose" image. The maximum quadtree depth was set at 6, with error tolerance 0.05, and the "Search for Best Domain" option set to "No". Two feature tolerance values were used for the feature extraction encoding: 0.25 and 0.05.

Fig. 4.1.4 compares the encoding times (200 MHz Pentium PC) for the two methods. The difference in encoding times is so great that a logarithmic scale is needed, otherwise the

FE times would appear as a flat line at the bottom of the graph. As expected from the results shown in Fig. 4.1.3, the feature tolerance value of 0.05 produces faster encoding times than the feature tolerance value of 0.25, though at the expense of producing more range cells (see Fig. 4.1.6), and hence somewhat poorer compression. Note that not only does the FE method produce much lower encoding times than the baseline method, but the rate of increase as the number of domains increases is also much lower. For example, with a feature tolerance value of 0.25, the encoding times increase from 57 seconds for 320 domains to 404 seconds for 125,707 domains, a factor of less than 10. However, for the same numbers of domains, encoding times for the baseline method increase from 959 seconds to over 130,000 seconds (over 36 hours), a factor of 135 (the encoding time for the baseline method for the case of 125,707 domains was not verified directly, but rather estimated from the average encoding time per range cell).

There is a certain amount of computational overhead associated with the FE method, namely the computation of feature vectors for each of the domains prior to the actual encoding process. The encoding times shown in Fig. 4.1.4 include the time needed for this computation. Fig. 4.1.5 shows the relative portion of the total encoding time that is devoted to this computation. Only for very large numbers of domains is this computation a significant fraction of the total encoding time.

The baseline method does generally produce somewhat fewer range cells, and hence slightly better compression, than the FE approach, as Fig. 4.1.6 shows. Fig. 4.1.7 shows that the difference in error in the decoded images is not significant. This is to be expected, since both methods are required to meet the same error tolerance when performing domain-range checks. One should not read too much into the variation in error in Fig. 4.1.7. The significant result is that both methods are meeting the 5% error requirement.

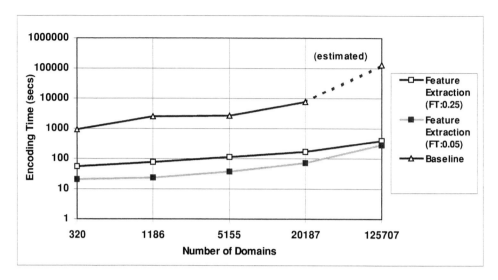

Fig. 4.1.4 Comparison of encoding times (200 MHz Pentium PC) for the feature-extraction (FE) encoding algorithm with encoding times for the baseline fractal image compression algorithm of the previous chapter. The image used is the 256×256 "Rose" image, with maximum quadtree depth set at 6, and error tolerance 0.05, and the "Search for Best Domain" option set to "No". Two feature tolerance (FT) values were used for the FE encoding: 0.25 and 0.05. The encoding time for the baseline method with 125,707 domains was estimated, from an average encoding time per range cell, to be approximately 130,000 seconds.

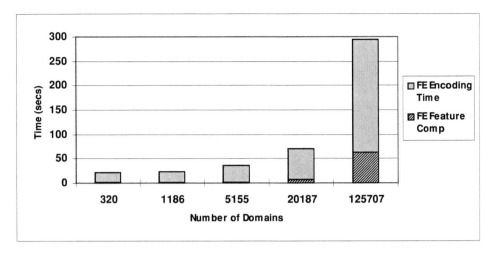

Fig. 4.1.5 Total encoding time, showing the computational overhead of computing feature vectors for all of the domains ("FE Feature Comp."). Encoding parameters are the same as in Fig. 4.1.4. The values shown here are for the case when the feature tolerance is 0.05. "FE Encoding Time" is encoding time without including the domain feature computation time. The total encoding time reported in Fig. 4.1.4 is the sum of these two times, represented by the total column height here.

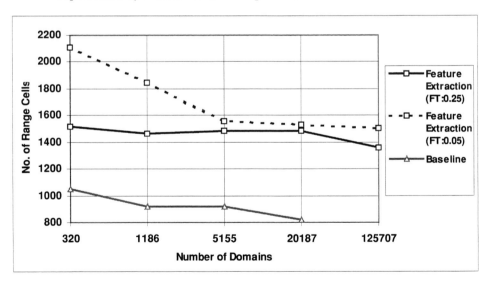

Fig. 4.1.6 Comparison of number of range cells versus number of domains, for feature extraction and baseline methods. Encoding parameters are the same as for Fig. 4.1.4.

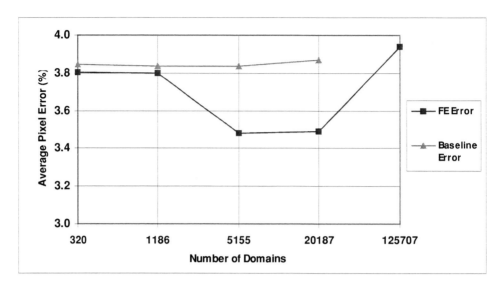

Fig. 4.1.7 Average pixel error for feature extraction and baseline
methods. Feature tolerance value is 0.25. Other encoding
parameters are the same as for Fig. 4.1.4.

As Figs. 4.1.4 - 4.1.7 show, feature extraction provides a significant speedup over the
baseline fractal encoding algorithm. The baseline method does tend to produce somewhat
better compression (i.e., fewer range cells). The FE method compensates for this by
producing smaller pixel errors. Fig. 4.1.8 shows there is no perceptual difference in
decoded image quality between the two methods. This figure provides a side-by-side
comparison of the decoded "Rose" image, encoded with the baseline fractal encoding
algorithm (a) and with the FE algorithm (b). The encoding parameters were: quadtree
level 7; error threshold 0.025; feature tolerance 0.25; number of domains 1186. The
"Search for Best Domain" option was turned off in both cases. Baseline encoding took
9,632 seconds (over two and a half hours) on a 200 MHz Pentium PC, while FE encoding
took just 180 seconds, an improvement of over 50 to 1. The baseline method did produce
better compression, 5.2:1 (3154 range cells) compared to 2.7:1 (5953 range cells). The
FE encoding produced a somewhat better quality decoded image (1.72% error compared
to 2.04% after 6 iterations), although the difference can be attributed to the higher number
of range cells.

(a)   **(b)**

Fig. 4.1.8 "Rose" image encoded using the baseline fractal encoding method (a) and the FE method (b). The baseline method here provides compression of 5.2:1 with pixel error of 2.04% (30.12 dB PSNR) after 6 decoding iterations, while the FE method provides 2.7:1 compression with pixel error of 1.72% (31.27 dB PSNR).

4.2 DOMAIN CLASSIFICATION

Long encoding times result from the need to perform a large number of domain-range matches. The total encoding time is the product of the number of matches and the time required to perform each match. The domain-range match is a computationally intensive pixel-by-pixel process of rotating, shrinking and fitting a domain cell to a range cell. The feature extraction encoding algorithm described above reduces encoding time by replacing this pixel-by-pixel process with the less demanding feature-distance computation. Only those domains that pass feature-distance tolerance checks make it through to the pixel-by-pixel comparison. Thus, many domain-range match computations are eliminated by this preliminary feature-distance check.

A further step that one can take to reduce the number of domain-range match computations is to perform classification on the domains and ranges. Domain-range matches are then performed only for those domains that belong to a class similar to the range. Actually, the feature-extraction approach of the previous section is a type of classification scheme. The feature computation serves to identify those domains belonging to the class of subimages whose feature vectors are within the feature tolerance value of the feature vector belonging to the range cell. More sophisticated classification schemes use a pre-defined set of classes. A classifier assigns each domain cell to one of these classes. During encoding, the classifier assigns the range cell to a class, and domain-range comparisons are then performed only against the domains in the same class (and possibly other similar classes) as the range cell. The savings in encoding time comes from the fact that fewer domain-range comparisons are performed.

The classification scheme described here is based on a self-organizing neural network that is trained on feature vector data extracted from domain cells obtained from a typical image. The features are the same five features described in the previous section. The advantage of using a self-organizing network is that we don't need to decide what the image classes should be for classification. The network organizes itself into clusters that represent image classes based on the image data presented to it. Moreover, the image used for training need not be (and usually isn't) the same image that is to be encoded. Thus, network training time is not part of the overall encoding time. For small numbers of domains, the classification approach provides a slight improvement in encoding time over the FE approach. However, for large numbers of domains (20,000 or more) the time savings is significant, and these large numbers of domains can provide better image quality at a given compression ratio. The approach discussed here was first presented in Welstead (1997). Other references (Bogdan and Meadows 1992; Hamzaoui 1995) have also discussed using a self-organizing neural network for domain classification.

4.2.1 Self-organizing neural networks

A fascinating feature of the brain is that its physical organization reflects the organization of the external stimuli that are presented to it. For example, there is a well defined relationship between the relative physical location of touch receptors in the skin surface and the relative location in the brain of the neurons that process the stimuli from those receptors. Nearby touch receptors correspond to nearby neurons. Areas of the skin that are densely populated with touch receptors, such as the hands and face, are assigned a proportionately larger number of neurons. This correspondence produces the so-called *somatotopic map*, which projects the skin surface onto the part of the brain, called the *somatosensory cortex*, corresponding to the sense of touch (Ritter, Martinez, and Schulten 1992).

Teuvo Kohonen, in the early 1980's, developed an algorithm to mimic the brain's ability to organize itself in response to external stimuli. He called his algorithm a *self-organizing feature map* (Kohonen 1984). Kohonen's algorithm represents a type of neural network that is capable of learning without supervision. This type of neural network is called a *self-organizing neural network*.

Self-organizing neural networks are characterized by a multi-dimensional array, or *lattice*, of nodes. Fig. 4.2.1 shows an example of such a network with a 2-dimensional lattice. Associated with each lattice node is a weight vector. The weight vector is the same dimension as the input vectors that will be used for training. The dimension of the lattice need not be the same as that of the weight vector. Complex relationships in problems requiring higher dimensional weight vectors usually require higher dimensional lattices to sort themselves out. However, biological inspiration and practical processing considerations typically limit the lattice dimension to 2 or 3.

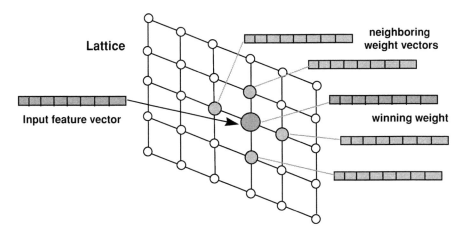

Lattice

neighboring weight vectors

Input feature vector

winning weight

Fig. 4.2.1 A self-organizing neural network. The weight vectors are attached to a lattice of nodes, such as the 2-dimensional lattice shown here. When an input vector is presented to the network, the weight vector that most closely resembles it is adapted to look more like the input vector. Neighboring weight vectors on the lattice are rewarded for their proximity by being adapted also, though not as much as the winning weight vector.

Network training is through unsupervised learning. The network of weight vectors is initialized to random values. An input feature vector is then presented to the network and we find the weight vector closest to the input vector. That is, we find i',j' such that

$$\|\mathbf{v} - \mathbf{w}_{i',j'}\| \le \|\mathbf{v} - \mathbf{w}_{i,j}\| \text{ for all } i,j$$

where $\mathbf{v}$ is the input feature vector and $\mathbf{w}_{i,j}$ is the weight vector at node i,j. Adapt the weights in the lattice neighborhood of the winning weight $\mathbf{w}_{i',j'}$ to look more like the input vector. This adaptation is summarized as:

$$\mathbf{w}_{i,j}^{\text{new}} = \mathbf{w}_{i,j}^{\text{old}} + \varepsilon \exp\left(\alpha \left\| \mathbf{v} - \mathbf{w}_{i,j}^{\text{old}} \right\|^2 \right)\left(\mathbf{v} - \mathbf{w}_{i,j}^{\text{old}} \right)$$

where i,j range over a neighborhood of i',j'. The size of this neighborhood is reduced during the course of the training iterations. The parameter ε is the iteration stepsize, and α is inversely proportional to the neighborhood size. Details of the algorithm are summarized in the sidebar "Training Algorithm for a Self-Organizing Neural Network".

Training Algorithm for a Self-Organizing Neural Network

1. Initialize the weight vectors.

2. Present input vectors to the network.

3. For each input vector **v**, determine the weight vector that is closest to the input vector:

Find i',j' such that

$$\|\mathbf{v} - \mathbf{w}_{i',j'}\| \le \|\mathbf{v} - \mathbf{w}_{i,j}\| \text{ for all } i,j$$

where **v** is the input vector, and i and j range over all the nodes in the lattice.

4. Adapt the weight vector and its lattice neighbors. The starting neighborhood size is a user-selectable parameter, and the neighborhood size is gradually reduced over the course of the iterations. The adaptation stepsize is also reduced over the course of the iterations. Also, weights within the neighborhood that are farther away from the winner are not adapted as strongly as weights close to the winner. This mechanism is accomplished through the use of a gaussian function applied to the distance of the weight vector from the winner. The adaptation can be summarized as:

$$\mathbf{w}_{i,j}^{\text{new}} = \mathbf{w}_{i,j}^{\text{old}} + \varepsilon \cdot \left(\mathbf{v} - \mathbf{w}_{i,j}^{\text{old}}\right) \exp\left(\alpha \left\|\mathbf{v} - \mathbf{w}_{i,j}^{\text{old}}\right\|^2\right)$$

where **v** is the input vector, and i and j range over just the neighborhood of i', j' as selected in step 3. Here, ε is the stepsize and α is a fixed coefficient that is set equal to the inverse of the neighborhood size.

The lattice serves to define a neighborhood topology for the weight vectors. That is, weight vectors whose lattice nodes are close to one another will share properties that are similar relative to the distribution of features in the input data. This neighborhood topology will be exploited in the domain search strategy described below.

4.2.2 Fractal image encoding using self-organizing domain classification

We use a classification scheme based on Kohonen self-organizing neural networks to classify the domains. The dimension of the feature vectors used here is 5. In the accompanying software, used to produce the examples shown here, the lattice dimension is fixed at 2, and the size (that is, number of rows and columns) is user-selectable. The examples discussed below use an 8×8 lattice. Each lattice node represents a class of domain cells, so it is desirable to keep the overall number of nodes fairly small. Table

4.2.1 shows the default values for the self-organizing neural network in the accompanying software. The starting neighborhood size should be approximately half the size of the rows and columns. A starting neighborhood size that is too small can lead to poor neighborhood topology in the trained network (that is, dissimilar weight vectors may appear close to one another in the lattice structure).

Lattice Rows:	8
Lattice Columns:	8
Starting Stepsize (ε):	0.25
Starting Neighborhood:	4
Iteration Blocksize:	100
Iteration Blocks:	10
Maximum Search Radius:	1

Table 4.2.1 Default parameter values for self-organizing neural network.

Once the network has been trained, the domain cells for the given image are classified by assigning them to the weight vector to which they are closest in feature space. Thus, each lattice node now has a weight vector and a list of domain cells attached to it. This list of domains belongs to the "class" associated with that weight vector. The class is, by definition, the set of all images that are closer in feature space to that weight vector than to any other weight vector on the lattice.

When a range cell feature vector is presented to the network, it is similarly assigned to a network weight vector. The range cell is then compared to those domain cells assigned to this weight vector, as well as to those domains assigned to the neighboring weight vectors on the network lattice, as shown in Fig. 4.2.2. The maximum search radius parameter, shown in Table 4.2.1, determines the size of this neighborhood. As before, we keep track of the best (minimum) feature distance obtained so far. If the new domain in the search list provides a smaller feature distance, we then check this distance value against the feature tolerance value, f_{tol}. If the distance passes this test, a complete pixel-by-pixel domain-range comparison is performed. The only difference between this algorithm and the FE algorithm of the previous section is that the number of domains upon which the feature-distance computation is performed is smaller. There is some overhead involved with the determination of the weight vector closest to the range cell feature vector (a series of feature-distance computations). The significance of this overhead decreases as the total number of domains increases. Fig. 4.2.3 shows the revised flow diagram incorporating self-organizing domain classification.

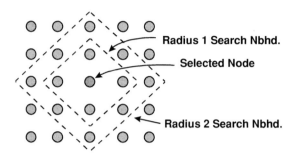

Fig. 4.2.2 Search neighborhoods around the selected node in the weight network.

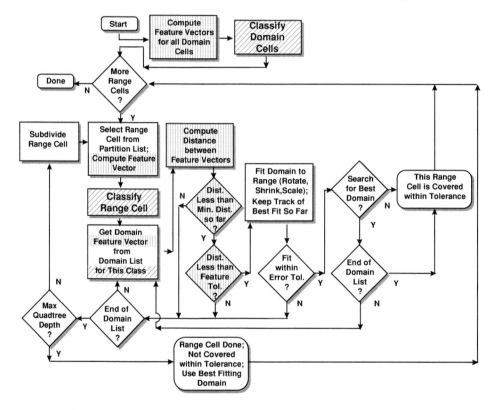

Fig. 4.2.3 Flow diagram for fractal image encoding with self-organizing domain classification. The diagonally shaded boxes indicate the additional steps required for using the self-organizing classifier to classify the range and domains.

4.2.3 Sample results using self-organizing domain classifier

Fig. 4.2.4 compares encoding times for the self-organizing domain classification method (referred to as the "SO method" for convenience) with the FE method of the previous section. The image and encoding parameters used here are the same as those in Fig. 4.1.4. The self-organizing network used here is an 8×8 network trained on 1186 domains extracted from the "Cat" image. This particular image was chosen for training to illustrate the fact that there does not need to be much similarity between the training image and the image to be encoded. The time required to train the network is not included in the encoding times shown below, since this training can be done once ahead of time and does not need to be repeated for different images. The network search neighborhood radius size was set to 1.

Fig. 4.2.4 shows that the advantage provided by the SO method over the FE method increases as the number of domains increases. This is in spite of the fact that the SO method has additional overhead. Not only must the SO method compute feature vectors for the domains, as the FE method does, but it must also assign each domain to one of the self-organizing network classes. For this example, there are 64 (8×8) such classes. Fig. 4.2.5 shows that this classification time becomes significant for large numbers of domains. However, comparison with Fig. 4.1.5 shows that the actual encoding times for the SO method are much lower than comparable times for the FE method, leading to the lower overall encoding times shown in Fig. 4.2.4.

The SO method does produce somewhat larger numbers of range cells, and hence somewhat worse compression, for a given error tolerance than either the FE or baseline methods, as shown in Fig. 4.2.6. This is offset by generally better error results, as shown in Fig. 4.2.7.

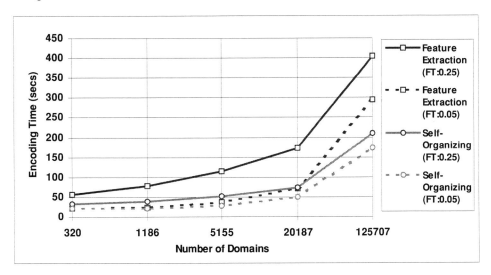

Fig. 4.2.4 Comparison of encoding times for the algorithm using self-organizing domain classification and the algorithm of the previous section using feature extraction only. The encoding parameters are the same as those used in Fig. 4.1.4. Results for feature tolerance (FT) values of 0.05 and 0.25 are shown.

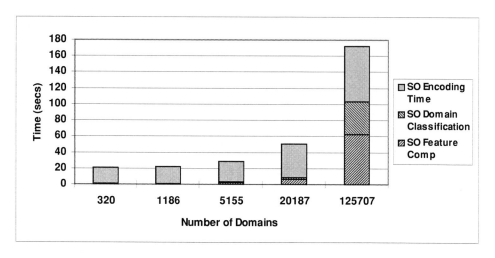

Fig. 4.2.5 Total encoding time for the self-organizing domain classification method includes computational overhead for computing feature vectors for the domains ("SO Feature Comp.") and also classifying the domains ("SO Domain Classification"). Encoding parameters are the same as in Fig. 4.2.4. The values shown here are for the case when the feature tolerance is 0.05.

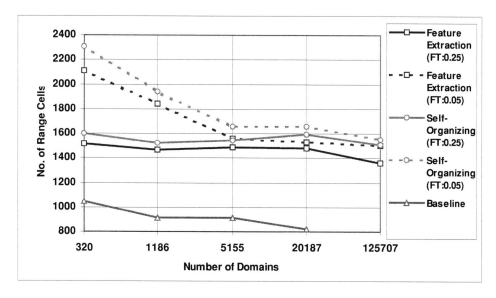

Fig. 4.2.6 Comparison of number of range cells versus number of domains, for SO, FE and baseline methods. Encoding parameters are the same as for Fig. 4.2.4.

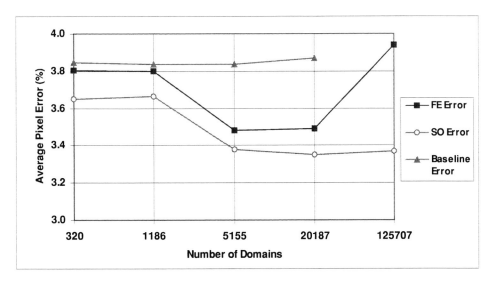

Fig. 4.2.7 Average pixel error for SO, FE and baseline methods. Feature tolerance value is 0.25. Other encoding parameters are the same as for Fig. 4.2.4.

Fig. 4.2.8 shows an example of an encoding of the "Leaves" image using the SO method. The self-organizing network used here is the same 8×8 network used in the preceding examples. The encoding parameters were: quadtree levels: 7; error tolerance: 0.05; feature tolerance: 0.25; number of domains: 5155 (3 levels, 0.5 overlap). The total encoding time was 118 seconds on a 200 MHz Pentium PC, about half of the 235 seconds required for FE encoding using the same parameters. The decoded error for this challenging image was 3.45% per pixel (25.61 dB PSNR) for FE and 3.19% per pixel (26.23 dB PSNR) for SO (using 6 decoding iterations in each case). The SO encoding produced 6592 range cells, which represents slightly worse compression than the 6241 range cells produced by FE encoding.

(a)   (b)

Fig. 4.2.8 (a) Original "Leaves" image. (b) "Leaves" image encoded
using self-organizing domain classification. Encoding parameters:
quadtree levels: 7; error tolerance: 0.05; feature tolerance: 0.25;
number of domains: 5155 (3 levels, 0.5 overlap). The total encoding
time was 118 seconds on a 200 MHz Pentium PC, compared with
235 seconds required for feature extraction encoding without
domain classification. The error is 3.18% per pixel (26.23 dB
PSNR).

The time advantage of domain classification encoding improves as the number of
domains increases. The number of feature distance computations for the SO method is
typically less than one-tenth the number for FE encoding. This is where most of the time
advantage comes from. The number of domain-range fittings using pixel operations is
approximately the same for each case and, in fact, remains roughly constant over a wide
range of domains, increasing slowly as the number of domains increases. Compared with
the baseline method, the advantage of using the SO and FE methods is that they allow one
to increase the number of domains without paying a large penalty in encoding time. This
leads to better compression performance and better quality in the decoded image.

4.3 OTHER APPROACHES FOR SPEEDING UP FRACTAL ENCODING

A number of other authors have proposed approaches for speeding up fractal encoding.
All of these approaches address one or both of the two contributors to long encoding
times, namely the complexity of the domain-range comparison and the number of domain-
range comparisons. Bogdan and Meadows (1992) applied a Kohonen self-organizing
network to the fractal encoding problem. Their approach differs from the one described
here in that they do not use feature extraction, but rather apply the network directly to the
domain pixel blocks. Thus, the complexity of the domain-range comparison is not
alleviated. Their approach also requires training the network on the image to be encoded,
so that network training time is part of the overall encoding time. McGregor, et al. (1994),
address both aspects of the encoding problem, using a K-D tree search on the domains,
combined with the extraction of a small number of image "characteristics" (what we call
features here), derived from Fourier coefficients. Saupe (1994) uses a nearest neighbor
search of the domains based on "multi-dimensional keys" that are versions of the domains
and ranges down-filtered to a small size (e.g., 8×8) for comparison purposes. Bani-Eqbal

(1995) proposes a tree search of domains. Hamzauoi (1995) modifies Bogdan and Meadows self-organizing network approach by introducing down-filtered versions of the domains and ranges as feature vectors. This approach, however, still requires training the network on the image to be encoded.

Finally, Ruhl and Hartenstein (1997) have shown that, in the context of computational complexity, fractal encoding is NP-hard. They show that, even with a finite number of admissible contrast and brightness factors (s and o), the number of feasible codes grows exponentially with the number of ranges or the image size. Moreover, they show that any code produced by standard fractal encoding methods (i.e., domain-range matching) is a suboptimal solution.

Part II

WAVELET IMAGE COMPRESSION

5

SIMPLE WAVELETS

We now turn our attention to an alternative approach to image compression that makes use of wavelets. Wavelet image compression belongs to the transform class of methods and as such differs from fractal methods. Nevertheless, there are fundamental connections between the two approaches. Fractal methods use self-similarity across different scales to reduce stored information. Wavelet methods exploit redundancies in scale to reduce information stored in the wavelet transform domain. Hybrid methods apply fractal techniques to information in the wavelet transform domain to provide even greater compression performance. This chapter introduces wavelet analysis through the use of the simple Haar wavelets. The following chapters look at wavelet image compression and more advanced wavelet topics.

5.1 INTRODUCTION

The idea behind wavelet image compression, like that of other transform compression techniques, is fairly simple. One applies a wavelet transform to an image and then removes some of the coefficient data from the transformed image. Encoding may be applied to the remaining coefficients. The compressed image is reconstructed by decoding the coefficients, if necessary, and applying the inverse transform to the result. The hope is that not too much image information is lost in the process of removing transform coefficient data. Fig. 5.1.1 illustrates this process.

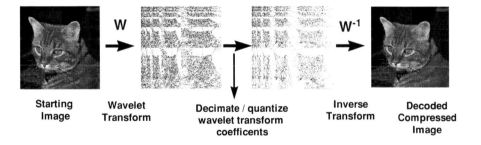

Starting Image — **Wavelet Transform** — **Decimate / quantize wavelet transform coefficents** — **Inverse Transform** — **Decoded Compressed Image**

Fig. 5.1.1 Wavelet image compression. The compression process involves application of a wavelet transform to the image, followed by some type of decimation and/or quantization, and possible encoding, of the resulting wavelet coefficients. The compressed image is reconstructed by decoding coefficients, if necessary, and applying the inverse wavelet transform.

The process of image compression through transformation and information removal provides a useful framework for understanding wavelet analysis. The literature contains a number of different approaches to the study of wavelets, some of which may seem daunting to the aspiring wavelet analyst. Mathematical references develop multiresolution analysis through the definition of continuous scaling and wavelet functions. Engineering papers introduce the topic through the use of highpass and lowpass filters and quadrature mirror filter pairs. As Fig. 5.1.2 shows, it is possible to relate these seemingly disparate approaches and see that they all lead to the idea of the wavelet transform and its inverse. The present chapter will start with the simple ideas of averaging and detail and show how these can be related to image compression. These simple ideas lead to scaling and wavelet functions, multiresolution analysis and the wavelet transform. The next chapter derives more advanced wavelets by generalizing the ideas of averaging and detail to introduce lowpass and highpass filters.

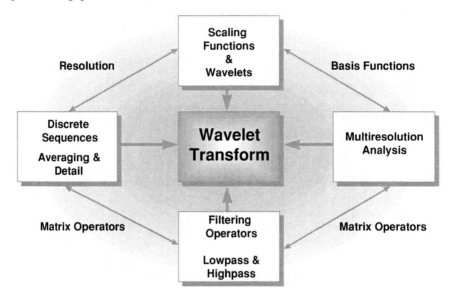

Fig. 5.1.2 There are a number of different entry points into wavelet analysis, all of which relate to one another and all of which lead to the wavelet transform.

5.2 AVERAGING AND DETAIL

As a simple-minded approach to image compression, one could replace an image by the average of its pixel values. This approach gives great compression (a single number represents the entire image!), but doesn't do much for image quality. To recover the original image from this average, you would need to know what detail was removed to arrive at the average. Consider an "image" with two pixels: $\{x_1, x_2\}$. These two values can be replaced by the average a and difference d of the values:

$$a = (x_1 + x_2)/2$$
$$d = (x_1 - x_2)/2.$$

(The factor of 1/2 is introduced in the definition of d for notational convenience.) Note that we can recover $\{x_1, x_2\}$ from $\{a, d\}$:

$$x_1 = a + d$$
$$x_2 = a - d.$$

The "wavelet transform" of the original sequence $\{x_1, x_2\}$ is $\{a, d\}$. No information is gained or lost in this representation. One might ask, then, what the advantage of replacing $\{x_1, x_2\}$ with $\{a, d\}$ might be. There is no advantage in particular, unless the two values x_1 and x_2 happen to be close to one another. In that case the difference d is small, and the "image" $\{x_1, x_2\}$ can be replaced by its approximation $\{a\}$. Note that this new "image" has fewer pixels than the original. We have achieved image compression! The reconstructed image is $\{a, a\}$, with error image $\{|x_1 - a|, |x_2 - a|\} = \{|d|, |d|\}$. Since d is small, the error is small.

Fundamental to wavelet analysis is the idea of extracting information at different levels of detail. Detail can also be thought of as scale or resolution information. The simple example above is of limited usefulness for real images, but it does illustrate the idea behind the application of wavelet analysis to image compression: Identify the detail information and remove the detail information that is small and does not contribute a great deal to the final image.

Let's look at a slightly bigger image $\{x_1, x_2, x_3, x_4\}$. As before, we consider averages:

$$a_{1,0} = (x_1 + x_2)/2$$
$$a_{1,1} = (x_3 + x_4)/2 \tag{5.2.1}$$

and differences:

$$d_{1,0} = (x_1 - x_2)/2$$
$$d_{1,1} = (x_3 - x_4)/2. \tag{5.2.2}$$

(The double subscripts here indicate that we are embarking on a multi-step process, of which this is the first step.) As before, we have a new representation $\{a_{1,0}, a_{1,1}, d_{1,0}, d_{1,1}\}$ for the original image that contains just as many pixels as the original. If we wanted to compress this image, we'd look at the size of the values $d_{1,0}$ and $d_{1,1}$ and decide if they could safely be eliminated. This would leave us with the compressed image $\{a_{1,0}, a_{1,1}\}$. Suppose, though, that we are not satisfied with this level of compression and want to further compress the image. We can apply the above procedure again to the remaining image $\{a_{1,0}, a_{1,1}\}$ to obtain its average and difference:

$$a_{0,0} = (a_{1,0} + a_{1,1})/2$$
$$d_{0,0} = (a_{1,0} - a_{1,1})/2. \tag{5.2.3}$$

If the difference $d_{0,0}$ is sufficiently small, we can replace the entire original image $\{x_1, x_2, x_3, x_4\}$ with the single pixel image $\{a_{0,0}\}$. Let's look at what $a_{0,0}$ really is:

$$\begin{aligned} a_{0,0} &= (a_{1,0} + a_{1,1})/2 \\ &= ((x_1 + x_2)/2 + (x_3 + x_4)/2)/2 \\ &= (x_1 + x_2 + x_3 + x_4)/4. \end{aligned} \tag{5.2.4}$$

Thus $a_{0,0}$ is just the overall average of all the pixels in the original image. If the original image is uniformly gray (i.e., all x_i equal to the same value), we can compress it by replacing it with a single value equaling that particular gray level. The value $a_{0,0}$ also represents the coarsest level of information in this image, that is, the information at the lowest resolution or coarsest scale. The values $a_{1,0}$ and $a_{1,1}$ together represent information at the next highest resolution level, or next finer scale. Note that we can recover $\{a_{1,0},a_{1,1}\}$ from $\{a_{0,0},d_{0,0}\}$ using the same procedure as above. The original pixel values $\{x_1,x_2,x_3,x_4\}$ represent the highest resolution and finest scale available for this image. These values can be recovered from $a_{1,0}$, $d_{1,0}$, $a_{1,1}$ and $d_{1,1}$. But since we can get $a_{1,0}$ and $a_{1,1}$ from $a_{0,0}$ and $d_{0,0}$, we can recover the original pixel values from the overall average $a_{0,0}$ and the differences $d_{0,0}$, $d_{1,0}$, and $d_{1,1}$. Thus the sequence

$$\{a_{0,0},d_{0,0},d_{1,0},d_{1,1}\} \tag{5.2.5}$$

is another representation of the original image consisting of an overall average and difference values representing two different levels of detail. The sequence (5.2.5) is a *wavelet transform* of the original sequence $\{x_1,x_2,x_3,x_4\}$. Note that we now have more choices for compression. If $d_{1,0}$ and $d_{1,1}$ are too large to ignore, it may be that we can eliminate the next level of detail, $d_{0,0}$. For larger images, we continue this process of averaging and extracting detail at coarser resolution levels.

5.3 SCALING FUNCTIONS AND WAVELET FUNCTIONS

The averaging and detail extraction of the previous section represent one node of the diagram in Fig. 5.1.2. In this section, we move clockwise on that diagram and show how resolution leads to the notion of scaling functions and wavelet functions.

Suppose now we consider our image $\{x_1,x_2,x_3,x_4\}$ as a function on the unit interval by writing

$$f(t) = x_1 \, X_{[0,1/4)}(t) + x_2 \, X_{[1/4,1/2)}(t) + x_3 \, X_{[1/2,3/4)}(t) + x_4 \, X_{[3/4,1)}(t) \tag{5.3.1}$$

where each $X_{[a,b)}$ is the characteristic function of the interval [a,b), that is,

$$X_{[a,b)}(t) = \{ 1 \text{ if } a \leq t < b; \ 0 \text{ otherwise} \}.$$

Fig. 5.3.1 shows how a graph of this piecewise-constant function might look for some arbitrarily chosen values of x_1, x_2, x_3, and x_4. Note that if we were using $f(t)$ to approximate a continuous function, then we would get a better approximation by using more characteristic functions over smaller subintervals. That is, we would get better approximation by using better *resolution*.

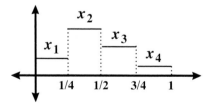

Fig. 5.3.1 The function $f(t)$ defined by equation (5.3.1).

Note that $X_{[1/4,1/2)}(t)$ is just a shifted version of $X_{[0,1/4)}(t)$, that is

$$X_{[1/4,1/2)}(t) = X_{[0,1/4)}(t - 1/4).$$

Similarly, $X_{[1/2,3/4)}(t)$ and $X_{[3/4,1)}(t)$ are shifted versions of $X_{[0,1/4)}(t)$. Also, $X_{[0,1/4)}(t)$ is a *scaled* version of the characteristic function of the unit interval, $X_{[0,1)}(t)$, that is,

$$X_{[0,1/4)}(t) = X_{[0,1)}(2^2 t).$$

Thus, all of the characteristic functions in (5.3.1) can be written as scaled and shifted versions of a single function, $X_{[0,1)}(t)$. We introduce the notation

$$\phi(t) = X_{[0,1)}(t), \tag{5.3.2}$$

and define

$$\phi_{k,j}(t) = \phi(2^k t - j) \quad j = 0,\dots,2^k\text{-}1. \tag{5.3.3}$$

Then:

$$\phi_{0,0}(t) = \phi(t)$$

$$\phi_{1,0}(t) = \phi(2t) = \{\, 1 \text{ for } 0 \le t < 1/2;\ 0 \text{ otherwise}\,\}$$

$$\phi_{1,1}(t) = \phi(2t\text{-}1) = \{\, 1 \text{ for } 1/2 \le t < 1;\ 0 \text{ otherwise}\,\}.$$

Figs. 5.3.2 (a) and (b) show some of these functions. Note that $\phi_{1,0}$ and $\phi_{1,1}$ are scaled and shifted versions of ϕ. We call ϕ the *scaling function*. The function f defined by (5.3.1) can be written in terms of these new functions as:

$$f(t) = x_1\, \phi_{2,0}(t) + x_2\, \phi_{2,1}(t) + x_3\, \phi_{2,2}(t) + x_4\, \phi_{2,3}(t). \tag{5.3.4}$$

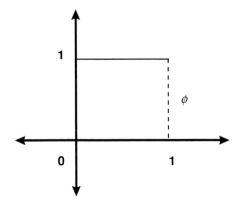

Fig. 5.3.2 (a) The scaling function ϕ.

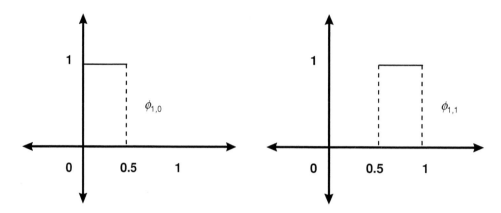

Fig. 5.3.2 (b) $\phi_{1,0}$ **and** $\phi_{1,1}$ **are scaled and shifted versions of** ϕ.

The interval over which the function $\phi_{k,j}$ is nonzero (and hence equal to 1) is called the *support* of the function. Note that the width of the support of $\phi_{k,j}$ decreases as k increases. In fact, the support of $\phi_{k+1,j}$ is half the width of the support of $\phi_{k,j}$. So, scale or resolution is determined by the value of k in $\phi_{k,j}$. If we want higher resolution, we use a higher value of k.

Suppose now that we want to go through a procedure similar to what we did in the preceding section. That is, we wish to represent the function $f(t)$ given by (5.3.4) in terms of averaging and differencing operations. Averaging is the same as going to lower resolution, so we can accomplish that by using $\phi_{k,j}$ with a lower value of k. This is equivalent to representing $f(t)$ in terms of $\phi_{1,0}$ and $\phi_{1,1}$. The coefficient of $\phi_{1,0}$ in this representation is $a_{1,0}$, given by (5.2.1), that is, this coefficient is the average of the first two coefficients of f. Similarly, the coefficient of $\phi_{1,1}$ is $a_{1,1}$, and so we obtain the following function:

$$g_1(t) = a_{1,0} \, \phi_{1,0}(t) + a_{1,1} \, \phi_{1,1}(t). \qquad (5.3.5)$$

It is clear, however, that g_1 is not identical to the function f. For example,

$$f(1/8) = x_1$$

while

$$g_1(1/8) = a_{1,0} = (x_1 + x_2)/2$$

which is not the same in general (unless $x_1 = x_2$). We have used only averaging in obtaining g_1 from f, so we should expect to lose information unless our original function has very little information to begin with. What's missing from our procedure of the previous section is the concept of identifying detail through some type of differencing operation. We need a function capable of expressing difference.

The function we seek is called a *wavelet function*. For the example here, the basic wavelet function is given by:

$$\psi(t) = X_{[0,\frac{1}{2})}(t) - X_{[\frac{1}{2},1)}(t)$$

$$= \begin{cases} 1 \text{ for } 0 \le t < \dfrac{1}{2}, \\[2mm] -1 \text{ for } \dfrac{1}{2} \le t < 1, \\[2mm] 0 \ \text{ otherwise.} \end{cases} \qquad (5.3.6)$$

Fig. 5.3.3 shows a graph of the wavelet function $\psi(t)$.

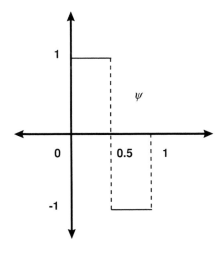

Fig. 5.3.3 The basic wavelet function $\psi(t)$

As we did for the scaling function $\phi(t)$, we now introduce scaled and shifted versions of $\psi(t)$. Define $\psi_{k,j}(t)$ by:

$$\psi_{k,j}(t) = \psi(2^k t - j), j = 0,\dots,2^k - 1.$$

Then, for example,

$$\psi_{0,0}(t) = \psi(t),$$

$$\psi_{1,0}(t) = \psi(2t) = \begin{cases} 1 \text{ for } 0 \le t < \dfrac{1}{4}, \\[2mm] -1 \text{ for } \dfrac{1}{4} \le t < \dfrac{1}{2}, \\[2mm] 0 \ \text{ otherwise}, \end{cases}$$

$$\psi_{1,1}(t) = \psi(2t - 1) = \begin{cases} 1 \text{ for } \dfrac{1}{2} \le t < \dfrac{3}{4}, \\[2mm] -1 \text{ for } \dfrac{3}{4} \le t < 1, \\[2mm] 0 \ \text{ otherwise}, \end{cases}$$

Fig. 5.3.4 shows graphs of $\psi_{1,0}$ and $\psi_{1,1}$.

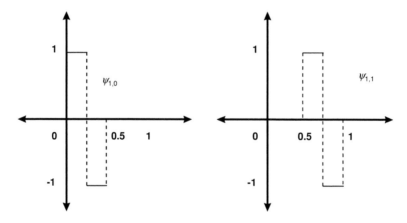

Fig. 5.3.4 The functions $\psi_{1,0}$ and $\psi_{1,1}$ represent scaled and shifted versions of the basic wavelet ψ.

Let's now reexamine the problem of expressing the function f in terms of averages and differences, or in our new terminology, in terms of scaling functions and wavelets. Since our finest resolution occurs on subintervals of length 1/4, we can examine $g_1(t)$ on each of the subintervals [0,1/4),...[3/4,1) to see where it fails at equaling the original function f. On [0,1/4) the difference is:

$$f(t) - g_1(t) = x_1 - a_{1,0} = d_{1,0}.$$

On [1/4,1/2) the difference is:

$$f(t) - g_1(t) = x_2 - a_{1,0} = -d_{1,0}.$$

Thus, for t in the interval [0,1/2) we can write:

$$f(t) = a_{1,0}\ \phi_{1,0}(t) + d_{1,0}\ \psi_{1,0}(t).$$

Similar analysis on $[1/2,3/4)$ and $[3/4,1)$ shows that

$$f(t) = a_{1,1}\ \phi_{1,1}(t) + d_{1,1}\ \psi_{1,1}(t)$$

for t in the interval $[1/2,1)$. Putting all of this together, we get a new representation for f on the entire interval $[0,1)$:

$$f(t) = a_{1,0}\ \phi_{1,0}(t) + a_{1,1}\ \phi_{1,1}\ (t) + d_{1,0}\ \psi_{1,0}(t) + d_{1,1}\ \psi_{1,1}(t). \tag{5.3.7}$$

We now have a representation of f as a sum of functions defined as averages on intervals of length $1/2$, plus whatever detail functions we need to make up the difference with the original function.

Following our steps in the previous section, we now introduce the average over the entire interval $[0,1)$, replacing the first two terms in (5.3.7) with $a_{0,0}\ \phi_{0,0}(t)$, and leaving the difference terms unchanged:

$$g_0(t) = a_{0,0}\ \phi_{0,0}(t) + d_{1,0}\ \psi_{1,0}(t) + d_{1,1}\ \psi_{1,1}(t).$$

On $[0,1/4)$ the difference between $f(t)$ and $g_0(t)$ is:

$$f(t) - g_0(t) = x_1 - a_{0,0} - d_{1,0} = d_{0,0},$$

while on $[1/4,1/2)$ we have

$$f(t) - g_0(t) = x_2 - a_{0,0} + d_{1,0} = d_{0,0}$$

also. Similarly, on $[1/2,1)$, $f(t) - g_0(t) = -d_{0,0}$, so that we can write $f(t)$ on all of $[0,1)$ as:

$$f(t) = a_{0,0}\ \phi_{0,0}(t) + d_{0,0}\ \psi_{0,0}(t) + d_{1,0}\ \psi_{1,0}(t) + d_{1,1}\ \psi_{1,1}(t). \tag{5.3.8}$$

Equation (5.3.8) is the functional analog of the sequence shown in (5.2.5).

5.4 MULTIRESOLUTION ANALYSIS

The process of decomposing a discrete sequence of values (such as a digital image) into blurred, or averaged, values, together with detail values at different scales, is called *multiresolution analysis*. In this section, we will illustrate multiresolution analysis with a simple example which forms the basis of the Haar wavelet. This section contains some mathematical detail regarding the function spaces where $\phi_{k,j}$ and $\psi_{k,j}$ live. Strictly speaking, this material is not necessary to apply wavelets to image compression. However, it is helpful in understanding the theory of wavelets in general, and as such it will help in understanding the topics in the following chapters where we look at advanced wavelets.

Let V^0 denote the space of all functions that are constant on the interval $[0,1)$. Then V^0 is a vector space of functions. That is, if we add two constant functions together, the result is certainly a constant function, and so is in V^0. Also, if we multiply a constant function by a number (scalar), the result is of course still constant, and so is also in V^0. The basic scaling function ϕ is a member of V^0. In fact, any member of V^0 can be obtained by multiplying ϕ by a suitable constant. Thus, $\{\phi\}$ forms a (rather trivial) basis for V^0.

Consider now a slightly more complicated space of functions. Let V^1 consist of all functions that are piecewise constant with constant pieces on $[0,1/2)$ and $[1/2,1)$. V^1 is also a vector space of functions. An example of an element of V^1 is the function $g_1(t)$ defined by equation (5.3.5). The scaling functions $\phi_{1,0}$ and $\phi_{1,1}$ are also elements of V^1. As suggested by (5.3.5), other elements of V^1 can be expressed as linear combinations of $\phi_{1,0}$ and $\phi_{1,1}$. One can show that $\{\phi_{1,0},\phi_{1,1}\}$ forms a basis for V^1. Also, note that a function constant on all of $[0,1)$ is trivially constant on each of the pieces $[0,1/2)$ and $[1/2,1)$, so that any element of V^0 is also an element of V^1, that is

$$V^0 \subset V^1.$$

We continue in this way, defining V^2 as the space of functions piecewise constant on the subintervals $[0,1/4)$, ..., $[3/4,1)$, and V^n the space of functions piecewise constant on the equally spaced subintervals of length $1/2^n$. Each V^n is a vector space, and the scaling functions $\{\phi_{n,j}; j=0,...,2^n-1\}$ form a basis for V^n. Moreover, the spaces V^n satisfy the nested sequence property:

$$V^0 \subset V^1 \subset ... \subset V^n \subset V^{n+1} \subset ...$$

Next we define an *inner product* for elements of V^n:

$$(f,g) = \int_0^1 f(t)g(t)dt. \tag{5.4.1}$$

A vector space equipped with an inner product is called an *inner product space*. Two functions are said to be *orthogonal* with respect to the inner product $(\cdot,\cdot)$ if

$$(f,g) = 0.$$

Orthogonality is of interest for several reasons. First of all, note that, for example,

$$(\phi_{1,0},\phi_{1,1}) = 0$$

so that $\{\phi_{1,0},\phi_{1,1}\}$ forms an orthogonal basis for V^1. In fact, for each k, and $j \neq l$, we have

$$(\phi_{k,j},\phi_{k,l}) = 0$$

so that $\{\phi_{k,j}; j = 0,...,2^k-1\}$ forms a set of mutually orthogonal basis vectors for V^k. Also, note that

$$(\psi_{k,j},\psi_{k,l}) = 0$$

for $j \neq l$.

Orthogonality is of interest for another reason. For a given inner produce space U contained within some larger inner product space S, we can talk about the set of vectors in S that are orthogonal to all of the vectors in U. This set is called the *orthogonal complement* of U in S, and is denoted $U^{\perp}$ (the shortcoming of this notation being its failure to display the implicit dependence on S, so sometimes this is also denoted $S\backslash U$). It is easy to check that $U^{\perp}$ is itself a vector space (and so is an inner product space as well).

We are interested in:

$$W^{k} \equiv \{h \in V^{k+1}: (h,f) = 0 \text{ for all } f \in V^{k}\}.$$

That is, W^{k} is defined as the orthogonal complement of V^{k} in V^{k+1}. We are already familiar with some members of W^{k}. Consider $\psi_{k,j}$. Note that the intervals where $\psi_{k,j}$ is constant are half the width of the intervals where members of V^{k} are constant. In other words, $\psi_{k,j} \in V^{k+1}$ for each j. Moreover, it is easy to convince yourself that $(\psi_{k,j},f) = 0$ for each $f \in V^{k}$, and thus $\psi_{k,j} \in W^{k}$ for each j and each k. For example, consider

$$f \equiv f_0 \phi_{1,0} + f_1 \phi_{1,1} \in V^{1},$$

where f_0, f_1 are scalar constants. Then

$$(\psi_{1,0},f) = f_0(\psi_{1,0},\phi_{1,0}) + f_1(\psi_{1,0},\phi_{1,1}) = 0 + 0 = 0,$$

since

$$(\psi_{1,0},\phi_{1,0}) = \int_0^{\frac{1}{4}} (1)(1)dt + \int_{\frac{1}{4}}^{\frac{1}{2}} (-1)(1)dt = 0$$

and

$$(\psi_{1,0},\phi_{1,1}) = \int_{\frac{1}{2}}^{1} (0)(1)dt = 0.$$

Thus, $\psi_{1,0} \in W^{1}$ and similarly $\psi_{1,1} \in W^{1}$. The argument for showing $\psi_{k,j} \in W^{k}$ is similar.

How big is W^{k}? Clearly it is no bigger than V^{k+1}, since $W^{k} \subset V^{k+1}$. Thus the dimension of W^{k} can be no more than 2^{k+1} (here we are talking about the vector space dimension, that is, the number of elements in a basis, as opposed to the fractal dimension discussed in earlier chapters). Since $\{\psi_{k,j}: j = 0,\ldots,2^{k}-1\}$ forms a set of 2^{k} mutually orthogonal, hence independent, vectors in W^{k}, the dimension of W^{k} is at least 2^{k}. But this is the most the dimension of W^{k} can be, for V^{k+1} is also home to another set of 2^{k} mutually orthogonal vectors, namely $\{\phi_{k,j}: j = 0,\ldots,2^{k}-1\}$, and each of these vectors is also orthogonal to each vector in $\{\psi_{k,j}: j = 0,\ldots,2^{k}-1\}$. Any vector in W^{k} not expressible in terms of $\{\psi_{k,j}\}$ would have to be expressible in terms of $\{\phi_{k,j}\}$, which is impossible. We have arrived at the following conclusion: the dimension of W^k is 2^k and $\{\psi_{k,j}: j = 0,...,2^k\text{-}1\}$ is a basis for W^k.

Isn't that interesting? The wavelet functions form a basis for W^k, the orthogonal complement of V^k in V^{k+1}. The previous section introduced wavelets as a means of restoring detail when moving to lower resolution. Here, wavelets arise as the basis for the orthogonal complement of the space of functions defined at a given resolution. This orthogonal complement can be thought of as the detail that is lost in going from one resolution level to the next lower resolution level. Wavelets can in fact be defined as any basis functions for this orthogonal complement.

A by-product of the above discussion is that we have stumbled upon an alternative basis for the higher resolution space V^{k+1}. We already know one basis for V^{k+1} is $\{\phi_{k+1,j}: j = 0,...,2^{k+1}\text{-}1\}$. The alternative basis is:

$$\{\phi_{k,0},...,\phi_{k,2^k\text{-}1},\psi_{k,0},...,\psi_{k,2^k\text{-}1}\}. \tag{5.4.2}$$

We can think of one step in the wavelet transform process, namely the step in going from the resolution of V^{k+1} to the lower resolution of V^k, as expressing an element $g_{k+1} \in V^{k+1}$ in the basis given by (5.4.2). Suppose $g_{k+1} \in V^{k+1}$ was originally expressed as

$$g_{k+1} = a_{k+1,0}\phi_{k+1,0} + ... + a_{k+1,2^{k+1}\text{-}1}\phi_{k,2^{k+1}\text{-}1}.$$

Then g_{k+1} can be expressed in terms of the basis (5.4.2), as, for example,

$$g_{k+1} = a_{k,0}\phi_{k,0} + ... + a_{k,2^k\text{-}1}\phi_{k,2^k\text{-}1} + d_{k,0}\psi_{k,0} + ... + d_{k,2^k\text{-}1}\psi_{k,2^k\text{-}1}.$$

The coefficients $\{d_{k,0},...,d_{k,2^k\text{-}1}\}$ become part of the wavelet transform. The next step in the process would express

$$g_k = a_{k,0}\phi_{k,0} + ... + a_{k,2^k\text{-}1}\phi_{k,2^k\text{-}1} \in V^k$$

in terms of $\{\phi_{k\text{-}1,j}\}$ and $\{\psi_{k\text{-}1,j}\}$.

5.5 NORMALIZATION

In what follows, it will be convenient to work with *normalized* scaling functions and wavelets. We define the *norm* of a vector f in an inner product space to be

$$\|f\| = \sqrt{(f,f)} .$$

A vector u in an inner product space is normalized if $\|u\| = 1$. A normalized vector u can be obtained from any non-zero vector f by dividing by the norm of the vector:

$$u = f/\|f\|.$$

Thus, to normalize $\phi_{k,j}$ and $\psi_{k,j}$ we need to determine their norms:

$$\left\| \phi_{k,j} \right\|^2 = \int\limits_0^1 \phi_{k,j}^2(t)\,dt = \int\limits_{\frac{j}{2^k}}^{\frac{j+1}{2^k}} dt = \frac{1}{2^k}.$$

Thus,

$$\left\| \phi_{k,j} \right\| = \frac{1}{\sqrt{2^k}}$$

for each $j = 0,\ldots,2^k\text{-}1$, and similarly,

$$\left\| \psi_{k,j} \right\| = \frac{1}{\sqrt{2^k}}$$

for each j. So, in order to work with normalized scaling functions and wavelets, a redefinition is necessary. From this point on, $\phi_{k,j}$ will be defined as:

$$\phi_{k,j}(t) \equiv \sqrt{2^k}\,\phi(2^k t - j),\ j = 0,\ldots,2^k - 1 \tag{5.5.1}$$

and $\psi_{k,j}$ will be defined as

$$\psi_{k,j}(t) \equiv \sqrt{2^k}\,\psi(2^k t - j),\ j = 0,\ldots,2^k - 1. \tag{5.5.2}$$

We will refer to the wavelets defined by (5.5.2) (with ψ defined by (5.3.6)) as the *normalized Haar wavelets*.

5.6 WAVELET TRANSFORM

Suppose we have a sequence consisting of 2^n points $\{x_1, x_2, \ldots, x_{2^n}\}$ for some integer $n > 0$. We can identify this sequence with the following function in V^n:

$$f(t) = x_1 \phi_{n,0}(t) + \ldots + x_{2^n} \phi_{n,2^{n-1}}(t). \tag{5.6.1}$$

The first step in computing the wavelet transform of the sequence $\{x_1, x_2, \ldots, x_{2^n}\}$ is to express $f(t)$ in terms of the alternative basis of the form (5.4.2) of V^n which has wavelets comprising half of its members:

$$\begin{aligned}
f(t) = a_{n-1,0}\phi_{n-1,0}(t) + \ldots + a_{n-1,2^{n-1}-1}\phi_{n-1,2^{n-1}-1}(t) + \\
d_{n-1,0}\psi_{n-1,0}(t) + \ldots + d_{n-1,2^{n-1}-1}\psi_{n-1,2^{n-1}-1}(t).
\end{aligned} \tag{5.6.2}$$

The coefficients $\{d_{n-1,0},...,d_{n-1,2^{n-1}-1}\}$ of the wavelet basis functions form half of the wavelet transform coefficients, so we will save these values. The transform process continues by applying the same basis transformation to the remaining terms in (5.6.2):

$$g_{n-1}(t) = a_{n-1,0}\phi_{n-1,0}(t) + ... + a_{n-1,2^{n-1}-1}\phi_{n-1,2^{n-1}-1}(t). \tag{5.6.3}$$

That is, g_{n-1} is an element of V^{n-1}, and so can be written in terms of an alternative basis consisting of scaling functions $\phi_{n-2,j}$ and wavelets $\psi_{n-2,j}$.

Before we continue too far down this path, one obvious question arises: How do we obtain the coefficients in (5.6.2) from the coefficients in (5.6.1)? This is what orthogonality lives for. Recall that each $\phi_{n-1,j}$ is orthogonal to each of the other $\phi_{n-1,k}$ as well as to all of the $\psi_{n-1,j}$, and similarly, each wavelet $\psi_{n-1,j}$ is orthogonal to the other wavelets $\psi_{n-1,k}$ and to all of the scaling functions $\phi_{n-1,j}$. Also, recall that each $\phi_{n-1,j}$ and each $\psi_{n-1,j}$ is normalized because of equations (5.5.1) and (5.5.2). To exploit this orthogonality and normalization, multiply both sides of (5.6.2) by $\phi_{n-1,j}(t)$ and integrate over t from 0 to 1. The result is

$$\int_0^1 f(t)\phi_{n-1,j}(t)dt = a_{n-1,j}. \tag{5.6.4}$$

Orthogonality is the reason there is only one term on the right side of (5.6.4) and normalization is the reason $a_{n-1,j}$ appears with no other multiplicative factors. Now substitute the right side of (5.6.1) for $f(t)$ in (5.6.4). For example, with $j = 0$, the left side of (5.6.4) becomes:

$$\int_0^{1/2^n} x_1\sqrt{2^n}\sqrt{2^{n-1}}dt + \int_{1/2^n}^{2/2^n} x_2\sqrt{2^n}\sqrt{2^{n-1}}dt = (x_1+x_2)\left(\frac{1}{\sqrt{2}}\right)2^n\left(\frac{1}{2^n}\right) \tag{5.6.5}$$

$$= (x_1 + x_2)/\sqrt{2}.$$

Combining (5.6.4) and (5.6.5), with $j = 0$, leads to

$$(x_1 + x_2)/\sqrt{2} = a_{n-1,0}. \tag{5.6.6}$$

The square root factor in (5.6.6) is a result of normalization. If we had used the non-normalized versions of the basis functions, then we would have recovered the two-point average seen in sections 5.2 and 5.3. The remaining coefficients $a_{n-1,j}$, $j = 1,...,2^n-1$, are computed similarly. Thus,

$$a_{n-1,j} = (x_{2j+1} + x_{2j+2})/\sqrt{2}, \quad j = 0,...,2^{n-1}-1. \tag{5.6.7}$$

Similarly, using the orthogonality and normalized properties of $\psi_{n-1,j}$, one determines the coefficients $d_{n-1,j}$ as

$$d_{n-1,j} = (x_{2j+1} - x_{2j+2})/\sqrt{2}, \; j=0,\ldots,2^{n-1}-1. \tag{5.6.8}$$

Once again, normalization is responsible for the square root factor in (5.6.8). Without normalization, we would have exactly the difference expressions derived in sections 5.2 and 5.3.

Equations (5.6.7) and (5.6.8) call out for expression as a single matrix equation:

$$\begin{bmatrix} \frac{1}{\sqrt{2}} & \frac{1}{\sqrt{2}} & 0 & . & . & . & . & 0 \\ 0 & 0 & \frac{1}{\sqrt{2}} & \frac{1}{\sqrt{2}} & 0 & . & . & 0 \\ . & . & . & . & . & . & . & . \\ 0 & . & . & . & . & 0 & \frac{1}{\sqrt{2}} & \frac{1}{\sqrt{2}} \\ \frac{1}{\sqrt{2}} & \frac{-1}{\sqrt{2}} & 0 & . & . & . & . & 0 \\ 0 & 0 & \frac{1}{\sqrt{2}} & \frac{-1}{\sqrt{2}} & 0 & . & . & 0 \\ . & . & . & . & . & . & . & . \\ 0 & . & . & . & . & 0 & \frac{1}{\sqrt{2}} & \frac{-1}{\sqrt{2}} \end{bmatrix} \begin{bmatrix} x_1 \\ . \\ . \\ . \\ . \\ . \\ x_{2^n} \end{bmatrix} = \begin{bmatrix} a_{n-1,0} \\ . \\ . \\ a_{n-1,2^{n-1}-1} \\ d_{n-1,0} \\ . \\ . \\ d_{n-1,2^{n-1}-1} \end{bmatrix}. \tag{5.6.9}$$

The matrix in (5.6.9) is a square matrix with 2^n rows and 2^n columns. Define

$$\mathbf{A}_n = \begin{bmatrix} \frac{1}{\sqrt{2}} & \frac{1}{\sqrt{2}} & 0 & . & . & . & . & 0 \\ 0 & 0 & \frac{1}{\sqrt{2}} & \frac{1}{\sqrt{2}} & 0 & . & . & 0 \\ . & . & . & . & . & . & . & . \\ 0 & . & . & . & . & 0 & \frac{1}{\sqrt{2}} & \frac{1}{\sqrt{2}} \end{bmatrix} \tag{5.6.10}$$

and

$$\mathbf{D}_n = \begin{bmatrix} \frac{1}{\sqrt{2}} & \frac{-1}{\sqrt{2}} & 0 & . & . & . & . & 0 \\ 0 & 0 & \frac{1}{\sqrt{2}} & \frac{-1}{\sqrt{2}} & 0 & . & . & 0 \\ . & . & . & . & . & . & . & . \\ 0 & . & . & . & . & 0 & \frac{1}{\sqrt{2}} & \frac{-1}{\sqrt{2}} \end{bmatrix}, \tag{5.6.11}$$

where $\mathbf{A}_n$ and $\mathbf{D}_n$ are $2^{n-1} \times 2^n$ matrices and $\mathbf{A}_n$ can be thought of as an averaging operator and $\mathbf{D}_n$ a differencing operator on $\mathbf{R}^{2^n} \rightarrow \mathbf{R}^{2^{n-1}}$. Let's also introduce the vector notation

$$\mathbf{x} = \begin{bmatrix} x_1 \\ \cdot \\ \cdot \\ \cdot \\ x_{2^n} \end{bmatrix}, \quad \mathbf{a}_{n-1} = \begin{bmatrix} a_{n-1,0} \\ \cdot \\ \cdot \\ \cdot \\ a_{n-1,2^{n-1}-1} \end{bmatrix}, \quad \mathbf{d}_{n-1} = \begin{bmatrix} d_{n-1,0} \\ \cdot \\ \cdot \\ \cdot \\ d_{n-1,2^{n-1}-1} \end{bmatrix}, \qquad (5.6.12)$$

where $\mathbf{x}$ is a column vector with 2^n components, and $\mathbf{a}_{n-1}$ and $\mathbf{d}_{n-1}$ are column vectors with 2^{n-1} rows. Then we can write (5.6.9) as

$$\begin{bmatrix} \mathbf{A}_n \\ \hdashline \mathbf{D}_n \end{bmatrix} \mathbf{x} = \begin{bmatrix} \mathbf{a}_{n-1} \\ \hdashline \mathbf{d}_{n-1} \end{bmatrix}. \qquad (5.6.13)$$

The matrix on the left side of (5.6.13) is a single $2^n \times 2^n$ matrix and the vector on the right side is a single $2^n \times 1$ column vector. At each step of the wavelet transform process, we collect detail coefficients and operate on average coefficients. In the case we are looking at here, the wavelet transform will have 2^n components. Equation (5.6.13) provides half of these as the detail coefficients in $\mathbf{d}_{n-1}$. Save these coefficients as half of the final wavelet transform. The next step in the wavelet transform is to apply the averaging and differencing operations at the next lowest resolution level to $\mathbf{a}_{n-1}$:

$$\begin{bmatrix} \mathbf{A}_{n-1} \\ \hdashline \mathbf{D}_{n-1} \end{bmatrix} \mathbf{a}_{n-1} = \begin{bmatrix} \mathbf{a}_{n-2} \\ \hdashline \mathbf{d}_{n-2} \end{bmatrix}. \qquad (5.6.14)$$

Here, $\mathbf{A}_{n-1}$ and $\mathbf{D}_{n-1}$ are $2^{n-2} \times 2^{n-1}$ matrices of the form shown in (5.6.10) and (5.6.11) and $\mathbf{a}_{n-2}$ and $\mathbf{d}_{n-2}$ are 2^{n-2}-dimensional column vectors. We keep $\mathbf{d}_{n-2}$ to form part of the wavelet transform, along with $\mathbf{d}_{n-1}$. We continue this process, applying averaging and differencing operations to $\mathbf{a}_k$ and keeping the resulting detail coefficients as part of the wavelet transform. At the final step, we keep the average $\mathbf{a}_0$, which is just a 1-component vector (in other words, a scalar) with the single component $a_{0,0}$. The resulting wavelet transform is:

$$\begin{bmatrix} \mathbf{a}_0 \\ \mathbf{d}_0 \\ \mathbf{d}_1 \\ \cdot \\ \cdot \\ \cdot \\ \mathbf{d}_{n-1} \end{bmatrix} \qquad (5.6.15)$$

which we can think of as a single column vector with $1 + 1 + 2 + \ldots + 2^{n-1} = 2^n$ components.

5.7 INVERSE WAVELET TRANSFORM

In order for the wavelet transform to be useful in applications such as image compression, we need to be able to undo the above process. That is, given a wavelet transform of the form (5.6.15), we need to be able to recover the original sequence $\{x_1, x_2, \ldots, x_{2^n}\}$ from which the transform was derived. We have actually gone through this inverse process previously in section 5.2, where we recovered x_1 and x_2 from the average and detail values. We follow a similar process here. The step in the wavelet transform going from resolution level k to k-1 looks like:

$$\begin{bmatrix} \mathbf{A}_k \\ \hline \mathbf{D}_k \end{bmatrix} \mathbf{a}_k = \begin{bmatrix} \mathbf{a}_{k-1} \\ \hline \mathbf{d}_{k-1} \end{bmatrix} \tag{5.7.1}$$

from which we obtain

$$\begin{aligned} (a_{k,0} + a_{k,1}) / \sqrt{2} &= a_{k-1,0} \\ (a_{k,0} - a_{k,1}) / \sqrt{2} &= d_{k-1,0}. \end{aligned} \tag{5.7.2}$$

For future reference, note also that (5.7.1) and (5.7.2) can be written as a pair of matrix-vector equations:

$$\begin{aligned} \mathbf{A}_k \mathbf{a}_k &= \mathbf{a}_{k-1} \\ \mathbf{D}_k \mathbf{a}_k &= \mathbf{d}_{k-1} \end{aligned} \tag{5.7.3}$$

for each $k = 1, \ldots, n$.

From (5.7.2) we can easily solve for the higher resolution terms $a_{k,0}$, $a_{k,1}$ from the lower resolution terms $a_{k-1,0}$ and $d_{k-1,0}$:

$$\begin{aligned} a_{k,0} &= (a_{k-1,0} + d_{k-1,0}) / \sqrt{2} \\ a_{k,1} &= (a_{k-1,0} - d_{k-1,0}) / \sqrt{2}. \end{aligned}$$

Similarly, for $j = 0, \ldots, 2^k$-1,

$$\begin{aligned} a_{k,2j} &= (a_{k-1,j} + d_{k-1,j}) / \sqrt{2} \\ a_{k,2j+1} &= (a_{k-1,j} - d_{k-1,j}) / \sqrt{2}. \end{aligned} \tag{5.7.4}$$

From a linear algebra point of view, we are solving equation (5.7.1) for the vector $\mathbf{a}_k$ by inverting the matrix that appears on the left side of that equation. That is, we have performed the following operation:

$$\mathbf{a}_k = \begin{bmatrix} \mathbf{A}_k \\ \hline \mathbf{D}_k \end{bmatrix}^{-1} \begin{bmatrix} \mathbf{a}_{k-1} \\ \hline \mathbf{d}_{k-1} \end{bmatrix}. \tag{5.7.5}$$

How do we know the inverse in (5.7.5) exists? Because we found it in (5.7.4)! In matrix form, this inverse looks like

$$
\begin{bmatrix} \mathbf{A}_k \\ \hline \mathbf{D}_k \end{bmatrix}^{-1} =
\begin{bmatrix}
\frac{1}{\sqrt{2}} & 0 & . & . & . & 0 & \frac{1}{\sqrt{2}} & 0 & . & . & . & 0 \\
\frac{1}{\sqrt{2}} & 0 & . & . & . & 0 & \frac{-1}{\sqrt{2}} & 0 & . & . & . & 0 \\
0 & \frac{1}{\sqrt{2}} & 0 & . & . & 0 & 0 & \frac{1}{\sqrt{2}} & 0 & . & . & 0 \\
0 & \frac{1}{\sqrt{2}} & 0 & . & . & 0 & 0 & \frac{-1}{\sqrt{2}} & 0 & . & . & 0 \\
0 & 0 & . & . & . & . & . & . & . & . & . & 0 \\
 & & & & & & & & & & & \\
. & . & . & . & . & . & . & . & . & . & . & . \\
0 & . & . & . & 0 & \frac{1}{\sqrt{2}} & 0 & . & . & . & 0 & \frac{1}{\sqrt{2}} \\
0 & . & . & . & 0 & \frac{1}{\sqrt{2}} & 0 & . & . & . & 0 & \frac{-1}{\sqrt{2}}
\end{bmatrix} .
\qquad (5.7.6)
$$

Comparison with (5.6.9) shows that this inverse matrix is just the transpose of the matrix used in the forward transform. In fact, the first 2^{k-1} columns of the matrix in (5.7.6) form exactly the transpose of $\mathbf{A}_k$, and the last 2^{k-1} columns form the transpose of $\mathbf{D}_k$. This convenient fact is due to the orthogonality and normalization of our scaling and wavelet basis functions. Thus, we can write the inverse in (5.7.6) as:

$$
\begin{bmatrix} \mathbf{A}_k \\ \hline \mathbf{D}_k \end{bmatrix}^{-1} = \begin{bmatrix} \mathbf{A}_k^* & \vdots & \mathbf{D}_k^* \end{bmatrix},
\qquad (5.7.7)
$$

where * denotes the matrix transpose.

We can now rewrite (5.7.5) as

$$
\begin{aligned}
\mathbf{a}_k &= \begin{bmatrix} \mathbf{A}_k \\ \hline \mathbf{D}_k \end{bmatrix}^{-1} \begin{bmatrix} \mathbf{a}_{k-1} \\ \hline \mathbf{d}_{k-1} \end{bmatrix} \\
&= \begin{bmatrix} \mathbf{A}_k^* & \vdots & \mathbf{D}_k^* \end{bmatrix} \begin{bmatrix} \mathbf{a}_{k-1} \\ \hline \mathbf{d}_{k-1} \end{bmatrix} \\
&= \mathbf{A}_k^* \mathbf{a}_{k-1} + \mathbf{D}_k^* \mathbf{d}_{k-1}.
\end{aligned}
\qquad (5.7.8)
$$

Equation (5.7.8) provides a practical formulation for obtaining $\mathbf{a}_k$ from $\mathbf{a}_{k-1}$ and $\mathbf{d}_{k-1}$: Apply $\mathbf{A}_k^*$ to $\mathbf{a}_{k-1}$ and $\mathbf{D}_k^*$ to $\mathbf{d}_{k-1}$ and add the result. This, in fact, rather than the direct inverse approach given by (5.7.5), is the approach used in the code in the accompanying software. Comparison with (5.7.3) shows the following to be true:

$$\mathbf{a}_k = \mathbf{A}_k^* \mathbf{A}_k \mathbf{a}_k + \mathbf{D}_k^* \mathbf{D}_k \mathbf{a}_k. \tag{5.7.9}$$

In fact, it is possible to show directly that the following relationship is true:

$$\mathbf{A}_k^* \mathbf{A}_k + \mathbf{D}_k^* \mathbf{D}_k = \mathbf{I}_{2^k} \tag{5.7.10}$$

where $\mathbf{I}_{2^k}$ is the $2^k \times 2^k$ identity matrix. The following relations also hold:

$$\begin{aligned}
\mathbf{A}_k \mathbf{A}_k^* &= \mathbf{I}_{2^{k-1}} \\
\mathbf{D}_k \mathbf{D}_k^* &= \mathbf{I}_{2^{k-1}}.
\end{aligned} \tag{5.7.11}$$

In the next chapter, we will require that relations analogous to (5.7.10) and (5.7.11) hold for the highpass and lowpass filters that lead to the definition of Daubechies wavelets.

5.8 WAVELET TRANSFORM IN TWO DIMENSIONS

So far, we have considered the wavelet transform only for one-dimensional sequences, and we have loosely referred to these sequences as "images". While it is true that we can always string out the rows and columns of an image into a single long sequence, that process results in a juxtaposition of information that is not representative of the arrangement of information in the original image. It is possible to extend the idea of the wavelet transform to higher dimensions. The easiest way to do this is to first transform the rows of the image, then transform the columns of the row-transformed image. This is easy to implement in code since the same one-dimensional transform can be used to transform both the rows and columns of the image.

To see why this works, consider the two-dimensional analog of the simple 4-element sequence treated in section 5.3. Suppose we now have a 4×4 image:

$$\begin{bmatrix}
x_{1,1} & x_{1,2} & x_{1,3} & x_{1,4} \\
x_{2,1} & x_{2,2} & x_{2,3} & x_{2,4} \\
x_{3,1} & x_{3,2} & x_{3,3} & x_{3,4} \\
x_{4,1} & x_{4,2} & x_{4,3} & x_{4,4}
\end{bmatrix} \tag{5.8.1}$$

which we can represent as a function on the unit square $[0,1] \times [0,1]$:

$$f(x,y) = \sum_{i=1}^{4} \sum_{j=1}^{4} x_{i,j} X_{I_i \times I_j}(x,y). \tag{5.8.2}$$

Equation (5.8.2) is the two-dimensional analog of equation (5.3.1). Here,

$$I_i \times I_j \equiv \left[\frac{i-1}{4}, \frac{i}{4}\right) \times \left[\frac{j-1}{4}, \frac{j}{4}\right)$$

$$= \{(x,y): x \in \left[\frac{i-1}{4}, \frac{i}{4}\right) \text{ and } y \in \left[\frac{j-1}{4}, \frac{j}{4}\right)\}$$

and

$$X_{I_i \times I_j}(x,y) = \begin{cases} 1 & \text{for } (x,y) \in I_i \times I_j \\ 0 & \text{otherwise} \end{cases}$$

$$= X_{I_i}(x) X_{I_j}(y) \qquad (5.8.3)$$

$$= \phi_{2,i-1}(x)\phi_{2,j-1}(y).$$

We can substitute (5.8.3) into (5.8.2) to obtain:

$$f(x,y) = \sum_{i=1}^{4}\sum_{j=1}^{4} x_{i,j}\phi_{2,i-1}(x)\phi_{2,j-1}(y)$$

$$= \sum_{i=1}^{4}\left\{\sum_{j=1}^{4} x_{i,j}\phi_{2,j-1}(y)\right\}\phi_{2,i-1}(x) \qquad (5.8.4)$$

$$= \sum_{i=1}^{4} \tilde{x}_i(y)\phi_{2,i-1}(x)$$

where

$$\tilde{x}_i(y) = \sum_{j=1}^{4} x_{i,j}\phi_{2,j-1}(y). \qquad (5.8.5)$$

Observe that for each $i = 1,\ldots,4$, equation (5.8.5) looks very much like equation (5.3.4). This means we can apply the one-dimensional wavelet transform just as before for each $i = 1,\ldots,4$, in (5.8.5). The result will be a new set of equations for $\tilde{x}_i(y)$ $i = 1,\ldots,4$, with coefficients in terms of the wavelet transform of $\{x_{i,1},\ldots,x_{i,4}\}$. Thus we arrive at the following:

$$\tilde{x}_i(y) = a_{0,0}^i\phi_{0,0}(y) + d_{0,0}^i\psi_{0,0}(y) + d_{1,0}^i\psi_{1,0}(y) + d_{1,1}^i\psi_{1,1}(y) \qquad (5.8.6)$$

for each $i = 1,\ldots,4$. This is the equivalent of applying the one-dimensional wavelet transform to each row of the original image (5.8.1). Now substitute (5.8.6) back into (5.8.4) and rearrange terms to obtain:

$$f(x,y) = \left\{\sum_{i=1}^{4} a_{0,0}^i \phi_{2,i-1}(x)\right\}\phi_{0,0}(y) + \left\{\sum_{i=1}^{4} d_{0,0}^i \phi_{2,i-1}(x)\right\}\psi_{0,0}(y) +$$

$$\left\{\sum_{i=1}^{4} d_{1,0}^i \phi_{2,i-1}(x)\right\}\psi_{1,0}(y) + \left\{\sum_{i=1}^{4} d_{1,1}^i \phi_{2,i-1}(x)\right\}\psi_{1,1}(y).$$

$$(5.8.7)$$

Each of the summation terms in brackets in (5.8.7) again looks very much like equation (5.3.4), and so the one-dimensional wavelet transform can be applied to each of these terms. This is the equivalent of applying the wavelet transform to each column of the original image (5.8.1).

To summarize the above discussion as it applies to images, one way to obtain a two-dimensional wavelet transform of a $2^n \times 2^n$ image is to first apply the one-dimensional wavelet transform to each of the 2^n rows, then apply the one-dimensional wavelet transform to each of the 2^n columns. This is not the only way to define two-dimensional wavelet transforms. This approach has the obvious implementation advantage of requiring no new development beyond the one-dimensional transform that is already available. It is quite effective for our image compression application.

5.8.1 What a wavelet transform looks like

What does the wavelet transform of an image look like? We can think of the averaging and detail extraction operations of the Haar wavelets as lowpass and highpass filtering operations. A lowpass filter allows low frequency information (i.e., low amount of detail) to pass through, while blocking high frequency (i.e., high detail) information, while a highpass filter allows high frequency information through while blocking low frequency information. Our 2-D wavelet transform applies a 1-D wavelet transform to each row, then a 1-D wavelet transform to the resulting information in each column. The diagram in Fig. 5.8.1 shows how to visualize this. Recall that the first step in the wavelet transform is to save the detail information from half of the coefficients. Thus fully a quarter of the 2-D transform coefficients result from a highpass filter (H) acting on the rows followed by a highpass filter operating on the resulting column information. This block of coefficients is indicated by HH_1 in the lower right corner of the diagram. Another quarter of the 2-D coefficients result from the lowpass filter (L) operating on the column information that has already passed through the row highpass filter. This block is indicated by LH_1 in the upper right corner of the diagram.[1] Similarly, the HL_1 block in the lower left corner of the diagram results from the lowpass row operation followed by the highpass column operation. The upper left corner of the diagram is subdivided into smaller blocks,

---

[1] The notation we are using here follows the mathematical convention for composition of operators. That is, if F and G are operators, then the mathematical notation for the operation of F followed by the operation of G is GF (i.e., G is applied to the result of applying F). Here, the notation for the composition of L followed by H is denoted LH. Unfortunately, this notation is not consistent with what appears in the wavelet literature, where this operator is usually denoted HL. The choice was made to use the mathematical notation because the next chapter will examine composition of operators extensively.

showing the wavelet transform operations acting on successively smaller numbers of coefficients, until the final coefficient in the upper left corner, which has had only lowpass operations performed on it.

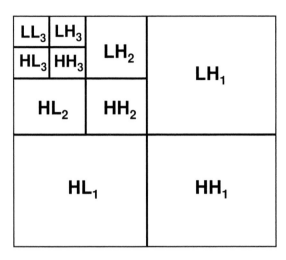

Fig. 5.8.1 Diagram of 2-D wavelet transform as a sequence of vertical and horizontal highpass (H) and lowpass (L) filtering operations. In the diagram, LH_x indicates a vertical highpass operation followed by a horizontal lowpass operation, while HL_x indicates a vertical lowpass operation followed by a horizontal highpass operation.

Figs. 5.8.2 (a)-(d) illustrate the effect of these highpass and lowpass operations acting on various types of images. Each pair of images shows an image together with a rendering of its two-dimensional Haar wavelet transform. The wavelet transform images were formed by decimating the array of wavelet coefficients by setting the smallest (in magnitude) 50% of the coefficients to zero. Pixels corresponding to the nonzero coefficients were then colored black, and pixels corresponding to zero coefficients were colored white. Since the wavelet transform itself may produce more than 50% zero coefficients, it is possible for more than 50% of the pixels to be white.

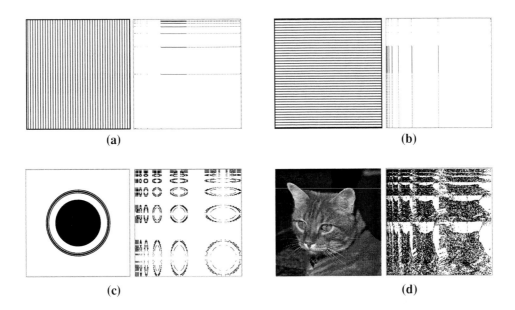

(a)   (b)

(c)   (d)

Fig. 5.8.2 Some images with their 2-D wavelet transforms. In each case, the image is on the left and its corresponding 2-D Haar wavelet transform is on the right. The wavelet transform images were formed by setting the smallest (in magnitude) 50% of the wavelet coefficients to zero and coloring the remaining nonzero coefficients black.

Fig. 5.8.2 (a) consists only of vertical lines, so any detail change occurs only when moving horizontally, that is, only when moving across the rows. There is no detail information when moving in the vertical direction along the columns. Thus, the H operator acting on rows will capture information, while the same operator acting on columns will destroy it. The effect of this is evident in the transform figure. All information in the lower half of the transform image is zero. This is because all of the coefficients in the lower half of the transform image have been subjected to a highpass operation on column information. The upper half of the transform image shows the detail information captured by moving across the rows. Only 3% of the coefficients are nonzero in this transform image. Fig. 5.8.2 (b) shows the converse situation when there is only vertical information and no horizontal information. Here, the right half of the transform image is zero. Once again, only 3% of the coefficients are nonzero.

Fig. 5.8.2 (c) shows a solid circle inside circular rings. The rings provide detail information in both the horizontal and vertical directions, and so nonzero coefficients appear in both the lower left and upper right blocks of the transform. Note that the circle itself contributes no detail information, except along its edge, and so there are no detail coefficients corresponding to the filled-in part of the circle. The single LL coefficient in the upper left corner of the transform provides all of the information needed to represent this part of the image. Approximately 9% of the coefficients are nonzero in this transform image.

Finally, Fig. 5.8.2 (d) shows a more realistic image with its 2-D wavelet transform. Notice that, as in the case of the circle image, the solid black background part of this image has no detail information and so results in zero values for coefficients in blocks away from the upper left corner of the transform. In this transform image, 50% of the coefficients are nonzero.

5.8.2 Simple wavelet compression scheme

A simple wavelet compression scheme is the following. Upon computing the wavelet transform, sort the wavelet coefficients and retain only the largest x% of the coefficients, setting the remaining smallest $(100-x)$% equal to 0, for some user-selectable value of x. Decode by applying the inverse wavelet transform to the decimated array of coefficients. Figs. 5.8.3 shows the result applying this scheme to the "Lena" image, using 10% and 5% of the wavelet coefficients. As you can see, good image quality can be obtained with a small fraction of the total number of wavelet coefficients. The 5% coefficient example shows a noticeable blockiness in the reconstructed images. This is a characteristic of using the Haar wavelet for image compression. The Daubechies wavelets developed in the next chapter will alleviate some of this blockiness.

Although Figs. 5.8.3 (a) and (b) use, respectively, 10% and 5% of the wavelet coefficients, these examples do not represent, respectively, 10:1 and 20:1 compression. This is because information about the location of the retained coefficients must also be stored, along with the actual coefficient values. Also, the wavelet coefficients tend to have significantly higher dynamic range than the original image pixels, and so require more bits for storage (or quantization that will degrade the quality of the decoded image). Chapter 7 discusses these issues, as well as more advanced coding techniques, in more detail.

(a)   (b)

Fig. 5.8.3 Simple wavelet compression of the "Lena" image, using the Haar wavelets. (a) Image reconstructed using just the largest 10% of the wavelet coefficients. (b) Image reconstructed using 5% of the wavelet coefficients. Average pixel error and PSNR: (a) 2.0376% and 30.9052 dB; (b) 2.8925% and 27.3918 dB. Compression ratio represented here is not 20:1 (5% case) or 10:1 (10% case) because information about the location of the retained coefficients must be stored and the wavelet coefficients require higher dynamic range than the original image.

6

DAUBECHIES WAVELETS

In the previous chapter, we saw that the ideas of simple averaging and differencing lead to the development of Haar wavelets and that these wavelets can be used for image compression. In this chapter we will see that we can extend these ideas to *weighted* averages and differences and that particular choices of weighting coefficients lead to different systems of wavelets. Ingrid Daubechies (1988) chose coefficients that lead to wavelet systems that are particularly well suited to compression of certain types of images. The wavelet image encoding techniques we will investigate in the next chapter can be used with either the Haar wavelets or the wavelets developed in this chapter.

6.1 WEIGHTED AVERAGES AND DIFFERENCES

Suppose we have a data sequence (e.g., an image): $\mathbf{x} = \{x_1, x_2, x_3, \ldots, x_n\}$ for some $n > 0$. Instead of the simple numerical average that led to the development of the Haar wavelets, we now consider a weighted average:

$$c_0 x_1 + c_1 x_2 + \ldots + c_{N-1} x_N$$

for some set of coefficients $c_0, c_1, \ldots, c_{N-1}$, $N \geq 2$. By convention, we define $c_k = 0$ for $k < 0$ or $k \geq N$. The analog of the simple difference operation is the following:

$$c_1 x_1 - c_0 x_2 + c_3 x_3 - c_2 x_4 + \ldots .$$

Note that this choice leads to the following orthogonality property:

$$(c_0, c_1, c_2, c_3, \ldots) \bullet (c_1, -c_0, c_3, -c_2, \ldots) = 0. \qquad (6.1.1)$$

6.1.1 Lowpass and highpass filtering

Let $n = 2^m$ for some $m > 0$ and extend the data sequence by wraparound to obtain a periodic sequence:

$$\ldots, x_1, x_2, \ldots, x_n, x_1, x_2, \ldots, x_n, x_1, x_2, \ldots, x_n, \ldots .$$

That is, $x_0 \equiv x_n$, $x_{-1} \equiv x_{n-1}$, $x_{n+1} \equiv x_1$, $x_{n+2} \equiv x_2$, and so on. Recall that $c_k = 0$ for $k < 0$ or $k \geq N$. Define the operator $\mathbf{L}_n: \mathbf{R}^n \to \mathbf{R}^{n/2}$ by:

$$(\mathbf{L}_n \mathbf{x})_i = \sum_{j=1}^{n} c_{j-2i+1} x_j, \quad i = 1, \ldots, \frac{n}{2}.$$

The operator $\mathbf{L}_n$ is called a *lowpass filter*.

Define the operator $\mathbf{H}_n: \mathbf{R}^n \to \mathbf{R}^{n/2}$ by:

$$(\mathbf{H}_n\mathbf{x})_i = \sum_{j=1}^{n} (-1)^{j+1} c_{2i-j} x_j, \ i = 1,\ldots,\frac{n}{2}.$$

The operator $\mathbf{H}_n$ is called a *highpass filter*. Together, $\mathbf{L}_n$ and $\mathbf{H}_n$ form a *quadrature mirror filter* (QMF) pair (see Gopinath and Burrus 1993).

6.1.2 Matrix representation

Let $\mathbf{L}_n[i,j]$ denote the i,j element of the matrix representation of the operator $\mathbf{L}_n$, where we assume wraparound of the data sequence $\mathbf{x}$. Then

$$\mathbf{L}_n[i,j] = \begin{cases} c_{j-2i+1} & \text{if } 0 \le j-2i+1 \le N-1 \\ c_{j-2i+1+n} & \text{if } j-2i+1 < 0 \\ 0 & \text{if } j-2i+1 \ge N \end{cases}.$$

Similarly, let $\mathbf{H}_n[i,j]$ denote the i,j element of the matrix representation of the operator $\mathbf{H}_n$, so that

$$\mathbf{H}_n[i,j] = \begin{cases} (-1)^{j+1} c_{j-2i+1} & \text{if } 0 \le 2i-j \le N-1 \\ (-1)^{j+1} c_{2i-j+n} & \text{if } 2i-j < 0 \\ 0 & \text{if } 2i-j \ge N \end{cases}.$$

$\mathbf{L}_n[i,j]$ and $\mathbf{H}_n[i,j]$ are defined for $i = 1,2,\ldots,n/2$ and $j = 1,2,\ldots,n$, so that $\mathbf{L}_n$ and $\mathbf{H}_n$ are $n/2 \times n$ matrices.

As an example, we can construct the matrices $\mathbf{L}_n$ and $\mathbf{H}_n$ for the case $n = 8$ and $N = 6$ (so the coefficients are $c_0, c_1,\ldots,c_5$). Here's what the matrices $\mathbf{L}_8$ and $\mathbf{H}_8$ look like:

$$\mathbf{L}_8 = \begin{bmatrix} c_0 & c_1 & c_2 & c_3 & c_4 & c_5 & 0 & 0 \\ 0 & 0 & c_0 & c_1 & c_2 & c_3 & c_4 & c_5 \\ c_4 & c_5 & 0 & 0 & c_0 & c_1 & c_2 & c_3 \\ c_2 & c_3 & c_4 & c_5 & 0 & 0 & c_0 & c_1 \end{bmatrix}$$

$$\mathbf{H}_8 = \begin{bmatrix} c_1 & -c_0 & 0 & 0 & c_5 & -c_4 & c_3 & -c_2 \\ c_3 & -c_2 & c_1 & -c_0 & 0 & 0 & c_5 & -c_4 \\ c_5 & -c_4 & c_3 & -c_2 & c_1 & -c_0 & 0 & 0 \\ 0 & 0 & c_5 & -c_4 & c_3 & -c_2 & c_1 & -c_0 \end{bmatrix}.$$

6.2 PROPERTIES AND CONDITIONS ON THE COEFFICIENTS

In Chapter 5, we saw that certain properties of the averaging and difference operators $\mathbf{A}_n$ and $\mathbf{D}_n$, such as orthogonality and the properties given by (5.7.10) and (5.7.11), followed from the definitions of these operators. In the present chapter, we will impose conditions on the coefficients $c_0, \ldots, c_{N-1}$ so that similar properties hold for $\mathbf{L}_n$ and $\mathbf{H}_n$.

From our construction of the matrices $\mathbf{L}_n$ and $\mathbf{H}_n$ and the orthogonality property (6.1.1), we have the following *orthogonality property*:

$$\mathbf{H}_n \mathbf{L}_n^* = \mathbf{L}_n \mathbf{H}_n^* = \mathbf{0}_{n/2},$$

where $\mathbf{0}_{n/2}$ is the $n/2 \times n/2$ matrix that is identically zero and * indicates the matrix transpose. We impose the following condition on $\mathbf{L}_n$ (and hence on the coefficients $c_0, \ldots, c_{N-1}$):

$$\mathbf{L}_n \mathbf{L}_n^* = \mathbf{I}_{n/2}, \tag{6.2.1}$$

where $\mathbf{I}_{n/2}$ is the $n/2 \times n/2$ identity matrix. Condition (6.2.1) is equivalent to:

$$\sum_{k=0}^{N-1} c_k c_{k+2m} = \delta_{0m}, \quad m = 0, \pm 1, \pm 2, \ldots, \tag{6.2.2}$$

where δ_{ij} is the Kronecker delta function:

$$\delta_{ij} = \begin{cases} 1 & \text{if } i = j \\ 0 & \text{if } i \neq j \end{cases}.$$

Condition (6.2.1) also implies:

$$\mathbf{H}_n \mathbf{H}_n^* = \mathbf{I}_{n/2}. \tag{6.2.3}$$

Note that

$$\begin{aligned}
\mathbf{H}_n(\mathbf{L}_n^* \mathbf{L}_n + \mathbf{H}_n^* \mathbf{H}_n) &= (\mathbf{H}_n \mathbf{L}_n^*)\mathbf{L}_n + (\mathbf{H}_n \mathbf{H}_n^*)\mathbf{H}_n \\
&= \mathbf{0}_{n/2}\mathbf{L}_n + \mathbf{I}_{n/2}\mathbf{H}_n \\
&= \mathbf{H}_n
\end{aligned}$$

and similarly,

$$\mathbf{L}_n(\mathbf{L}_n^* \mathbf{L}_n + \mathbf{H}_n^* \mathbf{H}_n) = \mathbf{L}_n.$$

Thus, the operator $\mathbf{L}_n^* \mathbf{L}_n + \mathbf{H}_n^* \mathbf{H}_n : \mathbf{R}^n \to \mathbf{R}^n$ is the identity operator:

$$\mathbf{L}_n^* \mathbf{L}_n + \mathbf{H}_n^* \mathbf{H}_n = \mathbf{I}_n. \tag{6.2.4}$$

The property (6.2.4) is analogous to property (5.7.10).

6.3 WAVELET TRANSFORM

The wavelet transform can be defined as a tree of lowpass and highpass filters, as shown in Fig. 6.3.1. As was the case for the averaging and difference operators of Chapter 5, the idea here is fairly simple. The lowpass filters $\{L_n\}$ reduce the amount of information in the signal $\mathbf{x}$. The highpass filters $\{H_n\}$ represent the information that is lost. Fig. 6.3.1 shows an example of the wavelet transform operating on an element $\mathbf{x}$ in $\mathbf{R}^8$. Recall that $L_n, H_n : \mathbf{R}^n \rightarrow \mathbf{R}^{n/2}$, that is, the filters decimate the dimension of the input vector by half. The wavelet transform is the element of $\mathbf{R}^8$ represented by $\{L_2L_4L_8\mathbf{x}, H_2L_4L_8\mathbf{x}, H_4L_8\mathbf{x}, H_8\mathbf{x}\}$. That is, the wavelet transform consists of the final weighted average $L_2L_4L_8\mathbf{x}$ plus all of the detail vectors collected at each step of the transform process.

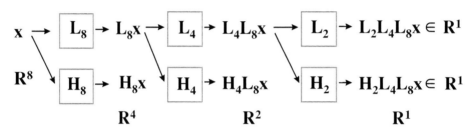

Fig. 6.3.1 Wavelet transform as a tree of lowpass and highpass filters. In this example, the transform is operating on an element x in $\mathbf{R}^8$. The output of the transform is an element of $\mathbf{R}^8$ consisting of the lowpass term $L_2L_4L_8\mathbf{x} \in \mathbf{R}^1$ together with the three highpass terms $H_8\mathbf{x} \in \mathbf{R}^4$, $H_4L_8 \in \mathbf{R}^2$, and $H_2L_4L_8 \in \mathbf{R}^1$.

Property (6.2.4) is the key to constructing the inverse wavelet transform. The inverse transform process is just the reverse of the steps that make up the transform process. Fig. 6.3.2 shows an example of how to recover the element $\mathbf{x} \in \mathbf{R}^8$ from its wavelet transform. For example,

$$L_2^* L_2 L_4 L_8 \mathbf{x} + H_2^* H_2 L_4 L_8 \mathbf{x} = (L_2^* L_2 + H_2^* H_2) L_4 L_8 \mathbf{x}$$
$$= L_4 L_8 \mathbf{x}$$

where we have used the fact that $L_2^* L_2 + H_2^* H_2 = I_2$, the identity operator on $\mathbf{R}^2$.

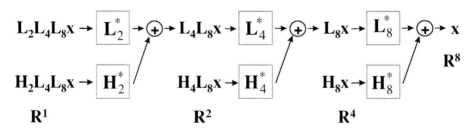

Fig. 6.3.2 Inverse wavelet transform.

6.4 SCALING FUNCTIONS AND WAVELET FUNCTIONS

We now extend the notion of scaling functions and wavelet functions, developed in the previous chapter for the Haar wavelet, to more general wavelets. The Haar scaling function $\phi(t)$ defined by (5.3.2) satisfies the following relation:

$$\phi(t) = \phi(2t) + \phi(2t - 1).$$

Suppose now, given a set of coefficients $c_0, c_1, \ldots, c_{N-1}$, we try to find a general scaling function $\phi(t)$ that satisfies the following property:

$$\phi(t) = s \bullet (c_0 \phi(2t) + c_1 \phi(2t - 1) + \ldots + c_{N-1} \phi(2t - (N - 1))). \tag{6.4.1}$$

Equation (6.4.1) is called the *dilation equation* (Strang 1989). The constant $s \neq 0$ is introduced to allow some flexibility in ensuring the existence of such a function ϕ satisfying (6.4.1) and the other properties we are about to impose. The constant s will in fact be determined by these properties.

We now introduce two additional properties, which are satisfied by the Haar scaling function, that we require of our general scaling function. The first of these is *normalization*:

$$\|\phi\|^2 \equiv \int_{-\infty}^{\infty} \phi^2(t) dt = 1. \tag{6.4.2}$$

The second property is *orthogonality* of translates:

$$\int_{-\infty}^{\infty} \phi(2t - j)\phi(2t - m) dt = \delta_{j,m}. \tag{6.4.3}$$

Integration of the dilation equation (6.4.1) leads to:

$$\int \phi(t) dt = s \sum_{j=0}^{N-1} c_j \int \phi(2t - j) dt = \left(\frac{1}{2}\right) s \sum_{j=0}^{N-1} c_j \int \phi(u) du,$$

from which we get:

$$\frac{2}{s} = \sum_{j=0}^{N-1} c_j \tag{6.4.4}$$

as a condition on the c_j's in order that such a function ϕ exists.

Then normalization (6.4.2) and orthogonality (6.4.3) applied to the dilation equation (6.4.1) lead to:

$$s^2 \left(\sum_{j=0}^{N-1} c_j^2 \right) \cdot \left(\frac{1}{2} \right) = 1,$$

and insertion of (6.2.2) with $m = 0$ provides a value for s:

$$s = \sqrt{2}.$$

Just as the Haar wavelet function is defined in terms of the difference operator, we can now define a more general wavelet function in terms of the highpass filter operator. For example, for $N = 4$, define the wavelet function $\psi(t)$ by:

$$\psi(t) = \frac{1}{\sqrt{2}}(c_3 \phi(2t) - c_2 \phi(2t - 1) + c_1 \phi(2t - 2) - c_0 \phi(2t - 3)). \qquad (6.4.6)$$

So, if we know the coefficients $c_0, c_1, c_2, \ldots$, we can find $\phi(t)$ and $\psi(t)$ recursively using (6.4.1) and (6.4.6). For example, if values of $\phi(t)$ are known at the integers, then we can easily find $\phi(1/2)$, $\psi(1/2)$, $\phi(1/4)$, and so on.

Equations (6.2.2) and (6.4.4) provide two conditions on the c_j's. For example, with $N = 2$, we get

$$c_0^2 + c_1^2 = 1, \qquad \sqrt{2} = c_0 + c_1,$$

as conditions for determining c_0, c_1. This leads to

$$c_0 = c_1 = \frac{1}{\sqrt{2}}$$

as the coefficients for the Haar scaling function and wavelets.

For $N > 2$, we need additional conditions to determine the c_j's.

6.5 DAUBECHIES WAVELETS

Daubechies (1988) chose the following conditions on the c_j's: Choose $\mathbf{W} = (c_3, -c_2, c_1, -c_0)$ so that the vectors $(1,1,1,1)$ and $(1,2,3,4)$ have zero components along $\mathbf{W}$. That is, the following should be true:

$$\begin{aligned} c_3 - c_2 + c_1 - c_0 &= 0 \\ c_3 - 2c_2 + 3c_1 - 4c_0 &= 0. \end{aligned} \qquad (6.5.1)$$

Conditions (6.5.1) are equivalent to saying that $\mathbf{W}$ has vanishing zeroth and first moments. This means that constant and linear signal information can be greatly compressed. For images that have large areas that are relatively smooth, such as the "Lena" image, this turns out to be advantageous for image compression. Not only is the overall error reduced for a given compression rate, but much of the blockiness associated with Haar wavelet compression is reduced as well.

Using conditions (6.5.1) along with the normalization and orthogonality conditions, you can find the Daubechies coefficients:

$$c_0 = \frac{1+\sqrt{3}}{4\sqrt{2}}, \qquad c_1 = \frac{3+\sqrt{3}}{4\sqrt{2}},$$

$$c_2 = \frac{3-\sqrt{3}}{4\sqrt{2}}, \qquad c_3 = \frac{1-\sqrt{3}}{4\sqrt{2}}.$$

These coefficients define the wavelets known as *D4 Daubechies wavelets*. Requiring vanishing higher moments leads to systems of Daubechies wavelets with more coefficients. For example, the *D6 Daubechies wavelets* are obtained by requiring a vanishing second moment:

$$1^2 c_5 - 2^2 c_4 + 3^2 c_3 - 4^2 c_2 + 5^2 c_1 - 6^2 c_0 = 0,$$

in addition to vanishing zeroth and first moments. There are other Daubechies wavelets, including systems with 12 and 20 coefficients.

There is a simple way to generate a graph of these wavelet functions by applying the inverse wavelet transform to a long (e.g., 1024 points) unit vector, that is, a vector with a 1 in one position and 0's in every other position (Press, et al., 1992). Fig. 6.5.1 shows graphs of the D4 and D6 wavelet functions generated in this way.

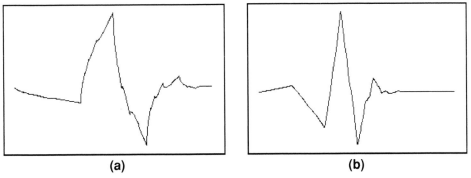

(a)   **(b)**

Fig. 6.5.1 The Daubechies D4 (a) and D6 (b) wavelet functions. These graphs were generated by applying the inverse wavelet transform to a unit vector of length 1024, with nonzero component in position 6 (a) and 11 (b), respectively.

The D4 wavelet function shown in Fig. 6.5.1 has some interesting properties. It is continuous, but not differentiable. Its derivative fails to exist at points $k/2^n$, where k and n are integers. At these points, it is left differentiable, but not right differentiable. It is 0 outside the interval [0,3]. A function whose nonzero values are restricted to a closed bounded interval is said to have *compact support*. All of the Daubechies wavelet functions have compact support. The D4 wavelet function is in fact fractal, in the sense that its discontinuities are independent of scale. The smoothness of the Daubechies wavelets increases with p, the number of vanishing moments, gaining about half a derivative for each increase in p. The D6 Daubechies wavelet function has a continuous first derivative, but higher derivatives fail to exist.

6.6 SIMPLE IMAGE COMPRESSION WITH DAUBECHIES WAVELETS

The vanishing moments property of the Daubechies wavelets means that they should be well suited to compression of images that have large smooth areas. For example, image segments that are of a nearly constant tone, or a linearly changing tone, should compress well with these wavelets. Figs. 6.6.1 - 6.6.2 show that the D4 Daubechies wavelets do a good job of compressing the "Rose" and "Lena" images. Comparison with Figs. 6.2.1 - 6.2.2 shows that D4 wavelet compression produces smaller errors than the corresponding Haar wavelet compression. In addition, block artifacts are reduced. In fact, the errors introduced by compression with the Daubechies wavelets tend to be of a blurry nature, as though one were looking at the image through an old glass window. This is less objectionable than the blockiness that occurs with Haar wavelet, or for that matter, fractal, image compression. Table 6.6.1 shows the actual error rates for the "Lena" image for the Haar and Daubechies wavelets. These values are plotted in Fig. 6.6.4.

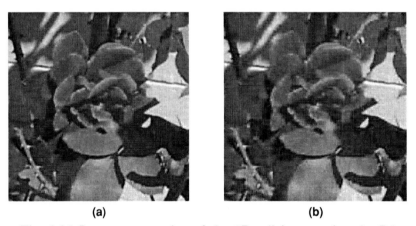

(a)   **(b)**

Fig. 6.6.1 Image compression of the "Rose" image using the D4 Daubechies wavelets. (a) 10% wavelet coefficients; average pixel error: 1.8929% (31.7549 dB PSNR). (b) 5% wavelet coefficients; average pixel error: 2.8264% (28.0999 dB PSNR).

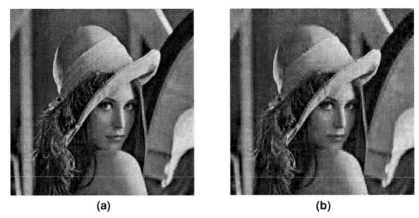

(a)   (b)

Fig. 6.6.2 Image compression of the "Lena" image using the D4 Daubechies wavelets. (a) 10% wavelet coefficients; average pixel error: 1.7066% (32.5803 dB PSNR). (b) 5% wavelet coefficients; average pixel error: 2.5006% (28.9101 dB PSNR).

While the Daubechies wavelets provide better compression performance for many images, Fig. 6.6.3 and Table 6.6.2 show that this advantage may not always be significant. The "Winter 1" image contains much more high frequency detail information than either the "Rose" or "Lena" images. The optimal choice of wavelets for compression is image dependent. Mandal, Panchanathan and Aboulnasr (1996) discuss this issue, and also suggest a way to quantify the detail content of an image in order to help choose an appropriate wavelet system.

(a)   (b)

Fig. 6.6.3 "Winter 1" image (a) and compressed version (b) using 10% of the D4 Daubechies wavelet coefficients. Average pixel error: 4.4540% (24.4362 dB PSNR). The same image compressed using 10% of the Haar wavelet coefficients yields 4.5452% average pixel error (24.2073 PSNR).

		10% Coefficients	5% Coefficients	1% Coefficients
Haar:	**Average Error**	**2.0376**	**2.8925 %**	**5.1009 %**
	PSNR	**30.9052**	**26.3918 dB**	**22.2369 dB**
D4:	**Average Error**	**1.7066 %**	**2.5006 %**	**4.6811 %**
	PSNR	**32.5803 dB**	**28.9101 dB**	**23.4130 dB**
D6:	**Average Error**	**1.6699 %**	**2.4530 %**	**4.7459 %**
	PSNR	**32.8309 dB**	**29.1049 dB**	**23.3612 dB**

Table 6.6.1 Error rates for compression of the "Lena" image, using 10%, 5% and 1% of the wavelet coefficients, for the Haar, Daubechies D4 and D6 wavelets.

		10% Coefficients	5% Coefficients	1% Coefficients
Haar:	**Average Error**	**4.5452 %**	**5.7742 %**	**8.1284 %**
	PSNR	**24.2073 dB**	**21.7420 dB**	**18.3067 dB**
D4:	**Average Error**	**4.4540 %**	**5.6570 %**	**6.8949 %**
	PSNR	**24.4362 dB**	**22.0399 dB**	**18.6811 dB**
D6:	**Average Error**	**4.4371 %**	**5.6506 %**	**6.8417 %**
	PSNR	**24.4696 dB**	**22.0911 dB**	**18.7611 dB**

Table 6.6.2 Error rates for compression of the "Winter 1" image, using 10%, 5% and 1% of the wavelet coefficients, for the Haar, Daubechies D4 and D6 wavelets.

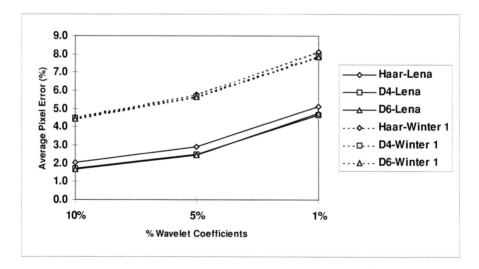

Fig. 6.6.4 Error rates for Haar and Daubechies D4 and D6 wavelets, for the "Lena" and "Winter 1" images. For the "Lena" image, the Daubechies wavelets provide a clear improvement over the Haar wavelets. However, for the more detailed "Winter 1" image, the error performance is virtually the same for all three wavelets.

6.7 OTHER WAVELET SYSTEMS

The Haar and Daubechies wavelets considered here are just a small sampling of a much larger universe of wavelet systems being used in signal and image processing applications. The Haar and Daubechies wavelet systems have the property of compact support, as discussed above, and are also orthogonal. That is, the scaling functions $\phi_{k,j}$ and wavelet functions $\psi_{k,j}$ satisfy:

$$\left.\begin{array}{l}(\phi_{k,j},\phi_{k,l})=0\\(\psi_{k,j},\psi_{k,l})=0\end{array}\right\} \text{ for } j \neq l. \tag{6.7.1}$$

In addition, these functions also satisfy

$$(\phi_{k,j},\psi_{k,l})=0 \text{ for all } j, l. \tag{6.7.2}$$

The Daubechies wavelet systems also have the properties of smoothness and vanishing moments.

There are other properties that might be desirable in a wavelet system. One such property is symmetry, that is, the scaling functions and wavelet functions are symmetric about their centers. The Haar wavelets satisfy this property, but the Daubechies wavelets do not. In fact, in turns out that the Haar wavelets are the *only* wavelets that are symmetric and orthogonal and compactly supported (Daubechies 1992).

So, for example, if we want smooth symmetric wavelets with compact support, we have to be willing to give up orthogonality. Many of the newer wavelet systems used in applications are not orthogonal, in the sense of satisfying properties (6.7.1) - (6.7.2), but rather satisfy some weakened form of orthogonality. One such property is *semiorthogonality* (Stollnitz, DeRose and Salesin, 1996). Semiorthogonal wavelet systems satisfy (6.7.2), but not (6.7.1).

Another weakened form of orthogonality is *biorthogonality* (Burrus, Gopinath and Guo, 1998) Biorthogonality is related to the concept of *duality*. Suppose $\{u_1,u_2,\ldots,u_n\}$ is a set of basis functions which are not orthogonal. It is possible to express a function f as a linear combination of these basis functions:

$$f(x) = \sum_{j=1}^{n} a_j u_j(x).$$

The lack of orthogonality makes it more difficult to determine the coefficients a_j. However, there is another basis $\{\tilde{u}_1,\tilde{u}_2,\ldots,\tilde{u}_n\}$ with the property that

$$a_j = (f,\tilde{u}_j).$$

The functions $\tilde{u}_j$ also satisfy the property

$$(u_k, \tilde{u}_j) = 0 \quad \text{for} \quad j \neq k.$$

The basis $\{\tilde{u}_1, \tilde{u}_2, \ldots, \tilde{u}_n\}$ is called the *dual basis* corresponding to $\{u_1, u_2, \ldots, u_n\}$. A *biorthogonal* wavelet system consists of four sets of functions: a scaling function basis $\{\phi_{k,j}\}$ and its dual basis $\{\tilde{\phi}_{k,j}\}$, and a wavelet function basis $\{\psi_{k,j}\}$ and its dual basis $\{\tilde{\psi}_{k,j}\}$. The condition of biorthogonality requires that these function sets satisfy the following property:

$$\left.\begin{aligned} (\phi_{k,j}, \tilde{\psi}_{k,l}) &= 0 \\ (\psi_{k,j}, \tilde{\phi}_{k,l}) &= 0 \end{aligned}\right\} \quad \text{for all } j, k, l.$$

In addition, duality implies

$$\left.\begin{aligned} (\phi_{k,j}, \tilde{\phi}_{k,l}) &= 0 \\ (\psi_{k,j}, \tilde{\psi}_{k,l}) &= 0 \end{aligned}\right\} \quad \text{for } j \neq l.$$

Biorthogonal wavelet systems have become a popular choice in the image compression applications. Villasenor, Belzer and Liao (1995) evaluated over 4300 biorthogonal wavelet systems for application to image compression.

7

WAVELET IMAGE COMPRESSION TECHNIQUES

In the previous two chapters, we looked at simple examples of wavelet image compression that consist of applying a wavelet transform to an image and then removing some of the information from the transformed array. These examples illustrate the potential of using wavelets for image compression. However, practical wavelet image compression techniques in use today use more sophisticated methods for encoding information in the wavelet domain than the simple sorting and decimation approach used for these examples. The present chapter examines some of the issues associated with wavelet image compression. It also introduces zerotree encoding, a technique that addresses these issues and forms the basis for most of the successful wavelet compression schemes in use today.

7.1 INTRODUCTION

The wavelet transform is easy to implement and fast to compute. It should not be surprising, therefore, that non-wavelet issues tend to dominate the implementation of wavelet image compression schemes. For example, in the simple compression scheme used in the previous two chapters, the process of extracting information about the relative significance of the coefficients, in order to decide which coefficients to decimate, takes up most of the encoding time. Fig. 7.1.1 shows the encoding times for a 256×256 image, using various percentages of Haar wavelet coefficients. The wavelet transform computation time remains constant at 3 seconds in each case. As the percentage of retained wavelet coefficients increases, the time required to select these coefficients increases and dominates the total compression time.

At first glance, one might think that a wavelet compressed image using 10% of the wavelet coefficients represents a 10:1 compression ratio. However, the situation is not quite that propitious. The problem is that, in addition to the values of the coefficients, we need to know *which* 10% of the coefficients are being used to represent the compressed image. For example, if we wish to store row and column information for a 256×256 image, we would need an additional 2 bytes per coefficient. Also, the wavelet coefficients of an 8-bit image tend to require more than 8 bits for representation. For example, the wavelet coefficients of the "Rose" image have a range of -2979 to 22,737, and so would require a full 2-byte integer for storage. So, we need roughly 4 bytes per stored coefficient (as before, without any special coding techniques being applied). A 10% wavelet compressed 256×256 image would have 6554 coefficients each requiring 4 bytes, for a compression ratio of approximately 2.5:1, rather than 10:1. The 5% wavelet compressed image represents a compression ratio of 5:1. Using more than 25% of the wavelet coefficients results in no compression at all.

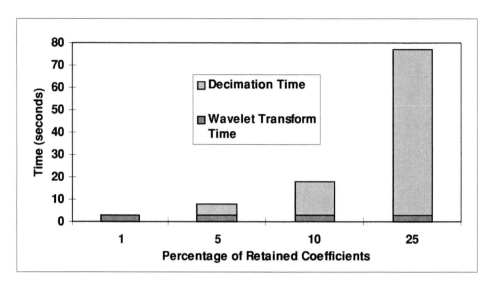

Fig. 7.1.1 Compression times (200 MHz Pentium PC) for a 256 × 256 image, using the Haar transform. As the decimation percent increases, the wavelet transform time remains constant, while the time required for selecting the coefficients to be retained ("Decimation Time") dominates the total compression time.

There are two areas to focus on when trying to improve the compression ratio for wavelet image coding. The first is storage of the coefficients themselves, and the second is the encoding of the coefficient location information.

Approaches for compressing coefficient values include:
   -Scalar quantization, either uniform or non-uniform.
   -Setting smallest $x\%$ of coefficient values to 0, with quantization of the remaining coefficients. This is a form of non-uniform quantization. Runlength coding can be applied to the 0 coefficients.
   -Entropy coding of the coefficients.

Approaches for compressing coefficient location information include:
   -Quantizing coefficients in place. Compression comes from the lower bit rate of the quantization. This can be combined with runlength coding.
   -Storing location information (row, column) with the coefficient value. Store this information only for those coefficients that survive the decimation process. This is feasible only if a small number of coefficients are retained.
   -Using a binary significance map. This is a structure with 1 bit per coefficient. A value of '1' indicates a significant coefficient; a value of '0' indicates a coefficient that has quantized to a value of 0. The size of the significance map depends only on the image size, not on the number of significant coefficients.
   -Using a wavelet zerotree structure.

The last of these items, using a wavelet zerotree structure, is where most of the current wavelet compression research is focused.

7.2 WAVELET ZEROTREES

We saw in Chapter 5 that we can think of the two-dimensional wavelet transform as a sequence of vertical and horizontal highpass and lowpass operators applied to the image. There are four types of composite operators: vertical highpass followed by horizontal highpass (HH_x); vertical highpass followed by horizontal lowpass (LH_x), vertical lowpass followed by horizontal highpass (HL_x); and finally, vertical lowpass followed by horizontal lowpass (LL_x)[1]. Fig. 7.2.1 diagrams the location within the wavelet transform array of the output of these operators. These blocks can be arranged in a tree structure, as Fig. 7.2.2 shows. Each coefficient in a block has 4 "children" in the corresponding block at the next level. For example, if Fig. 7.2.1 represents the wavelet transform of an 8×8 image, then LL_3, HH_3, HL_3 and LH_3 are 1×1 blocks, HH_2, HL_2, and LH_2 are 2×2 blocks, and HH_1, HL_1 and LH_1 are 4×4 blocks.

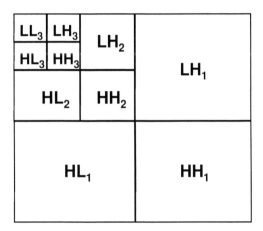

Fig. 7.2.1 Wavelet subtree structure. LH_x indicates a vertical highpass operation followed by a horizontal lowpass operation, while HL_x indicates a vertical lowpass operation followed by a horizontal highpass operation.

The significance of this tree structure is that there typically is a great deal of similarity in coefficients in a block from one level to the next. That is, the children at one level are likely to resemble their parents in the previous level. This is evident in the examples shown in Fig. 5.8.2 in Chapter 5 and Fig. 7.2.3 below. In particular, it is quite often the case that if a coefficient quantizes to zero, then its children quantize to 0 as well. This observation is the basis for what is known as *wavelet zerotree encoding*, first introduced by Lewis and Knowles (1992).

---

[1] Once again, the notation here is that of composition of operators. Thus, LH_x means that the H operator is applied first, followed by the L operator.

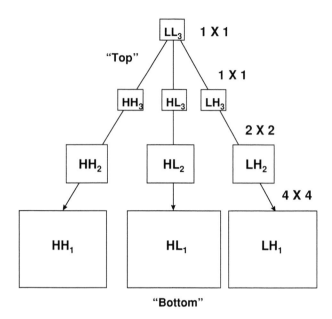

Fig. 7.2.2 The wavelet subtree blocks from Fig. 7.2.1 are arranged here in a tree structure. Each coefficient in a block has 4 "children" in the corresponding block at the next level. For example, if Fig. 7.2.1 represents the wavelet transform of an 8×8 image, then LL_3, HH_3, HL_3 and LH_3 are 1×1 blocks, HH_2, HL_2, and LH_2 are 2×2 blocks, and HH_1, HL_1 and LH_1 are 4×4 blocks. "Top" and "Bottom" are indicated as these terms are used in the zerotree algorithm described below.

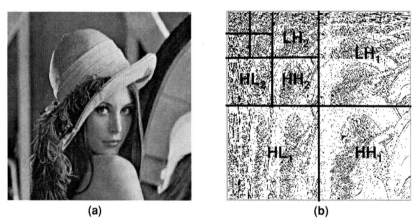

Fig. 7.2.3 The "Lena" image (a) and its wavelet transform (b). The image in (b) is formed by rendering the largest 50% of the Haar wavelet coefficients black and the remaining coefficients white. The wavelet subtree structure is superimposed here, with some of the highpass and lowpass operators identified. Note the similarity in corresponding blocks from one level to the next.

The original wavelet zerotree implementation of Lewis and Knowles (1992) assigned 0 to all of the descendants of a coefficient that quantized to 0. This can be thought of as a form of runlength coding. In fact, it is even more efficient than traditional runlength coding since there is no need to code the length of the run of 0's. However, while it is true that a coefficient that quantizes to zero in the wavelet subtree structure is likely to have children that also quantize to zero, it is also possible for that coefficient to have significant nonzero children. This possibility contributes to errors in the Lewis and Knowles zerotree approach. Shapiro (1993) proposed a modified zerotree encoding approach that accommodates the possibility of isolated zeros. Said and Pearlman (June 1996 and September 1996) introduced a refined version of zerotree coding called Set Partitioning in Hierarchical Trees (SPIHT). In the next section, we develop an implementation of zerotree coding that is similar to the methods introduced by Shapiro and Said and Pearlman.

7.2.1 An implementation of wavelet zerotree coding

In this section we'll develop an encoding algorithm that takes advantage of the wavelet subtree structure shown in Figs. 7.2.2 and 7.2.3. This algorithm is fast, provides good compression and decoded image quality, and has the desirable property of accommodating *progressive transmission*. Progressive transmission means that encoded information is stored, and hence transmitted, in such a way that intermediate versions of the transmitted image contain complete approximations of the final image. This is a desirable property for applications such as the Internet, where impatient users can observe intermediate images and decide whether to wait for a complete image download, or move on to something more interesting.

The particular implementation developed here is based on the zerotree ideas used by Lewis and Knowles (1992), Shapiro (1993), and Said and Pearlman (June 1996). However, the implementation details are this author's own, and any performance measures provided here refer only to this implementation and should not be taken as indicative of the referenced zerotree algorithms. The implementation given here is intended only to illustrate the ideas involved and is not intended as a complete compression system. For example, entropy encoding of the symbols that result from the algorithm, incorporated in all of the referenced algorithms, is not included here.

7.2.1.1 Terminology: Which way is up?

First, we need to define some terminology for maneuvering through the tree structure of Fig. 7.2.2. "Top" refers to the top of Fig. 7.2.2, as shown, that is, near the lowest resolution wavelet coefficients. "Bottom" refers to the part of the tree structure at the bottom of the figure, where the high-detail coefficient terms are located. We will work with the three subbands, LH, HH and HL as shown in the figure. The lowpass (LL) term tends to be among the largest of the coefficients in magnitude. Rather than try to encode this term, we will simply write its entire value as is.

Moving from top to bottom in Fig. 7.2.2, each block in the next lower level in each band has twice as many rows and columns as the block in the level above it. Thus, each block at the next lower level has four times as many coefficients as the block in the level above it. Each coefficient in a given block, except for the lowest block, has four "children" in the corresponding location in the block below it. The four immediate children of the coefficient at location (i,j) are located at $(2i-1,2j-1)$, $(2i-1,2j)$, $(2i,2j-1)$ and $(2i,2j)$. This relationship is shown in Fig. 7.2.4. All of the descendants in the subtree below a coefficient will be referred to as children of that coefficient (that is, its immediate children, the children's children, and so on). Similarly, a coefficient is a parent to all of the children in the subtree below it.

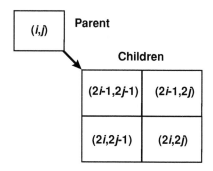

Fig. 7.2.4 Each coefficient in blocks higher than the lowest level has four children in the next lower level.

The notion of what is meant by a "significant" coefficient is important in the implementation of zerotree encoding. A coefficient is *significant* with respect to a given threshold if its magnitude (i.e., absolute value) exceeds that threshold. This brings up the question of how to choose such a threshold. In the implementation presented here, we will extract the binary representation of each wavelet coefficient, so we will choose a sequence of thresholds that are powers of 2.

To keep track of where we are in the processing of an image, we set up a symbol array of the same size as the image. Each element of the symbol array is initialized to 0 at the start of each threshold comparison pass to indicate that that element has not yet been processed. We will use a set of five symbols to indicate a processed element. These are:

POS: the corresponding wavelet coefficient on this threshold pass is significant and positive;

NEG: the corresponding wavelet coefficient on this threshold pass is significant and negative;

IZ: an *isolated zero*, that is, the corresponding wavelet coefficient on this threshold pass is not significant, but does have a significant child somewhere in the subtree below it;

ZR: a *zerotree root*, that is, the corresponding wavelet coefficient on this threshold pass is not significant and the entire subtree of children of this coefficient contains no significant coefficients;

ZT: an insignificant child of a zerotree root.

Only four symbols, POS, NEG, IZ and ZR, are written to the output file. On decoding, the ZR symbols are expanded to fill out their zero subtree, so there is no need to write out the corresponding ZT symbols. Thus, we can use two bits each for the four symbols (of course, a complete system would use entropy coding to achieve lower overall bit rates). The use of a two-dimensional symbol array differs from the approaches taken by Shapiro (1993) and Said and Pearlman (June 1996), who use auxiliary lists to keep track of significant coefficients. Because we do not do entropy coding, we can write out the symbols on each threshold pass, and thus need to maintain only one symbol array in memory, rather than one array for each threshold value.

7.2.1.2 Handling the insignificant coefficients

The significant coefficients are easy to handle: If the magnitude of the coefficient exceeds the threshold, simply assign either a POS or NEG symbol, depending on the coefficient's sign. The insignificant coefficients present more of a challenge. Before we can assign one of the symbols IZ, ZR or ZT to an insignificant coefficient, we need to know not only about that coefficient, but everything about all of its children and parents as well. That means we need information about coefficients both above and below the current coefficient in the tree structure.

We obtain this information by making two passes over the coefficients: a "Bottom-Up" pass to identify the parents of significant children, and a "Top-Down" pass to identify the zerotree roots. Within a subband (LH, HH or HL), the bottom-up pass is applied first. Fig. 7.2.5 shows a block diagram of this process. Starting in the lowest block of the subband, identify the significant coefficients, and assign the corresponding elements in the symbol array POS or NEG symbols. We now also have information about the parents of these coefficients: None of the parents of these significant coefficients can be zerotree roots (ZR) or children of zerotree roots (ZT); they must all be coded as POS, NEG or IZ. At this point, mark all of the parents of this significant coefficient as IZ. That is, assign the symbol IZ to all of the elements in the symbol array corresponding to the parents of this coefficient. Later on, as we move up the tree, these elements may be found to correspond to significant coefficients themselves, in which case the IZ symbol will be overwritten with either POS or NEG. Listing 7.2.1 shows the member function `mark_parents` from the `tzerotree` C++ class in the accompanying software.

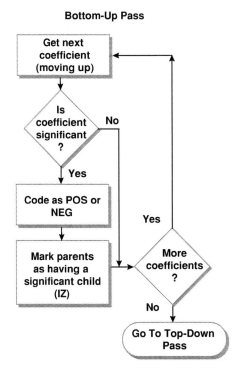

Fig. 7.2.5 The "Bottom-Up" process used in the zerotree algorithm.

Listing 7.2.1 The `mark_parents` member function of the C++ class `tzerotree`, from the accompanying software.

```
void tzerotree::mark_parents (int row,int col,short symbol)
{
  // Mark the parents of this position (row,col) as having a
  // significant child.
  // The four "children" of position (i,j) in the subtree
  // are: (2i-1,2j-1),(2i-1,2j),(2i,2j-1) and (2i,2j).
  // Here, we need to move "backward", or up the tree, and
  // determine the parent of a given (row, col) position.
    int ichild = row,jchild = col;
    int iparent = ichild,jparent = jchild;
    while ((iparent > 1)&&(jparent > 1)) {
       if ((ichild/2)*2 == ichild) // even
          iparent = ichild/2;
       else // odd
          iparent = (ichild+1)/2;
       if ((jchild/2)*2 == jchild) // even
          jparent = jchild/2;
       else // odd
          jparent = (jchild+1)/2;
       set(iparent,jparent,symbol);
       ichild = iparent;
       jchild = jparent;
       } // end while
    return;
    }
```

At the conclusion of the bottom-up pass for a given subband, all of the significant coefficients have been identified and coded as POS or NEG, and all of the isolated zeros have been identified and coded as IZ. All of the remaining coefficients are either zerotree roots (ZR) or children of zerotree roots (ZT). The top-down pass identifies which is which. Starting at the top of the subband, we check the symbol array to see which coefficients have been coded. Because we start at the top, any coefficient that has not yet been coded must be a zerotree root. This is true for all but the lowest block in the subtree. Coefficients in the lowest block have no children, and so by definition cannot be zerotree roots. Coefficients in this block that have not yet been coded are assigned the IZ symbol, rather than ZR. When a zerotree root is identified, all of its children in the subtree below it are marked as ZT. Listing 7.2.2 shows the code for the `tzerotree` class member function `mark_children` which accomplishes this.

The top-down pass also writes the symbols to the binary output file. When a POS, NEG, IZ or ZR symbol is encountered, it is written out with the appropriate 2-bit code. ZT symbols are not written to the output file. Fig. 7.2.6 shows the block diagram for the top-down process.

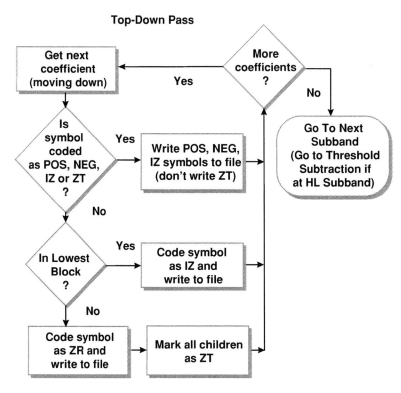

Fig. 7.2.6 The "Top-Down" process used in the zerotree algorithm.

Listing 7.2.2 The `mark_children` member function of the C++ class `tzerotree`, from the accompanying software.

```
void tzerotree::mark_children (int row,int col,int nrows,
            int ncols,short symbol) {
   int child_end_row,child_end_col,child_rows,child_cols;
   // The four "children" of position (i,j) in the subtree
   // are: (2i-1,2j-1),(2i-1,2j),(2i,2j-1) and (2i,2j).
   child_end_row = 2*row;
   child_end_col = 2*col;
   child_rows = 2;
   child_cols = 2;
   while ((child_end_row<=nrows)&&(child_end_col<=ncols)) {
      for (int i=child_end_row-child_rows+1;
                             i<=child_end_row;i++)
         for (int j=child_end_col-child_cols+1;
                                j<=child_end_col;j++)
             set(i,j,symbol);
      child_end_row *= 2;
      child_end_col *= 2;
      child_rows *= 2;
      child_cols *= 2;
      } // end while
   return;
   }
```

7.2.1.3 The zerotree encoding algorithm

We're now ready to put the entire encoding algorithm together. Fig. 7.2.7 shows a block diagram of the algorithm. The first step, not surprisingly, is to apply the two-dimensional wavelet transform to the image. Any of the three wavelets that we have developed so far, Haar, Daubechies D4 or D6, can be selected in the accompanying software. Other wavelets can also be used with this algorithm. Next, set the initial threshold T equal to the largest power of 2 that is less than the maximum magnitude wavelet coefficient. The accompanying software automatically keeps track of this maximum as it computes the wavelet transform. It is often the case that the lowpass LL coefficient value (the single coefficient in the upper left corner of the transform array) has the largest magnitude in the transform array. This coefficient is not one of the three subbands LH, HH and HL and so is excluded from consideration when determining the transform maximum. This lowpass value is written to the output file as is. In addition, some other items that the decoder will need are written to the beginning of the output file: wavelet type (Haar, D4, D6), row size (the algorithm works only for square images), and $\log_2(T)$.

The algorithm now enters the threshold loop. The symbol array is initialized to 0 at the start of each pass through the loop. For each subband, the algorithm performs the bottom-up and top-down passes, as described above. The subbands are processed in the order LH, HH, HL. Recall that the symbols are written to the output file as part of the top-down pass. At the end of the loop, the threshold value T is subtracted from all of the significant coefficients (i.e., all coefficients that have POS or NEG symbols). The threshold is then cut in half, so that the new threshold value is $T/2$. The next pass through the loop compares the new wavelet coefficients with this new threshold. The resulting symbols are written to the output file. The loop continues until $T = 1$. There is also an option to stop sooner than this, which we will discuss below.

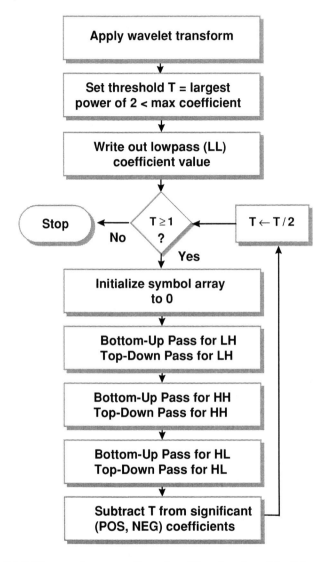

Fig. 7.2.7 The zerotree encoding algorithm developed in this section.

7.2.1.4 Bit planes

Examination of the above algorithm reveals that the encoding is actually constructing a sequential bit-plane representation of the wavelet transform of the image. Notice that nowhere have we stored explicit information about the actual values of the significant coefficients at each threshold level (other than their sign). However, by successively subtracting powers of 2 from these coefficients, the algorithm is extracting a binary representation of the values of these coefficients. The result is that each pass through the threshold loop in Fig. 7.2.7 produces a bit plane, starting with the most significant bits and ending with the least significant bits, as shown in Fig. 7.2.8.

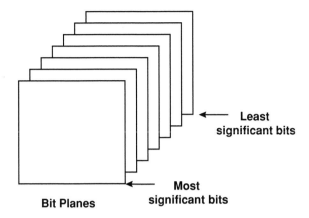

Bit Planes

Least significant bits

Most significant bits

Fig. 7.2.8 Bit planes. The zerotree encoding algorithm produces a sequence of bit planes corresponding to a binary representation of the wavelet transform of the image. The most significant bits are encoded first and the least significant bits are encoded last.

Actual examples of symbol-encoded bit planes are shown in Fig. 7.2.9. These bit planes are from zerotree encoding of the "Lena" image, using Daubechies D4 wavelets. The images in Fig. 7.2.9 are rendered so that the four symbols (POS, NEG, IZ, ZR) that are encoded and written to the output file appear in various shades of gray, while the ZT symbol is rendered in white. Notice that most of bit planes 1 through 7 are white, which means that these bit planes don't require much storage. In fact, the first three bit planes combined require less than 30 bytes, and the first 7 bit planes require only about 1 Kb of storage. This is good news for compression schemes, since these first bit planes contain the most significant bits, and hence most of the significant information in the image. The later bit planes, such as 13 and 14, are densely packed with encoded symbols. However, these planes contain the least significant bits, and so it may be possible to safely ignore these bit planes in a compression scheme. We'll need to decode the encoded image to see the effect of removing some of this information.

7.2.2 Decoding a zerotree encoded image

Decoding a zerotree encoded image is easier than encoding it. A block diagram for decoding is shown in Fig. 7.2.10. The header information contains the wavelet type, number of rows (which equals the number of columns and so provides image size), the lowpass value, $N = \log_2(\text{threshold})$, and number of bit planes, whose use will be explained below. Just as for encoding, we use a symbol array of the same size as the image to store the symbols. The symbol array is an instantiation of the same `tzerotree` C++ class used for encoding. The symbol array is initialized to 0 on each threshold pass. For each threshold value, we read the symbols for the LH subband, the HH subband and the HL subband from the top down into the symbol array. Whenever a zerotree root symbol, ZR, is encountered, it is expanded into its full zero subtree by assigning the ZT symbol to all of its children in the symbol array. This expansion is accomplished using the same mark_children (Listing 7.2.2) member function of the tzerotree class as was used for encoding.

A separate array maintains the wavelet transform values. This wavelet transform array is initialized to 0 at the start of the decoding process. Once the symbol array has been completely filled in for a particular threshold pass, the values in the wavelet transform array are updated by adding the threshold value T to each array location corresponding to a POS symbol and subtracting T at each location corresponding to a NEG symbol. Thus the wavelet transform values are built up from their binary representations, using the most significant bits first and progressing to the least significant bits. The decoded image is obtained by applying the inverse wavelet transform after the final bit plane has been constructed.

It is this ordering of the bit planes of the transform image, from the most significant bit plane to the least significant bit plane, that provides zerotree decoding with its progressive transmission property. To see how much information is transmitted after each bit plane, it is instructive to apply the inverse transform after each bit plane is constructed. Fig. 7.2.11 shows an example of this technique. The images in Fig. 7.2.11 were constructed by applying the inverse Daubechies D4 wavelet transform to the bit planes of Fig. 7.2.9.

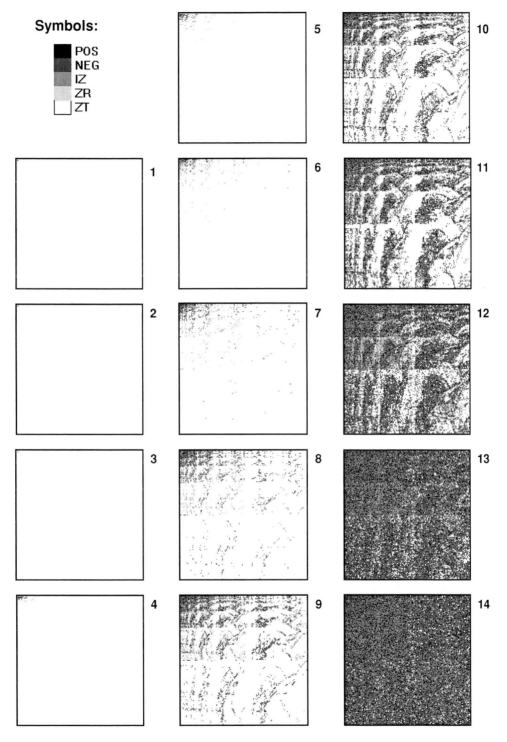

Fig. 7.2.9 Bit planes 1-14 during zerotree encoding of the "Lena" image, using Daubechies D4 wavelets.

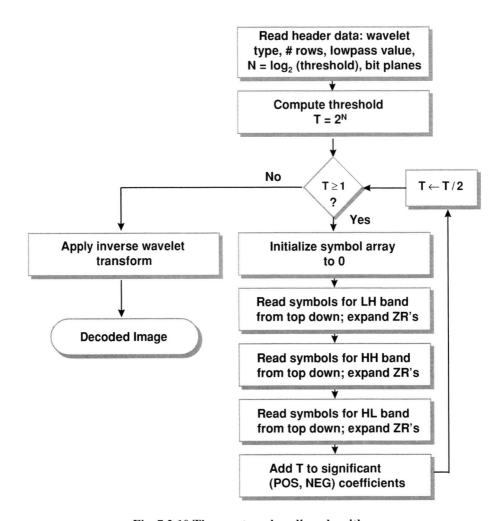

Fig. 7.2.10 The zerotree decoding algorithm.

Fig. 7.2.12 shows (a) PSNR and (b) pixel error % as a function of bit plane number for the images shown in Fig. 7.2.11. Note that the zerotree encoding-decoding algorithm described thus far is nearly a lossless algorithm, when all of the bit planes are incorporated. This is expected, since the algorithm attempts to encode the entire binary representation of the transform coefficients, without throwing away any information. However, as it turns out, a small quantization error is introduced since the wavelet coefficients are floating point values and the algorithm encodes only the integer part of these floating point values. There is also a small numeric error introduced in applying the wavelet transform and inverse transform operations. This is the reason for the pixel error (0.99%; 36.4 PSNR) which remains after decoding is applied to all of the bit planes.

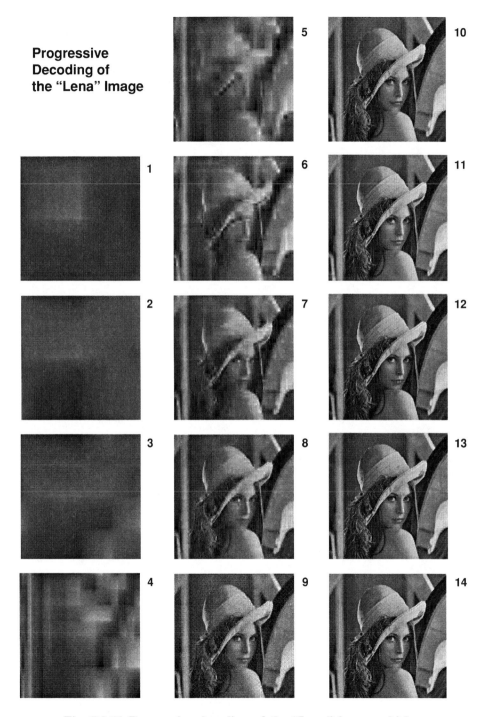

Progressive Decoding of the "Lena" Image

Fig. 7.2.11 Progressive decoding of the "Lena" image, which was encoded with the zerotree algorithm using Daubechies D4 wavelets. Each image here results from decoding the corresponding bit plane in Fig. 7.2.9.

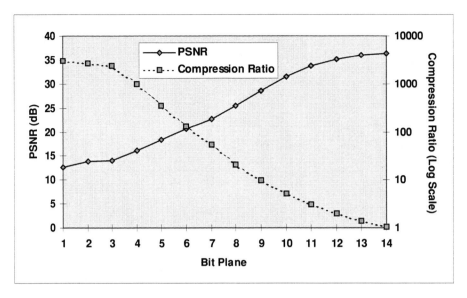

(a) PSNR and Compression Ratio vs. Bit Plane

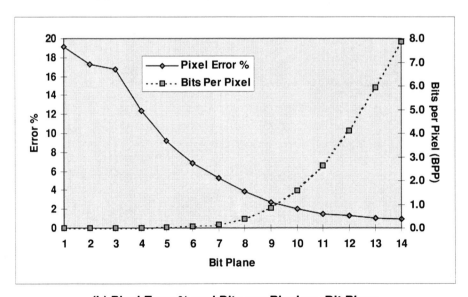

(b) Pixel Error % and Bits per Pixel vs. Bit Plane

Fig. 7.2.12 Two views of error and compression as a function of bit plane number. The numbers here correspond to the 256×256 "Lena" image encoded with the zerotree algorithm, using the Daubechies D4 wavelets, as shown in Figs. 7.2.9 and 7.2.11.

7.2.3 Where is the compression?

Fig. 7.2.12 also shows the effective compression ratio at each level of bit plane decoding. Unfortunately, the algorithm as implemented here, without entropy encoding of the symbols, provides essentially no compression when all of the bit planes are used. However, if we eliminate the last few bit planes, we can obtain very good decoded image quality with modest compression. For example, at bit plane 10, the decoded image has 2.0 % pixel error (31.4 PSNR) with a compression ratio of 5.16:1 (1.5 bits per pixel). This is the reason for including the number of bit planes in the header information for the stored encoded image. The decoder can stop at the designated bit plane to achieve better compression.

There is another way to achieve additional compression. We can combine the decimation technique of the previous two chapters with the zerotree algorithm. The decimation is applied to the wavelet coefficients before the zerotree encoding. If all the bit planes are retained, the results are approximately the same as for the basic decimation algorithm, both in terms of decoded image error and compression ratio. For example, when 10% of the Daubechies D4 wavelet coefficients are retained from the wavelet transform of the "Lena" image, each algorithm provides a compression ratio of approximately 2.5:1 and 31-32 dB PSNR. We can improve the compression ratio of the zerotree encoded image for a small price in decoded image error by retaining only 10 bit planes. Fig. 7.2.13 compares the basic decimation algorithm with the zerotree algorithm using decimation and 10 bit planes. With 10 bit planes and 10% retained wavelet coefficients, the compression ratio of the zerotree encoded image is 7.35:1 with a PSNR of 30.3 dB.

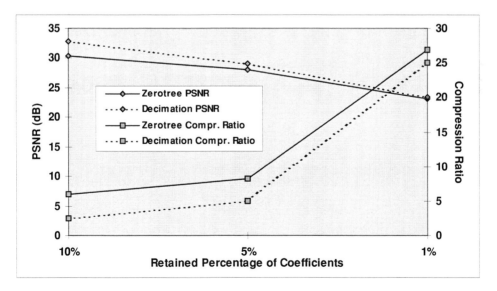

Fig. 7.2.13 Comparison of PSNR and compression ratio for the decimation algorithm and the zerotree algorithm using decimation and 10 bit planes. The zerotree algorithm provides better compression for a small cost in PSNR. The image is 256×256 "Lena" and the wavelets are Daubechies D4.

7.2.4 Encoding speed

A significant advantage of the zerotree algorithm, particularly when compared to fractal algorithms, is encoding speed. Fig. 7.2.14 compares encoding times for the zerotree algorithm with the basic decimation algorithm. The zerotree algorithm in this case includes no decimation. Compression comes from reduced bit planes only. The decimation process involves a sorting operation that dominates the encoding time. The wavelet transform by itself takes approximately 3 seconds for a 256×256 image. The zerotree algorithm with no decimation takes just a second or two in addition to this transform time. This time includes writing the symbols to a file. The decimation time increases with the percentage of retained coefficients. For 1% retained coefficients (25:1 compression ratio) this time is negligible, and so the total encoding time approximately equals the wavelet transform time of 3 seconds. For 10% retained coefficients (2.5:1 compression ratio), the decimation time increases to 15 seconds, which is the predominant portion of the total encoding time of 18 seconds.

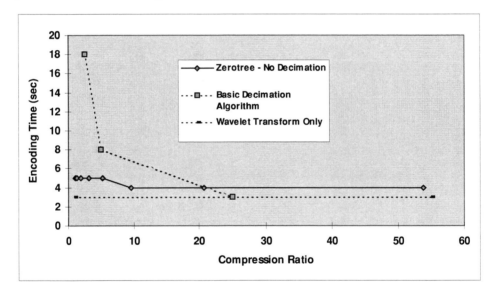

Fig. 7.2.14 Encoding time vs. compression ratio for zerotree encoding with no decimation and the basic decimation algorithm (200 MHz Pentium PC processor). Decimation includes a sorting operation that accounts for most of the encoding time for that algorithm.

7.3 HYBRID FRACTAL-WAVELET CODING

Self-similarity in scale is the defining characteristic of fractals. Wavelets, with their ability to extract scale information, are a natural tool for analyzing fractals. It should not be surprising, therefore, that recent research activities have focused on combining wavelet and fractal techniques for image compression. Davis (1995, 1996, 1998) has proposed an image compression approach that uses elements of both fractal and wavelet image compression and provides a framework that ties these two approaches together. Asgari, et al. (1997) use a wavelet transform to construct non-affine transformations for a compression scheme based on iterated function systems. Hebert and Soundararajan (1998) perform domain-range matching in the wavelet transform domain to achieve very high compression ratios.

The idea behind most hybrid fractal-wavelet coding approaches is to apply a wavelet transform to the image and then use fractal methods in the wavelet domain. However, the distribution and dynamic range of the wavelet coefficient values can cause problems with this approach. The very properties that make the wavelet transform advantageous for image compression make manipulation of the image in the wavelet transform domain difficult. Remember, we can throw away 90% or more of the wavelet transform values and still get a good rendering of the original image when the inverse transform is applied. This is telling us that most of the image information is concentrated in a small number of transform values. We have seen that the significant coefficients of the wavelet transform array are located primarily in the upper left corner among the lowpass filter values. This is evident, for example, in Fig. 7.2.9, where the first 6 bit planes of the significant coefficients are nearly all zero, except for a few values in the upper left corner.

Fig. 7.3.1 shows two different quantizations of the wavelet transform of the "Lena" image. Part (a) of this figure shows uniform quantization (256 gray levels). Nearly all of the image quantizes to the same level (corresponding to the transform value of 0 – the transform contains both negative and positive values). This is because of the large dynamic range of the wavelet values, as well as the fact that many of the values cluster near zero (which is why the wavelet transform provides such good compression!). The dynamic range increases approximately by a factor of two at each wavelet level. In part (b) of this figure, each wavelet level was quantized separately, in an attempt to bring out more detail in the transform image. More detail is visible, but there is still a preponderance of wavelet values that quantize to zero at each level.

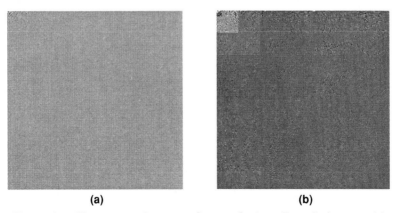

(a)   **(b)**

Fig. 7.3.1 Haar wavelet transform of the "Lena" image. (a) Uniform quantization. (b) Separate quantization for each wavelet level.

A problem with applying fractal image compression to a wavelet transform image, such as Fig. 7.3.1 (a) or (b) is that there is not enough image information for the fractal algorithm to latch onto. The domain-range matching process of fractal encoding does not apply special attention to one region of the image versus other regions. Thus, the standard fractal algorithm would not supply sufficient encoding fidelity to the critical information in the upper left corner of the wavelet transform array.

7.3.1 Operator approach to hybrid fractal-wavelet coding

Davis (1995, 1996, 1998) proposed a hybrid approach that develops an operator framework in the wavelet domain. This operator framework is similar to the operator representation of fractal encoding that we developed in Chapter 3. However, instead of operating on block subimages, as was the case for fractal encoding, Davis introduces "get subtree" and "put subtree" operators that operate on subtree structures in the wavelet domain (Fig. 7.3.2).

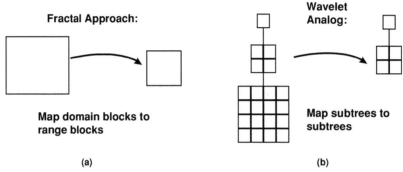

Fig. 7.3.2 Fractal encoding maps domain blocks to range blocks (a). Davis (1995, 1996, 1998) proposed an analogous operation in the wavelet domain that maps subtrees to subtrees (b).

Given an image $F \in \mathfrak{I}^N$ with wavelet transform $W(F)$, the algorithm maps domain subtrees to range subtrees to obtain an operator G such that

$$W(F) \approx G(W(F)) + H. \tag{7.3.1}$$

The solution of (7.3.1) is given by

$$\widetilde{F} = W^{-1}(I - G)^{-1}(H) \tag{7.3.2}$$

which exists provided $\|G\| < 1$. Note the similarity to the operator formulation of standard fractal image coding. As for the fractal case, (7.3.2) can be solved by first iteratively obtaining $W(\widetilde{F})$ and then applying the inverse wavelet transform W^{-1}.

To summarize the steps in Davis' hybrid approach:
To encode an image F:
    1. Apply wavelet transform: $F \rightarrow W(F)$. Reorganize the coefficients of $W(F)$ into wavelet subtrees.
    2. Set up a system of domain subtrees and disjoint range subtrees (similar to fractal domain and range blocks). Determine composite mapping operator G from domain subtrees to range subtrees to minimize error in wavelet domain.

3. Apply quantization and entropy coding.

To decode an image:
1. Extract operator G and offset H from quantized entropy-coded coefficient values.
2. Start with an arbitrary image $Y^{(0)}$ and iterate:

$$Y^{(n)} = G(Y^{(n-1)}) + H .$$

3. Apply inverse wavelet transform:

$$\widetilde{F} = W^{-1}(Y).$$

Operating on wavelet subtrees rather than directly on image subblocks provides the advantage of removing blocking artifacts in the decoded image. This leads to decoded images that are more acceptable from a visual perception point of view, even when standard error measures are comparable to those of standard techniques. Davis (1998) achieves quite good results using his self-quantization of subtrees (SQS) approach. He reports 65:1 compression of the 512×512 "Lena" image, with a PSNR of nearly 30 dB. On the downside, the computational complexity of this method produces encoding times in excess of an hour on a 133 MHz Pentium PC.

7.3.2 Other hybrid approaches

Hebert and Soundararajan (1998) use a special scan order to transform the two-dimensional image into a one-dimensional vector. This vector is then subdivided into range subvectors of fixed equal length. A system of overlapping domain subvectors, each of twice the size of the range subvectors, is also established. The one-dimensional wavelet transform of each range and domain vector is then computed. Domains and ranges are compared on the basis of their wavelet transforms. Speed is attained by comparing low resolution coefficients first and eliminating matches that fail a threshold test. (The authors report encoding times in the range of several minutes on a Pentium PC for a 256×256 grayscale image). Once the best domain-range match is found, the domain is mapped onto the range using an affine transformation that shrinks the domain by a factor of two and applies optimal scaling and offset values determined by a least squares fitting. The algorithm achieves high compression ratios (greater than 100:1) because of its relative inflexibility. There is no adaptation of ranges, for example. The number of ranges is fixed, and so the number of transformations is fixed. The location of the transformation in the list determines the range to which it applies. There is a relatively small number of domains (the authors use 255 in their example), so the domain index takes up a small number of bits. The only transformation information that needs to be stored is the domain index and scaling and offset values. The price for this inflexibility, as you might expect, is relatively low PSNR values for the decoded images (on the order of 21 dB). However, the scan order approach eliminates blocking artifacts, which leads to visually acceptable decoded images in spite of the low PSNR.

8

COMPARISON OF FRACTAL AND WAVELET IMAGE COMPRESSION

The preceding chapters have examined techniques for compressing images using fractal and wavelet approaches. This final chapter will compare these two approaches and discuss the relative advantages of each. The results shown here were generated with the accompanying software. As mentioned previously, this software was developed to illustrate the ideas of the book and was not developed with performance as a primary goal. Also, the systems compared here are not complete compression systems. In particular, there is no entropy coding on the output of the fractal or wavelet algorithms. The presence of entropy coding might alter the results presented here. For example, one or the other of these algorithms might produce output that is more compressible under entropy coding. The results shown here should be used to compare the relative merits of the fractal and wavelet algorithms presented here and should not be compared, for example, to research or commercial quality compression software.

8.1 RATE DISTORTION

Rate distortion compares the tradeoffs between compression and distortion of the decoded image in lossy compression schemes. Rate is defined as the average number of bits needed to represent each pixel value (Sayood 1996). It is usually expressed as bits per pixel (bpp). Distortion is usually measured in terms of PSNR, although this is not always a good measure of perceived image quality. Rate-distortion curves normally plot bpp versus PSNR. However, the fractal encoding literature more commonly reports rate distortion in terms of compression ratio versus PSNR, rather than bpp versus PSNR. This may be due to the fact that fractal encodings are not tied to an image size in pixels, as are other encoding methods. The discussion that follows will also report rate distortion in terms of compression ratio versus PSNR. For fractal methods, the encoded image size is determined by assuming 4 bytes for each range cell. The compression ratio is determined by dividing the size of the original bitmap image, in bytes, by the number of bytes in the encoded image. Distortion, as measured by PSNR, is determined by decoding the image at the same size as the original bitmap, and comparing the decoded image to the original. For wavelet methods, the encoded image size is the size of the actual binary zerotree file, as discussed in Chapter 7.

Fig. 8.1.1 shows compression ratio vs. PSNR curves for various fractal and wavelet compression techniques applied to the 256×256 "Lena" image. These curves plot compression ratio versus image quality, as represented by PSNR. The most desirable real estate on this graph is the upper right quadrant, where high compression ratios and good image quality live. In reality, all encoding algorithms reside closer to the lower left region, where they must manage a tradeoff between compression ratio and image quality.

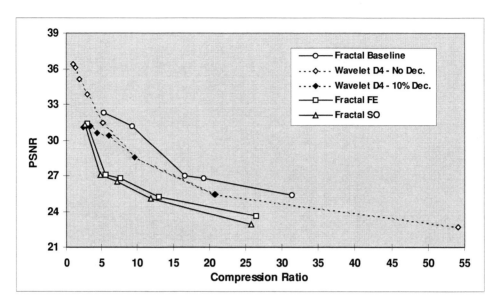

Fig. 8.1.1 Compression ratio vs. PSNR curves for fractal and wavelet compression applied to the "Lena" image (256 × 256).

There is a fundamental difference in how the fractal and wavelet algorithms presented in this book handle compression versus image quality. The fractal methods use an adaptive quadtree partitioning scheme which is driven by a preset error tolerance. The tighter the error tolerance, the better the decoded image quality. However, this leads to worse compression since it results in more range cells. Thus, the user picks image quality in advance and settles for whatever compression results from that. It is possible to design a non-adaptive partitioning scheme, in which the user designates in advance the range cell partitioning, usually uniform over the entire image. This allows the user to control compression, however the uniform partitioning leads to much poorer decoded image quality for most images.

The wavelet methods, on the other hand, give the user control over compression by allowing the designation of bit planes or decimation percent, or both. In this case, the user picks compression in advance and settles for whatever decoded image quality results from that. You should keep in mind these differences between fractal and wavelet compression when comparing rate-distortion curves for these algorithms.

Three fractal algorithms were used for this comparison: the "Baseline" method of Chapter 3, and the feature extraction ("FE") and self-organizing ("SO") domain classification methods of Chapter 4. In each case, 1186 domains were used (level 2, with horizontal and vertical overlap set to 0.5). The "Search for Best Domain" option was set to "Yes", which improves image quality (at the expense of compression time, as we'll see below). To get a variety of compression ratios and image qualities, five combinations of quadtree level and error tolerance were used:

       1. Quadtree level 5; error tolerance 0.05;
       2. Quadtree level 6; error tolerance 0.05;

3. Quadtree level 7; error tolerance 0.05;
4. Quadtree level 6; error tolerance 0.025;
5. Quadtree level 7; error tolerance 0.025.

As expected, a tight error tolerance (e.g., 0.025) combined with a large quadtree depth (e.g., 7) leads to good image quality, but not very good compression.

The wavelet algorithm is the zerotree algorithm of Chapter 7, using the Daubechies D4 wavelets, and implemented both with no decimation of coefficients ("No Dec.") and decimation of all but 10% of the coefficients ("%10 Dec.").

The baseline fractal algorithm actually works best in this case, providing better image quality for comparable compression ratio than either the wavelet algorithms or the FE or SO fractal algorithms. The next best performers are the wavelet algorithms. Note that for compression ratios of about 10:1 or greater, the two wavelet algorithms merge, providing essentially the same performance. Thus, there is no point in doing the time-consuming decimation operation at this level of compression, since it adds no benefit to compression (and certainly not image quality). The zerotree algorithm with no decimation is essentially a lossless algorithm when using large numbers of bit planes. Thus it is not surprising to see the compression ratio vs. PSNR curve for this algorithm reaching high along the PSNR axis. The catch, of course, is that this curve is also asymptotically approaching the vertical line where the compression ratio equals one.

The worst performers are the FE and SO fractal algorithms. These algorithms were designed with speed in mind, and Fig. 8.1.1 shows that some performance has been sacrificed in terms of compression and image quality. The gap between the compression ratio vs. PSNR curves for these algorithms and that of the baseline fractal algorithm indicates that improvement could be made in the selection of features used by these algorithms. No attempt has been made to optimize the choice of these features. Other researchers have considered Fourier (McGregor et al. 1994) and wavelet features (Hebert and Soundararajan 1998).

For a second example of compression ratio vs. PSNR curves, we'll look at results obtained for the "Leaves" image. This image is shown in Fig. 8.1.2 along with a fractal-encoded version. As it turns out, this image is fairly challenging for our compression algorithms, as can be seen from the compression ratio vs. PSNR curves shown in Fig. 8.1.3.

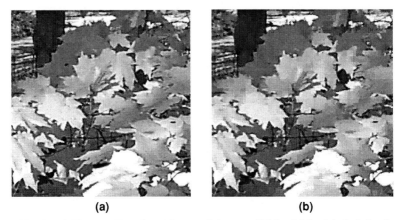

(a)   (b)

Fig. 8.1.2 The challenging "Leaves" image (256 × 256). (a) Original image. (b) Image compressed with baseline fractal algorithm to 3.8:1 with 3.1% pixel error (25.9 PSNR).

Comparison with Fig. 8.1.1 shows that all of the algorithms perform significantly worse on this image than on "Lena". The wavelet zerotree algorithm with no decimation does provide high PSNR for cases where there is a large number of bit planes, but compression is nearly nonexistent at these levels. Note that performance for this algorithm is quite close to that of the baseline fractal algorithm. In fact, the compression ratio vs. PSNR curves for these algorithms cross at a compression ratio of approximately 5:1, with the image quality of the wavelet algorithm rising above that of the fractal algorithm for compression ratios to the left of this point. The FE and SO fractal algorithms fare somewhat better here, out-performing the 10% decimation wavelet algorithm for small compression ratios.

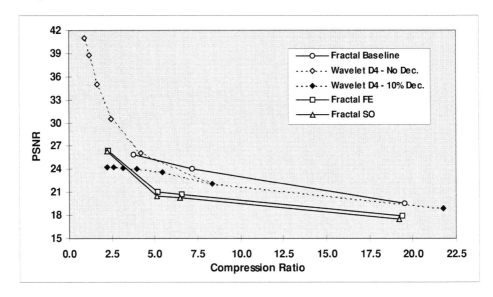

Fig. 8.1.3 Compression ratio vs. PSNR curves for fractal and wavelet compression applied to the "Leaves" image (256 × 256).

8.2 ENCODING SPEED

In addition to compression ratio and image quality, there is a third parameter, namely encoding speed, which should be considered when comparing compression algorithms. This is where the baseline fractal algorithm, which held its own quite nicely under the wavelet assault in the previous section, would like to avoid further scrutiny. Fig. 8.2.1 compares compression ratio and encoding time (on a 200 MHz Pentium PC). The time scale on the vertical axis is logarithmic, otherwise the baseline fractal times would flatten all of the other curves. The times here correspond to the encodings shown in Fig. 8.1.1 for the "Lena" image.

Recall that the fractal algorithms used for Fig. 8.1.1 all used the "Search for Best Domain" option. With this option in effect, the domain-range matching operation checks all of the domains, even if a match has been found that is within the error tolerance. This provides slightly better rate-distortion performance, but it carries the expense of increased encoding time. As we saw in Table 3.3.2, in Chapter 3, this option can triple the encoding times for the baseline algorithm. The situation is not quite as bad for the FE and SO fractal algorithms, where this option only doubles encoding times.

Fig. 8.2.2 shows encoding times for the baseline algorithm with the "Search for Best Domain" option turned on ("Fractal Baseline") and with this option turned off ("Fractal Baseline - No Best Domain"). In addition, for the latter case, the number of orientation transformations was reduced from 8 to 4 to provide a further time improvement. These two modifications decreased encoding times by a factor of 5, but also decreased PSNR by 2 dB for these cases.

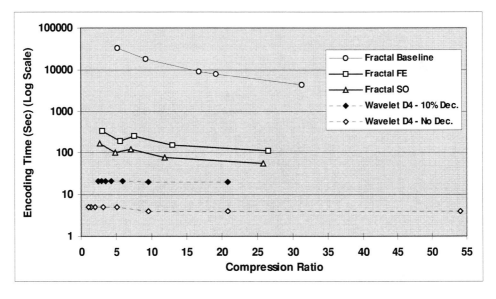

Fig. 8.2.1 Encoding time (on a 200 MHz Pentium PC) vs. compression ratio for the "Lena" image (256 × 256).

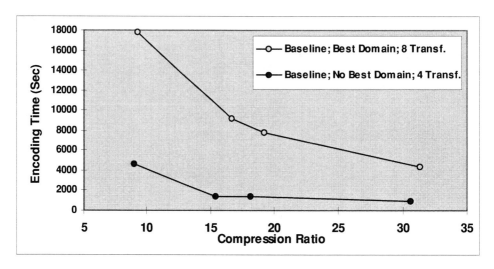

(a) Encoding Time vs. Compression Ratio

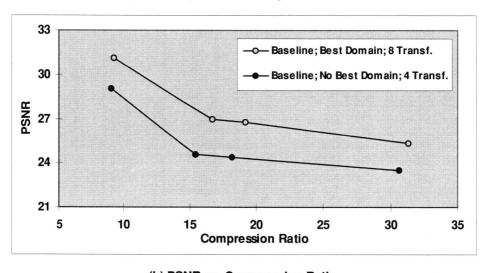

(b) PSNR vs. Compression Ratio

Fig. 8.2.2 (a) Encoding time vs. compression ratio for the 256 × 256 "Lena" image. This figure compares the effect of using the "Search for Best Domain" option, as well as reducing the number of orientation transformations from 8 to 4. (b) PSNR vs. compression ratio for the same cases.

8.3 LARGER IMAGES

All of the examples we have looked at so far have been 256 × 256 images. These smaller images are convenient to work with. However, many image compression references report results for larger images, with 512 × 512 being a standard size. Larger images are usually easier to compress. This is particularly true when they represent larger versions of the same image, such as when comparing the 512×512 "Lena" image to the 256×256 version. This is not surprising, since the information content of the larger image has increased very little. Fractal methods, in particular, can take advantage of this lack of increase in information to provide much greater compression ratios for larger images.

Fig. 8.3.1 compares the rate-distortion curves for fractal encoding of the 512×512 and 256×256 "Lena" images. Note that for the larger image, the curves shift significantly to the right, indicating greater compression for the same PSNR levels. In fact, if you draw a horizontal line through a PSNR value you will see that it intersects the compression ratio vs. PSNR curves for the larger image at compression ratios approximately 4 times greater than the same curves for the smaller image. The dashed line in Fig. 8.3.1 shows one example of this. The horizontal line at the level of approximately 26 dB PSNR intersects the FE and SO curves for the 256×256 image at a compression ratio of 10:1 and intersects the 512×512 curve at 40:1.

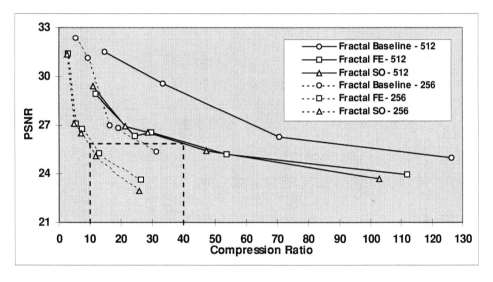

Fig. 8.3.1 Compression ratio vs. PSNR curves for fractal encoding of the 512×512 "Lena" image and the 256×256 "Lena" image. The dashed line shows an example where, for a given PSNR level, the compression ratio is approximately 4 times greater for the larger image.

In fact, for the same quadtree depth and error tolerance level, the fractal encoding methods give nearly the same number of range cells for either image size. This can be seen in Fig. 8.3.2, which plots PSNR vs. number of range cells for both image sizes. There is very little difference in the number of range cells for the two image sizes.

The fact that the number of range cells does not increase with image size is the same phenomenon that produces the resolution independence property of fractal encoding that was discussed in Chapter 3. Fractal encoding looks for information in an image. It does not care about image size.

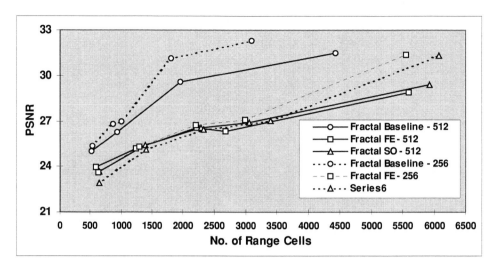

**Fig. 8.3.2 PSNR vs. number of range cells for fractal encoding of
the 512 × 512 and 256 × 256 "Lena" images.**

The situation is similar for wavelet encoding. Here, as for the fractal methods, as Fig.
8.3.3 shows, we get nearly a factor of 4 increase in compression ratio when going from a
256 × 256 image to a 512 × 512 image. The examples in Fig. 8.3.3 represent wavelet
zerotree encoding of the "Lena" image using Daubechies D4 wavelets with no
decimation. The dashed line in Fig. 8.3.3 shows a horizontal line intersecting the
compression ratio vs. PSNR curve for the smaller image at a compression ratio of 20:1,
and intersecting the curve for the larger image at nearly 80:1.

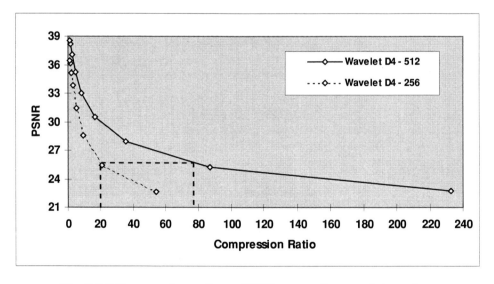

**Fig. 8.3.3 Compression ratio vs. PSNR curves for wavelet zerotree
encoding of the 512 × 512 "Lena" image and the 256 × 256 "Lena"
image.**

The increased compression ratios that are possible for larger images do not come without a price. Encoding times, as one might expect, increase for the larger images. For the fractal methods, encoding times are approximately twice as long for the 512×512 image as for the 256×256 image. This situation is not quite as bad as it could be, since there are 4 times as many pixels in the larger image. For the wavelet zerotree approach, with no decimation, the encoding times actually increase by a factor of 5-6 for the larger image, although total encoding times are still only on the order of 30 seconds (200 MHz Pentium PC). With decimation, encoding times are significantly longer, due to the sorting operation that is involved.

8.4 CONCLUSIONS

In this book, we have examined fractal and wavelet techniques for image compression. It has not been the intention of this book to "sell" one or the other of these techniques, either compared to each other or compared to the standards now in use. Rather, the intention has been to equip you, the reader, with the tools and information to further pursue these techniques on your own.

Fractal and wavelet methods provide an alternative to Fourier-based compression techniques, such as JPEG. As mentioned in Chapter 1, standards such as JPEG and MPEG should not stifle further research in image compression. Rather, by encouraging the use of digital images in communication, these standards help to uncover new uses and needs for compression technology. New technologies such as fractals and wavelets should not be viewed as competitors but as allies in establishing new standards. In fact, wavelets are at the core of the new JPEG 2000 standard. The International Standards Organization (ISO) JPEG Committee, in collaboration with the Digital Imaging Group (DIG), have recognized the need to update the original JPEG standard to address digital imaging's enormous growth due to the Internet and also to address the changing needs of those who create and use digital images. For the last three years they have been developing JPEG 2000 as a new digital image compression standard. According to the DIG JPEG 2000 white paper (1999), the wavelet technology of JPEG 2000 can provide a 20% improvement in compression efficiency over previous JPEG DCT compression methods. JPEG 2000 also takes advantage of the progressive transmission property of wavelets, covered here in Chapter 7, to provide the end user of the image with progressive access to resolution quality and color depth. Release of JPEG 2000 is planned for early in the year 2000, with formal adoption as an international standard later that year.

The baseline fractal encoding method can provide better rate-distortion performance, that is, better compression and image quality, than the wavelet approach. However, this performance comes at great expense in encoding time. Better performance could be obtained using more domains, but that only exacerbates the time problem. We addressed the time problem through the use of feature extraction and domain classification. This brought encoding times down to a level more competitive with the wavelet methods, but at the expense of decreased rate-distortion performance. As mentioned above, this suggests that the features used, which were not subjected to any sort of optimization, could be improved upon. One encouraging aspect of the fractal encoding process is that it is completely parallelizable. Domain-range matching can proceed simultaneously on multiple image segments on multiple processors, with no communication required among the processors. Specialized parallel hardware can therefore provide significant reduction in encoding times. Such hardware is currently in use at Iterated Systems, Inc.

With current implementations, such as those described in this book, fractal methods are probably best suited to archival applications, such as digital encyclopedias, where an image is encoded once and decoded many times. Wavelet methods are better suited to applications requiring fast encoding, such as communication across the Internet, or from a missile seeker to ground control.

Our understanding of images as information sources is far from complete. Fractal methods represent a step in a new direction toward furthering our understanding of images. Unlike wavelet and Fourier transform methods, which essentially throw information away to achieve compression, fractal methods attempt to reconstruct the image using relationships among subimages. The domain-range matching approach that is the basis for most fractal methods is a far from optimal implementation of the theory of fractal representation of images. Recall from Chapter 2 the "fern" image that is the quintessential example of an IFS image. This image is generated using just 4 affine transformations. What would happen if we applied our fractal encoding to a bitmap image of this same fern? We would get hundreds or thousands of transformations, and the decoded image would not be as good as the one generated with the original 4 transformations. Rather than condemning fractal encoding, this simple example should point out that there is need for further research to unlock its potential.

Appendix A

USING THE ACCOMPANYING SOFTWARE

The software accompanying this book is intended to illustrate the ideas introduced here. It can be found at **http://www.spie.org/bookstore/tt40/**. While every effort has been made to provide stable software with a functional user interface, you will not find all of the features you might expect in commercial-grade software. Source code is also provided so that you can build on this software and do your own explorations in fractal and wavelet compression techniques. The source code is not optimized for speed, but rather has been written with clarity of style in mind. Appendixes B and C discuss the source code in more detail.

System Requirements. The software is designed to run on a Pentium (or better) PC with a 32-bit Windows operating system (Windows 95, 98 or NT; you can also use Windows 3.1 augmented with WIN32S). The executables (*.exe) run without any additional dynamic link libraries (DLL's), other than what is available in a standard Windows configuration.

Software Systems. There are three software systems supplied:
- IFS System: Create and run iterated function systems
- IMG System: Fractal image compression
- WAV System: Wavelet image compression and plotting

A.1 IFS SYSTEM

The IFS System creates iterated function systems (IFS's), using specified points and affine transformations between sets of points. Fig. A.1.1 shows the main frame window for the IFS System, with the menu showing the options for opening various window types. The program provides an interface for placing points on a 2-dimensional grid and using these points to specify affine transformations. These affine transformations define an IFS. The program computes and stores the coefficients for the affine transformations in a file.

The steps to produce an IFS attractor image are the following:

1. Define the points.
2. Define the affine transformations.
3. Save the coefficients to a file.
4. Open the coefficient file and run the IFS.

The next sections discuss these steps in more detail.

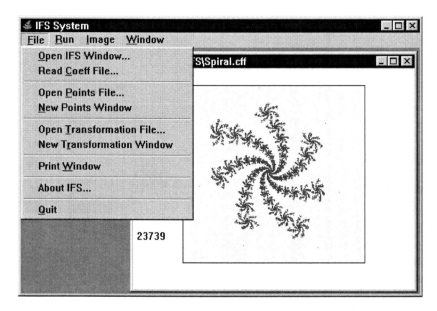

Fig. A.1.1 Frame window for IFS System, showing main menu options, and an IFS window.

A.1.1 Points window

The points window provides a grid for specifying the locations of points that will be used to define the affine transformations. The program provides the option of importing a bitmap image ("Image" menu) that will be superimposed on the grid to aid in defining the point locations. Fig. 2.4.1 shows an example of the grid with an imported bitmap image. You should define your x-y points at easily identified image points, such as the tips of leaves, or corners of block letters. You need to know in advance what your transformations are going to be, and what points are going to define those transformations. Remember, you are trying to implement the Collage Theorem (section 2.3.2) here. Your transformations must be contractions (i.e., transformations that map large areas to smaller areas) and they must cover the image without too much overlap and without missing too much of the image. The closer your collage of transformations comes to accomplishing this, the better your final IFS image will be.

To add a new point, click on the "Add New Points" item in the "Edit" menu, then click on the grid in the approximate location where you want to locate the point. The "X-Y Point" dialog, as shown in Fig. A.1.2, then appears, allowing you to fine tune the numeric values of the x and y coordinates of the point. When you click "OK" on this dialog, you will see the new point on the grid with its consecutively assigned numeric label. You will remain in "Add New Points" mode as long as that menu item is checked.

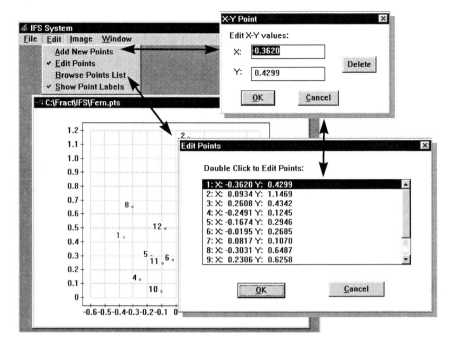

Fig. A.1.2 The points window, showing its "Edit" menu and the dialogs for editing the points list.

To edit an existing point, select the "Edit Points" menu item, then click on the point you want to edit. You can now drag the point to its desired location. You can also edit points by selecting the "Browse Points List" menu item, which brings up a list box dialog containing the current points list. Double-clicking an item in this list summons the "X-Y Point" dialog for numeric editing. Fig. A.1.2 shows the points window, with its "Edit" menu, and the list box and "X-Y Point" dialogs.

When you are satisfied with your points list, save the list to a file, using either the "Save Points File" or "Save Points File as…" menu items under the "File" menu. (By the way, the ellipses ("…") on a menu item means that that item summons a dialog box. This is a user interface convention that goes back at least as far as the earliest Macintosh.) Close the points window when you are done.

A.1.2 Transformation window

The transformation window creates, edits and saves affine transformations, using a previously created points file. To open a transformation window, select either "New Transformation Window" to create new transformations, or "Open Transformation File…" to edit an existing list of transformations. In either case, you will be asked for the name of a points file that will supply the points list upon which the transformations will be defined.

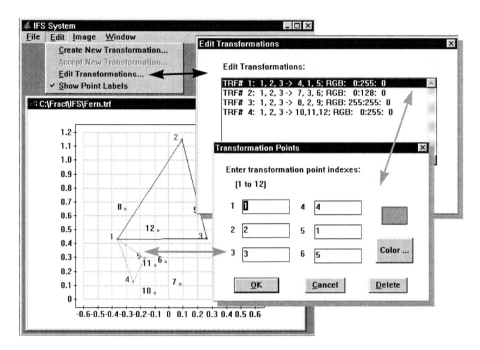

Fig. A.1.3 The transformation window, with its "Edit" menu and dialogs for editing the transformations.

The transformation window displays the points on the same grid that was used for their creation by the points window. However, you cannot edit the points in the transformation window. Fig. A.1.3 shows the transformation window, with its "Edit" menu and dialogs for editing the transformations. You can import a bitmap image here, to be superimposed on the grid, just as for the points window, to aid in drawing the transformations.

Select "Create New Transformation…" to begin creating a new transformation. An affine transformation is defined by six points, mapping the first three points onto the last three points. The left mouse button selects a point, the right mouse button deselects it. As you select the points, lines will appear between the selected points, with a triangle defining the first three points, and a second triangle defining the last three points. Remember, as mentioned in the previous section, you are trying to implement the Collage Theorem of section 2.3.2. The second triangle should be smaller than the first, so that you have a contraction, and the collection of second triangles from all of the transformations should cover the desired image without missing too much and without too much overlap. When you have selected the sixth and final point defining the transformation, select "Accept New Transformation…" from the "Edit" menu. The "Transformation Points" dialog will appear, as shown in Fig. A.1.3. This dialog allows you to edit your point selections, and also to specify a color for the transformation, using the standard Windows color chooser dialog. This color selection determines the color of the range of the transformation (i.e., the region determined by the second triangle of the transformation) in the final IFS image.

You can edit your list of transformations using the "Edit Transformations…" menu item, which brings up the list dialog shown in Fig. A.1.3. You can also use this dialog to view a transformation by selecting it from the list. The two triangles for the selected transformation are displayed on the grid, with the second triangle shown in the color for that transformation.

When you are finished creating and editing your transformations list, save the list to a file, using either the "Save Transformation File" or "Save Transformation File as..." menu items under the "File" menu. With points and transformations defined, you are now ready to create your IFS. Select "Create Coeff File..." under the "File" menu to create a file with the coefficients of the IFS. You will be prompted for a file name ("*.cff"). Once this has been specified, the program calculates the affine coefficients from your transformation definitions. The program checks to see that each transformation constitutes a contraction mapping. If it encounters a transformation that is not a contraction mapping, it displays a warning message identifying the offending transformation. It will, however, generate the affine coefficients and save them to the designated file. A system with a non-contractive transformation will most likely diverge when you attempt to display the IFS image.

A.1.3 IFS window

The IFS window runs the IFS and displays the resulting attractor image. The image can be generated using either the deterministic algorithm, as described in section 2.4.3.1, or the random algorithm, as described in section 2.4.3.2. Fig. A.1.4 shows IFS windows displaying both random and deterministic images. "Run IFS" iterates the IFS and displays the resulting attractor image. Stop the iterations by clicking the left mouse button anywhere on the window, or hitting the "Esc" key. The random algorithm runs by default. You can choose the deterministic algorithm by checking the "Use Deterministic System" menu item. Pick from among a square, a circle, or a point as the starting image for the deterministic image, using the dialog summoned from the "Change Det Start Image..." menu item.

Fig. A.1.4 IFS window, showing a fern IFS generated with the random (right) and deterministic (left) algorithm. The starting image for the deterministic algorithm is a circle in this example.

The "Graph Setup" dialog can be used to change various graphing parameters, such as the x-y window and the background color. Changing the x-y window effectively zooms in on the attractor image (this feature works only with the random IFS attractor), as shown in Fig. A.1.5. The clipboard feature allows you to import the image directly into other Windows applications for printing or display.

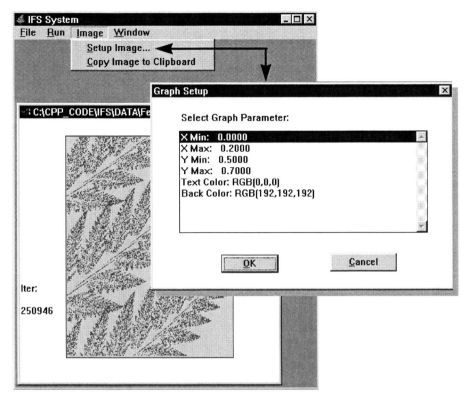

Fig. A.1.5 The "Graph Setup" dialog can be used to change the *x-y* window and the background color.

A.2 IMG SYSTEM: FRACTAL IMAGE COMPRESSION

The IMG System implements fractal image compression, as described in Chapters 3 and 4. It has the following capabilities:

- Encode grayscale images using:
    - i) standard fractal quadtree encoding;
    - ii) fractal quadtree encoding with feature extraction;
    - iii) fractal quadtree encoding with feature extraction and a self-organizing neural network for domain classification;
- Store encoded image as either text or binary range file;
- Decode images stored as text or binary range files;
- Compare decoded image with original and provide error performance using image subtraction;
- Plot grayscale image as a two-dimensional surface in three-dimensional space.

Fig. A.2.1 shows the "File" menu options for opening the various window types. The encode windows read in image files in Windows bitmap (BMP) format. Numerous utility programs are available for translating other image formats, such as TIFF, GIF or JPEG, into BMP format (since we're trying to do image compression here, it would be counterproductive to start with an already compressed format, such as GIF or JPEG!). The program can actually read and display color BMP images. These images will be transformed into grayscale images prior to encoding.

A.2.1 Encode window

The encode window implements basic fractal quadtree image encoding. The domain-range matching can be based on extracted features or on direct pixel comparison. When you open an encode window, you will see a file dialog asking for a bitmap file. This is the image to be encoded. Fig. A.2.2 shows the encode window with two of its menus. The "Image" menu provides information about the image, such as its size ("Bitmap Info…") and overall feature values ("Show Image Features…"). These are the same features that are extracted for each domain and range, as discussed in Chapter 4, when the feature extraction encoding mode is selected. "Stretch Bitmap" enlarges or shrinks the image to fit the window. "Copy Image to Clipboard" copies the window contents (as a bitmap) to the Windows clipboard, for importing into other Windows applications. The "Run" menu runs the application. "Gray Image" converts the screen bitmap image into an internal grayscale array (even if the original image is color). "Encode Image" will do this step automatically before encoding. Image comparisons (such as the image subtraction window) are done with this internal array, so sometimes it is necessary to run "Gray Image" without the encoding process. "Remove Redundant Domains" compares domains and removes redundant domains from the list. A domain is redundant if it can be mapped onto another domain with a fit that is within the selected error tolerance.

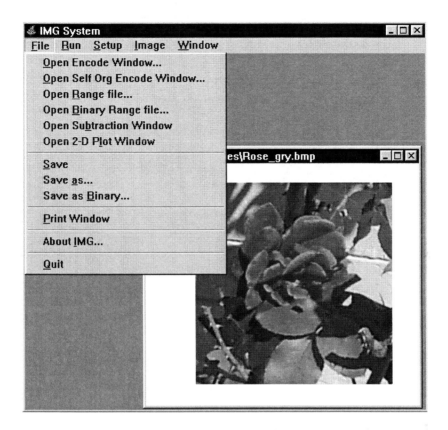

Fig. A.2.1 The IMG System for fractal image compression. The system can encode grayscale images using the fractal methods of Chapters 3 and 4 and can decode images stored as range files. The subtraction window provides error performance.

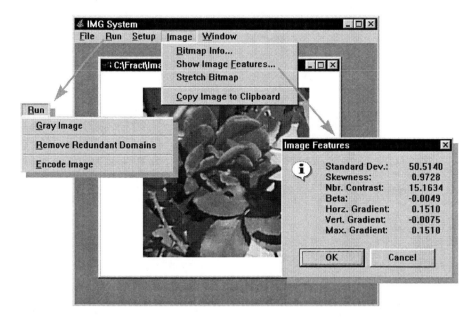

Fig. A.2.2 The encode window, showing the "Run" menu, "Image" menu, and "Image Features" message dialog.

A.2.1.1 Encode setup

The "Setup Image Encoding…" item under the "Setup" menu summons the "Encode Setup" dialog, as shown in Fig. A.2.3. This dialog is an example of a data object list dialog. Double-clicking on an item in the list will bring forth a dialog that is appropriate for editing the value of that item. For example, there are numeric items that are updated through dialogs that accept only numeric values and can do max-min bounds checking. "Yes-No" items are updated through radio-button dialogs that allow only a yes or no answer. There are also file name items and color items that are updated through standard Windows dialogs for selecting file names and colors, respectively. The advantage of this type of list dialog is that it is easy for the developer (and you, after all, are now the developer!) to add items, without redesigning the user interface.

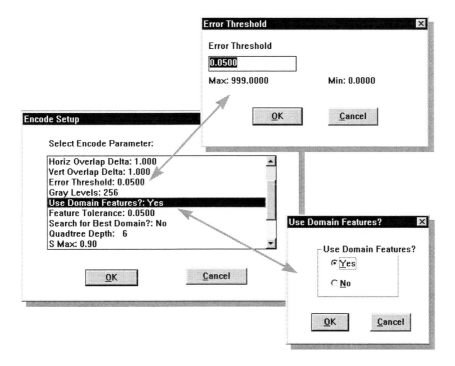

Fig. A.2.3 The "Encode Setup" dialog is an example of a data object list dialog. Double-clicking on an item brings up a dialog appropriate for editing that item's data.

The parameters in the setup dialog allow you to control the performance (both speed and decoded image quality) of the fractal encoding. Default values are provided that give reasonable performance for 256×256 grayscale images. Here is a list of the parameters and the impact that they have:

Domain Rows, Columns: Determine the basic domain block size. Default is 8×8.

Domain Levels: The basic domain size is halved with each level. If the basic domain size is 8×8, then levels = 2 means that there are 8×8 and 4×4 domain blocks in the pool.

Horizontal and Vertical Overlap Delta: This parameter designates fraction of domain overlap, with a smaller value resulting in more domains. A value of 1.0 indicates no overlap, while a value of 0.0 is complete overlap (the program forces a minimum 1 pixel "overhang" so that there will be a finite number of domains!).

Error Threshold: This is the primary quality control parameter. The domain-range match must be less than this value in order for the match to be accepted. A smaller value leads to better image quality, but longer encoding times and worse compression.

Gray Levels: This is the number of gray levels used when converting the screen image to the internal grayscale array.

Use Domain Features?: This turns feature extraction on or off. When this is off ("No"), then domain-range matching is done on a pixel-by-pixel basis (i.e., baseline fractal image encoding). Be prepared for encoding times of hours or more when this is off.

Feature Tolerance: This is the feature "gatekeeper" parameter, as discussed in Chapter 4. When in feature extraction encoding mode, the first domain-range check is done on the basis of feature values. If the difference in feature space is less than this feature tolerance value, then a pixel-by-pixel comparison is done, using the error tolerance parameter. A small feature tolerance value leads to fast encoding times, but may reject too many domains. A large value negates the speed advantage of using feature comparisons.

Search for Best Domain?: If this is "No", then domain-range comparison stops for that range as soon as a match is found within the error threshold. If this is "Yes", then all domains are compared, and the best one is kept (if the match is within error threshold, then no further quadtree subdivision is done on that range).

Quadtree Depth: This sets the maximum quadtree depth for the ranges. A large value (e.g., 7 for a 256×256 image) leads to good image quality, but worse compression.

S Max: Maximum allowable contrast factor used in affine transformations. Should be close to 1. A value larger than 1 can be used, but may jeopardize contractivity of transformations. Too small a value increases the number of iterations required for decoding.

Number of Transformations: Number of allowed combined rotations and reflections for affine transformations. Maximum value of 8 allows 4 rotations for each of two reflections. Encoding can be sped up by reducing this number to 4 or 2, without a noticeable impact on compression performance.

Display graphics during encoding?: Turns the display graphics on/off. The program displays the quadtree partition over the image as this partition is adapted during encoding. This provides visual feedback on the progress of the encoding. The time overhead for this option is only a second or two, but if you're going for an absolute speed record, you have the option of turning the graphics off.

Write features to file?: You have the option of saving the feature vectors computed for each domain cell. The program will write the seven features shown in Table 4.1.1 (and in the dialog shown in Fig. A.2.2) to a text file, seven columns of data, one line of text for each domain cell (for example, if there are 320 domains, then 320 lines of feature vector data will be written). Note that only five features are actually used for domain-range comparison, since maximum gradient is used in place of horizontal and vertical gradient.

Feature File Name: The name of the feature data file. This item brings up a file browser dialog.

A.2.1.2 Running image encoding

Once you have selected the appropriate setup parameters, you are ready to run image encoding. From the "Run" menu, "Encode Image" runs the fractal encoding. Encoding will take anywhere from less than a minute, if you have selected feature extraction, to several hours or more, if you have elected to go with "classic" fractal image compression. The quadtree partition is displayed as it is adapted during encoding, providing visual feedback on the progress. You can stop encoding at any time by hitting the "Esc" key. At the termination of encoding, you will see the message dialog shown in Fig. A.2.4, displaying the statistics of the encoding process. You can save the encoded image as a text range file or a binary range file ("Save as Binary...").

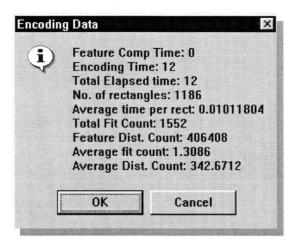

Fig. A.2.4 This message dialog is displayed at the end of encoding, showing the statistics of the encoding process.

A.2.2 Self-organizing encoding window

The self-organizing encoding window implements fractal encoding using a self-organizing neural network for domain classification, as discussed in Chapter 4. This window includes all of the same options for encoding as the regular encoding window, plus additional options for setting up and training the self-organizing neural network. Fig. A.2.5 shows this window, with the "Weights" menu and the setup dialog for the self-organizing neural network.

A.2.2.1 Setting up the self-organizing network

The first step in setting up the self-organizing network is to set the parameters, which are shown in the dialog in Fig. A.2.5. The values shown in Fig. A.2.5 are the default values, and these will work fine in most situations. Here is a list of the parameters and their meaning, if you want to experiment with changing them:

Lattice Rows, Cols: The number of rows and columns in the weights lattice. Their product is the number of nodes in the lattice, which corresponds to the maximum number of domain classes. There is a balance between the number of nodes and the number of domains per class, since the algorithm must search over both the lattice nodes and the domains within the selected class. More nodes means fewer domains per class; fewer nodes means a quicker lattice search, but more domains within the selected class.

Starting Stepsize: This is the starting value for the stepsize ε used in training the network. It controls the speed of adaptation during training iterations. A small value will slow down training iterations, while too large a value may cause the adaptation to "overshoot" and fail to converge.

Fig. A.2.5 The self-organizing encode window includes a menu for training and saving the neural network weights and a dialog for setting the parameters associated with neural network training.

Starting Nbhd: This is the size of the starting lattice neighborhood used for training adaptation. When a lattice node is selected as the "winner" during a training iteration, the weight vector for that node as well as the weight vectors attached to each node in the neighborhood of that node are adapted to look more like the input vector. If the starting neighborhood size is too small, the weights lattice can tie itself in a knot during training, leading to poor neighborhood topology in the trained network (that is, dissimilar weight vectors may appear close to one another in the lattice structure) See Welstead (1994) for an example of this phenomenon. As a rule of thumb, the starting neighborhood size should be half the number of rows (or columns) in the lattice.

Iter Blocksize: The training iterations are divided into blocks. At the end of one iteration block, the adaptation stepsize and neighborhood size are reduced, and training continues with the next iteration block.

Iter Blocks: The total number of iteration blocks. The total number of training iterations is therefore the number of blocks times the blocksize. Larger networks require more training iterations.

Max Search Radius: This is a search parameter, rather than a training parameter. When the network is operating as a classifier and an input is presented to the network, the search algorithm selects the lattice node whose weight vector most closely resembles the input. The algorithm will search through the domains associated with that node and will also search the nodes within the search radius, as shown in Fig. 4.2.2.

Read weights from file?: The algorithm does not necessarily need to train on the same image that is being encoded. If you want to read in a weights file trained on a different image, then specify "Yes" here and supply the weights file name as the next item in the list. If this option is "No", the algorithm will automatically train on the image to be encoded, as part of the encoding process.

Weights File Name: The name of the weights file. This is the file that will be read in, if the preceding item is "Yes" or the name of the file to which the weights will be written, if the preceding item is "No".

A.2.2.2 Running self-organized image encoding

The only difference between this encoding and the previous encoding window is the presence of the self-organizing neural network and its weights file. If you elected to use a previously trained weights file, the program will read in that file and proceed with encoding. If you have elected to not read in a weights file, the program will train the weights on the image currently loaded in the window. You can separate the training and encoding steps by selecting "Train and Save Weights to File…" from the "Weights" menu. A progress bar dialog appears during training to indicate where you are in the training process.

A.2.3 Decode window

Use either "Open Range File…" or "Open Binary Range File…" to open a window for decoding. Fig. A.2.6 shows the decode window with its "Run" menu. As this figure shows, you can view the quadtree partition that was generated during encoding. For step-by-step decoding, "Decode Image" runs one iteration of decoding. To view the resulting image, select "Gray Image". To automate the decoding process, use "Iterate Decoding".

You will be asked for an iteration number (the default is 6 iterations). The program will automatically cycle through that number of iterations, displaying the resulting image at each step.

Fig. A.2.6 The decode window, showing a quadtree partition and a decoded image.

Recall that the contraction mapping theorem asserts that you can use any starting image and still converge to the attractor of the system. The options under the "Image" menu, shown in Fig. A.2.7, allow you to determine the starting image. The default starting image is uniformly gray. The program will fill its internal grayscale image array using the gray level value shown as "Starting Image No." in the decode setup dialog shown in Fig. A.2.7. You change this value through the setup dialog. You also have the option of importing a bitmap image as the starting image ("Use Starting Bitmap Image..."). This option will present you with a file browser dialog for selecting the bitmap file and will load the selected bitmap image and display it in the window. The starting image does not have a significant impact on the speed of decoding or the quality of the decoded image, but it is interesting to observe a validation of the contraction mapping theorem in action. Figs. 3.2.4 and 3.4.1 show examples of this.

Note that the setup parameters also allow you to specify the number of rows and columns for the decoded image. The decoder has no knowledge of the size of the original encoded image and indeed has no need for such knowledge. The decoded image size, and in fact shape, is independent of the dimensions of the encoded image. You can decode at a larger or smaller size, or a different rectangular shape, than the encoded image. The default image size for decoding is 256×256. If, for example, you want to decode at 512×512, you would change the number of rows and columns in the image setup parameters to 512.

The "Image" menu also includes options for corrupting the domains and transformations. These options are available for studying transmission robustness issues, as discussed in Chapter 3. The domain corruption randomly modifies a percentage of the domain indexes. The percentage is one of the setup parameters. Similarly, you can corrupt a percentage of the rotation/reflection transformations. Once the corruption has been done, it can't be undone without reloading the range file. Obviously, this corruption is not something you want to do on a routine basis.

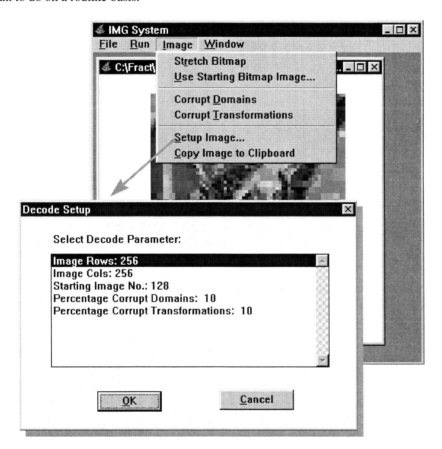

Fig. A.2.7 The "Image" menu and setup dialog for the decode window.

A.2.4 Subtraction window

The subtraction window compares the decoded image to the original image. To open a subtraction window, you must have an open encode window and an open decode window. The image in the encode window must be loaded into the program's internal grayscale image array. If this has not already been done as a result of encoding, then you can run "Gray Image" on the encode window to accomplish this. Run image subtraction simply by selecting that option from the "Run" menu on the subtraction window. There are no setup parameters. Fig. A.2.8 shows an example of a subtraction window. The program reports average pixel error and peak signal-to-noise ratio (PSNR) and also displays the subtraction image. Grayscale is reversed in this image so that zero error shows up as white, and large errors show up as dark gray levels. The less this image looks like the original image, the less error you have. The subtraction window operates on the most recently opened encode and decode windows. To avoid confusion, it is best to just have one open encode window and one decode window prior to opening the subtraction window.

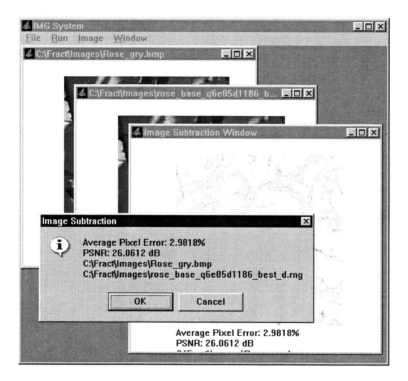

Fig. A.2.8 The subtraction window subtracts a decoded image from the original encoded image and computes the average pixel error and power signal-to-noise ratio (PSNR).

A.2.5 Plot window

The final capability of the IMG system is the two-dimensional plot window. This window plots an image as a two-dimensional surface in three-dimensional space. This plotting window works in conjunction with an encode window. To run this window, you must first open an image bitmap file using an encode window and convert the image to a grayscale array. Fig. A.2.9 shows a plot window with its corresponding encode window, and setup dialog.

The setup parameters control the appearance of the plot. The elevation and rotation angles control the viewing angle. The pixel averaging and decimation factors control the density of the grid lines used in the graph. The pixel averaging factor reduces the size of the image array by averaging adjacent pixels in the original image. The reduced image is the array that is actually plotted. The x and y decimation factors reduce the number of grid lines that are used in plotting in the x and y directions. There are thus two ways of reducing the grid density. Setting either the pixel averaging factor to 4 and the decimation factors to 1, or the pixel averaging factor to 1 and the decimation factors to 4, results in the same number of grid lines. A higher value for the averaging factor, however, tends to produce a smoother graph.

The projection coordinates determine the location of the virtual central projection point. This is the point where the virtual observer is located. Changing the x or y values will skew the graph sideways, while the z value determines the distance of the observer from the graph. A large z value (e.g., 100) will reduce the projection effect, while a small value (e.g., 2) will exaggerate it.

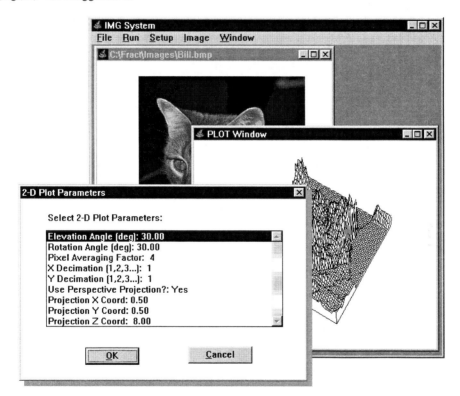

Fig. A.2.9 The 2-D plot window, with its setup parameters dialog.

A.3 WAV SYSTEM: WAVELET IMAGE COMPRESSION

The WAV System performs wavelet image compression on Windows bitmap images, using Haar and Daubechies D4 and D6 wavelets. It can also plot wavelet functions, as well as display two-dimensional wavelet transforms of images. The WAV System implements two different compression algorithms: the basic decimation algorithm described in Chapters 5 and 6, and the zerotree algorithm described in Chapter 7. The "Wavelet Compression Window" implements the basic decimation algorithm, and both compresses and decodes the image. The zerotree algorithm is implemented by an encoding window and a decoding window, and the system can save zerotree encoded images to a file. Fig. A.3.1 shows the WAV System frame window, with its "File" menu for opening the various window types.

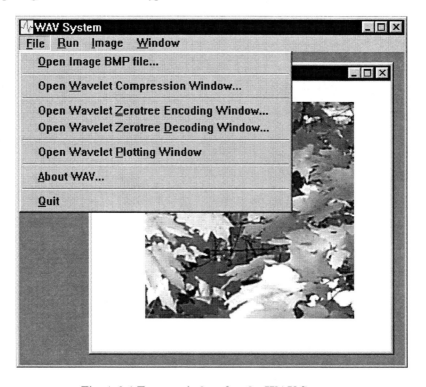

Fig. A.3.1 Frame window for the WAV System.

A.3.1 Wavelet compression window

The wavelet compression window can display either the compressed image ("Show Wavelet Compressed Image") or the wavelet transform of the image ("Show Wavelet Transform"), as shown in Fig. A.3.2. You can select from among three wavelet types: Haar, and Daubechies D4 and D6 wavelets. You can specify the compression percent via a numeric dialog ("Compression Percent..." under the "Setup" menu). This is the percentage of wavelet transform coefficients that will not be set equal to zero prior to applying the inverse transform. Thus, if compression percent is 10%, then the largest 10% of the wavelet transform coefficients will be retained, and the remaining 90% will be set equal to zero. However, if this percentage is 0%, then no decimation is performed. Recall that a compression percent of 10% does not represent 10:1 compression, however, since information about the location of the retained 10% of the coefficients must be stored as well. The processing that is performed when you select "Show Wavelet Compressed Image", with compression percent equal to $x\%$, is the following:

1. The wavelet transform is applied to the image, using the selected wavelet type.
2. The largest (in magnitude) $x\%$ of the transform coefficients are retained, the remaining $(100-x)\%$ are set equal to zero, leaving a decimated two-dimensional array of transform coefficients.
3. The inverse wavelet transform is applied to this decimated array. The resulting image is displayed.

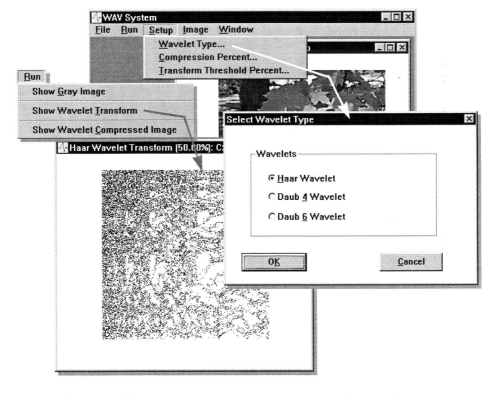

Fig. A.3.2 The wavelet compression window can display either the compressed image ("Show Wavelet Compressed Image") or the wavelet transform of the image ("Show Wavelet Transform"). The example here shows the largest 50% of the Haar wavelet transform coefficients of the "Leaves" image. The wavelet type, the compression percent and the transform threshold percent (for displaying the wavelet transform coefficients) are user-selectable via dialogs.

You can check the error performance of this compression by opening an image subtraction window, just as was the case in the fractal image compression system. As before, the subtraction window requires a window displaying the original image to be open ("Open Image BMP file…"), as well as an open wavelet compression window. Each window must contain a grayscale image array ("Gray Image").

This wavelet compression window also has the capability of displaying a binary version of the wavelet transform of the image, as shown in Fig. A.3.2. This option displays the largest $x\%$ of the wavelet transform coefficients in black, and the remaining $(100-x)\%$ of the coefficients in white. This option typically takes a minute or two to display the binary image, since a sorting operation is involved in selecting the coefficients.

A.3.2 Wavelet zerotree encoding

The wavelet zerotree encoding window encodes bitmap images using the zerotree algorithm described in Chapter 7. Fig. A.3.3 shows an example of this window, with its "Setup" and "Run" menu options displayed. As for the basic wavelet compression window, you can select one of three wavelet types, and also the compression percent. Compression percent is the percentage of wavelet coefficients that are retained after decimation. However, the default value of 0 indicates that no decimation is to be performed. In addition, zerotree encoding has a "Set Max Bit Plane…" option.

Zerotree encoding can achieve compression in two ways. The first way is through decimation of coefficients, which is controlled by setting the compression percent. The second, and more efficient, way is to restrict the maximum number of bit planes used by the encoder. When this value is 0, all bit planes (typically 14-16) are used. When a nonzero number is entered here, the encoder stops when that number of bit planes have been encoded. The progressive decoding example in Chapter 7 gives an idea of decoded image quality at various bit plane levels.

When you are ready to encode, select "Wavelet Zerotree Encoding…" from the "Run" menu. The zerotree encoding window saves the encoded image as a "*.wvz" file. You will be asked to specify the file name at this time. The bit planes are displayed with the four coded symbols rendered with four grayscales, and the ZT symbol displayed in white, as shown in the example in Fig. A.3.3. Checking the menu item "Show Bit Planes During Encoding" will display each symbol bit plane during encoding. When this item is not checked, only the final bit plane is displayed. The time used to do the actual display of these bit planes is not included in the encoding time summary that is provided at the conclusion of encoding. Similar to the wavelet compression window, this window also has the capability to display the wavelet transform, using the "Transform Threshold Percent…" setting (this value is not used during encoding).

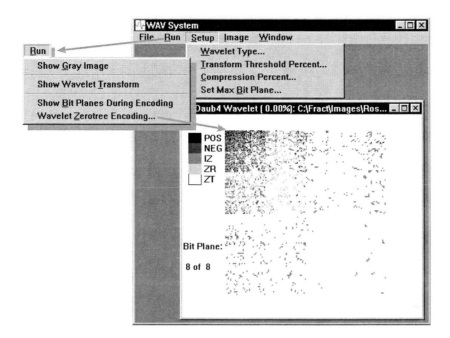

Fig. A.3.3 The zerotree encoding window. This window has options to select wavelet type, compression percent, and maximum bit plane used during encoding. The window displays the symbol array for each bit plane during encoding.

A.3.3 Wavelet zerotree decoding

The zerotree decoding window reads in a file of type "*.wvz", containing data recorded during zerotree encoding. Wavelet type, image size and number of bit planes are all included in the file information, so there are no options to select that will impact the final decoded image. There is a menu option to "Show Progressive Decoding", located under the "Run" menu, which will display each bit plane as it is built up during decoding. This takes longer, but the process is instructive to observe. When this option is off, only the final decoded image is displayed. Fig. A.3.4 shows an example of the zerotree decoding window during progressive decoding.

Fig. A.3.4 The zerotree decoding window. When "Show Progressive Decoding" is selected, each bit plane will be displayed during decoding. When this option is turned off, only the final decoded image will be displayed.

A.3.4 Image subtraction with the WAV System

The WAV System has a subtraction window option so that you can compute the errors in decoded images. The subtraction window requires the original image to be displayed in a window. This is done using the "Open Image BMP File…" option from the "File" menu. The image must be converted to an internal gray image prior to opening the subtraction window. There must also be a decode image displayed in a window. This can be either a basic wavelet compression window or a zerotree decoding window. When both an image window and a decode image window are open, you can open a subtraction window and run image subtraction to compute the errors. To avoid confusion and unpredictable results as to which decode image is subtracted from which original image, you should have only one image window and one decode window open when doing image subtraction.

A.3.5 Wavelet plotting window

The wavelet plotting window graphically displays the Haar, Daubechies D4 or Daubechies D6 wavelet functions. Fig. A.3.5 shows an example of this window with some of its menu options. The method for generating the graphs is a simple algorithm, taken from Press, et al. (1992), that makes efficient use of code already developed for the wavelet compression part of the system. This algorithm simply applies the one-dimensional inverse wavelet transform to a unit vector consisting of all 0's except for a single component set to 1. You can set which component is nonzero using the "Setup" menu option "Set Starting Component…". The graph in Fig. A.3.5 was produced using a vector of length 1024 with the 11th component set equal to 1.

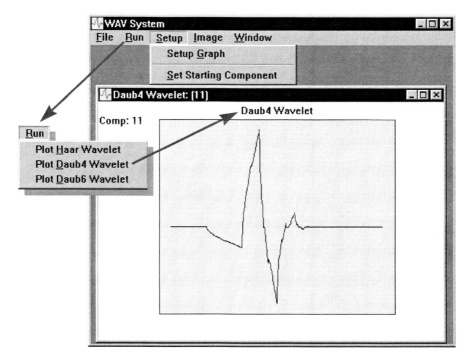

Fig. A.3.5 The wavelet plotting window can display the Haar, Daubechies D4 or Daubechies D6 wavelet functions.

Why does this algorithm produce a graph of the wavelet function? Recall that a one-dimensional wavelet transform vector represents the coefficients of a basis-expansion of some function, using scaled and shifted versions of the wavelet function as basis functions. What kind of function would have an expansion with only a single non-zero coefficient? It would have to be one of the basis functions, that is, one of the scaled and shifted wavelet functions. If you specify larger starting components, such as 50 or 100, you will see the graph of the wavelet function slide to the right and become compressed, that is, it has been shifted and scaled.

A.3.5.1 Setting up the graph parameters

The graph setup dialog (Fig. A.3.6) controls the appearance of the graph, allowing you to turn on or off various options such as grid lines and tic marks. You can modify the x-y window of the graph, implementing a crude "zoom" functionality, by setting "Scale Window from Data?" to "No", and then changing the values of "X Min", "X Max", "Y Min" and "Y Max".

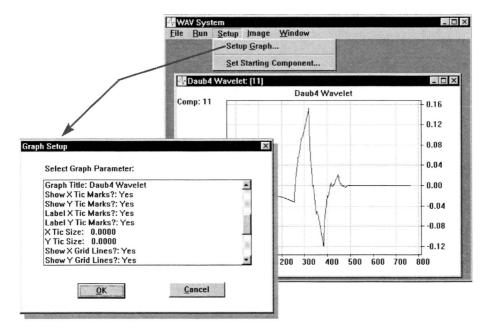

Fig. A.3.6 The graph setup dialog controls the appearance of the graph, such as the inclusion of grid lines, tic marks and axis labels.

Appendix B

UTILITY WINDOWS LIBRARY (UWL)

This appendix gives a brief overview of Windows programming, and describes the Utility Windows Library (UWL), a C++ object-oriented framework that is the basis for the application systems in the accompanying software.

B.1 WINDOWS PROGRAMMING

From a programming point of view, the Windows environment is defined by the Windows Application Programming Interface (API), which consists of over a thousand function definitions, as well as defined types, structures, and constants. To program for Windows using C, you can write code that directly calls the API functions. There are also several C++ class libraries that have been developed to deal with Windows programming, the most prevalent of which is the Microsoft Foundation Classes (MFC), which today effectively defines the C++ Windows interface. The software accompanying this book uses its own self-contained C++ class library, called the Utility Windows Library (UWL), for interfacing with the Windows environment. This library provides a framework for easily implementing a subset of the Windows API. Complete source code for UWL is provided with the software.

Why develop a class library when MFC is available? For one thing, MFC was not mature at the time of initial development of this software. There were several competing libraries at that time, including an early version of MFC and Borland's Object Windows Library (OWL). It appears that MFC has won out. Having a self-contained class library, however, ensures that the code with this book can be compiled with any compiler that supports the Windows API. This code has been compiled and tested with Borland C++ 3.1 (16-bit only), 4.5 and 5.0, Symantec C++ 7.2, and Microsoft Visual C++ 4.1. Another advantage of UWL is that it produces small executables, typically less than 300 Kb in size (without requiring any of its own Dynamic Link Libraries, or DLL's), compared with 1.5 Mb or more for a typical MFC-produced executable.

Where possible, the computational aspects of the application code have been separated from the Windows-specific code. This allows you to interface these computational code modules with another Windows library, such as MFC, or even another windows platform, such as X-Windows in a UNIX environment.

The best reference for basic Windows programming is (Petzold 1992), or the updated version for Windows 95 (Petzold 1996).

UWL addresses the two primary needs that the applications in this book require of a Windows interface: (i) the ability to display multiple windows with graphical information; (ii) the ability to communicate with the user via dialog boxes. The following two sections discuss these two aspects of Windows in more detail.

B.1.1 Multiple Document Interface (MDI)

Most commercial Windows applications, such as Microsoft Word and Visual C++, use some variation of what is known as the Multiple Document Interface (MDI). MDI allows multiple windows to be open at the same time. The user can move freely among these windows. Fig. B.1.1 shows the main components of a MDI application. The MDI frame controls the menus and defines the region of the screen that contains the application's windows. The MDI frame controls the opening of new windows, and also shuts the application down when the user exits the application. The MDI client window is the actual "window" contained within the frame (the dark gray background in Fig. B.1.1). Functionally, the MDI client window controls the initial placement of the child windows, and can also automatically arrange the child windows through commands such as "Tile" or "Cascade", selected from the "Window" menu.

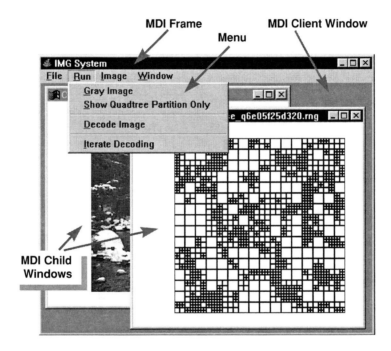

Fig. B.1.1 The main components of a MDI system include the frame window, the client window, the menu, and multiple child windows.

In most commercial MDI applications, each child window has the same behavior. For example, in MS Word, each window is an editor window for entering text. However, it is possible for a MDI application to have different types of child windows and this is in fact true of each of the applications in the software accompanying this book. For example, the IMG System has several types of encoding and decoding windows, as well as image subtraction and plotting windows.

B.1.2 Dialogs

Dialog boxes are the primary means by which application programs communicate with the user. Dialog boxes accept input from the user, and can also display information back to the user. Dialog boxes are distinguished both by their appearance and by their functionality. Resource scripts define how the dialog looks. Callback functions define what the dialog does. In Fig. B.1.2, for example, a resource script defines the size of the dialog box, and the location and appearance of its components, including the "OK" and "Cancel" buttons, the groupbox containing the "Yes" and "No" radio buttons, and the text ("Use Domain Features?"). Resource scripts typically are created with a visual resource editor, although it is possible to edit manually the resulting text file.

Once the resource script has been defined for a dialog, its functionality can be defined using a callback procedure. The callback procedure is provided to Windows as a function that defines actions to be performed in response to events associated with the dialog. Examples of such events include the user hitting the "OK" button or selecting one of the radio buttons. Each component of the dialog has an identifier, i.e., a defined constant, associated with it so that the program knows when an event affects that component.

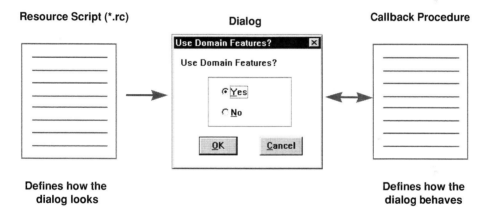

Resource Script (*.rc)   **Dialog**   **Callback Procedure**

Defines how the   **Defines how the**
dialog looks   **dialog behaves**

Fig. B.1.2 Resource scripts define the appearance of a dialog box, while its behavior is defined by a callback procedure.

B.1.2.1 Modal vs. modeless dialogs

Windows provides two types of dialogs. By far the most frequently used type of dialog is the so-called *modal* dialog. When a modal dialog is open, it demands undivided attention from the user. The user cannot communicate with any other user interface component outside the dialog until the dialog has been dismissed, usually by clicking on its "OK" or "Cancel" button. From a programming point of view, modal dialogs are easy to deal with. Program execution effectively halts while the dialog is open. So, if you have a line of code that executes the dialog, then you can depend on the next line of code having available to it the latest input from the user via that dialog.

The other type of dialog in Windows is the less commonly used *modeless* dialog. Modeless dialogs allow communication with other components of the application while the modeless dialog is open. A modeless dialog is more like an ordinary window than a typical modal dialog. The spell-check dialog in MS Word is an example of a modeless dialog, since you can leave the dialog and actually correct an errant word in the text window while the dialog remains open. From a programming point of view, modeless dialogs are somewhat more difficult to deal with. For one thing, the *WinMain* function must be modified to capture messages intended for the modeless dialog and route them to that dialog. Also, once the dialog is open, the calling program must know when to check back with the dialog while its own processing continues. The only place in the accompanying software where a modeless dialog is used is in the IMG system, which uses a modeless dialog to display a progress bar during training of the self-organizing network.

B.1.2.2 Windows Common Dialogs

Windows includes a set of pre-defined dialogs for performing commonly occurring tasks, such as selecting file names or colors. These dialogs, called *Windows Common Dialogs*, do not require resource scripts or callback functions. Fig. B.1.3 shows two of the common dialogs, *ChooseColor* and *GetOpenFileName*. There are also Common Dialogs for printing and font selection. You should take advantage of Windows Common Dialogs whenever possible in your Windows code development. For one thing, they are easier to use than defining your own dialogs. Also, they automatically incorporate upgrades that appear with new releases of Windows. For example, the file dialogs that are included with Windows 95 and later, as well as the recent versions of Windows NT, have the capability of handling file names longer than 8 characters, and also have a new look, as shown in Fig. B.1.3. If your code used the Windows file dialog, it would automatically benefit from the new functionality and appearance, without even the need to recompile (the dialogs are accessed through a DLL). However, if you had developed your own file browser dialog, that dialog would remain with the functionality you had originally provided for it.

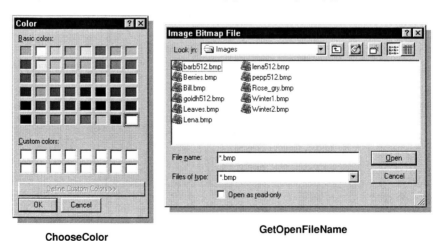

ChooseColor   GetOpenFileName

Fig. B.1.3 *ChooseColor* **and** *GetOpenFileName* **are two of the Windows common dialogs. These dialogs do not require a resource script or callback procedure, and can be used with a single call to the appropriate API function.**

B.2 UTILITY WINDOWS LIBRARY (UWL)

The Utility Windows Library (UWL) is a C++ class library that handles the basics of MDI window management and dialogs. Windows user-interface development is an ideal candidate for an object-oriented language such as C++. Mundane tasks that are common to all windows and dialogs can be assigned to base classes and then needn't be dealt with again. Some of the references at the end of this appendix provide more details about the approach used here for MDI window management (Welstead 1996) and dialogs (Welstead 1995). Fig. B.2.1 shows the class hierarchy for the classes in UWL that deal with MDI window management.

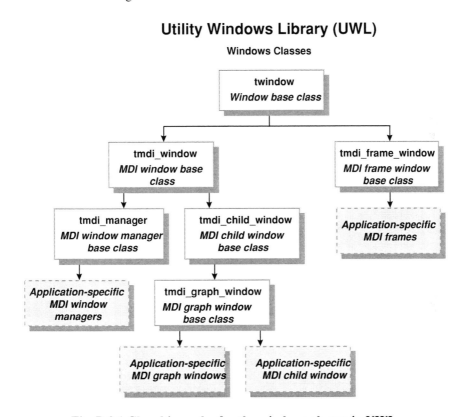

Fig. B.2.1 Class hierarchy for the windows classes in UWL.

B.2.1 The *twindow* class

The *twindow* class is the basic window class from which all other windows, including MDI frame and child windows, are derived. This class takes care of the routine tasks and behavior common to all windows.

Windows is an event-driven program environment. User actions, such as moving the pointing device or entering keystrokes through the keyboard, generate events. Windows responds to these events by sending messages to the application program. In fact, the main program in any Windows application program (called *WinMain*) simply executes a loop that looks for messages from the Windows environment and dispatches them to the application's windows. One application differs from another only in the way that it responds to these messages.

The base class *twindow* responds to Windows messages through its *handle_message* member function. Listing B.2.1 shows the code for this function. Functions such as *respond_wm_paint* define the response for a particular Windows message, in this case WM_PAINT. In *twindow*, this response is not functional. However, descendant window classes need only redefine the individual message response functions. In most cases, it is not necessary to redefine *handle_message* itself. Note that *handle_message* returns 0 in most cases. Returning 0 to Windows tells it to continue processing the message; a nonzero value would tell Windows to do no further processing. It is usually best to let Windows continue to process a message after you are done with it, since there may be functionality that you are not aware of (some of which may be introduced in later versions of Windows).

How do Windows messages get to the *handle_message* function? Windows provides for a procedure (the *callback* procedure) to be associated with each window type. This association occurs by assigning the address of the procedure to the window during window registration, which occurs as part of the application *WinMain* function. Ideally, we'd like to assign the address of the *handle_message* member function. However, C++ doesn't allow the assignment of the address of a member function, since this address is not known until a particular class object is instantiated at run time. This is why *twindow* has a s*et_global_ptr* member function. In descendant window classes, this member function is redefined to set the value of a global pointer to a particular instantiation of the window class (using the class's "*this*" pointer). That global pointer then defines a particular instance of the *handle_message* function that is called from a global function, whose address is provided to Windows as the callback procedure associated with that window type.

Listing B.2.1 The *handle_message* member function of the *twindow* class.

```
LRESULT CALLBACK twindow::handle_message (HWND hwnd,
    UINT message, WPARAM wParam, LPARAM lParam) {
  /* If "respond_..." procedure actually does
     something,then return, otherwise drop through to
     default. */
    hwindow = hwnd;
    switch (message)
        {
      case WM_CREATE:
            if (respond_wm_create (hwnd)) return 0;
            break;
      case WM_COMMAND:
            if (respond_wm_command (wParam,lParam))
            return 0;
            break;
      case WM_PAINT:
            if (respond_wm_paint ()) return 0;
            break;
      case WM_MDIACTIVATE:
            if (respond_wm_mdiactivate(hwnd,wParam,lParam))
            return 0;
            break;
      case WM_SIZE:
            if (respond_wm_size(lParam)) return 0;
            break;
      case WM_HSCROLL:
            if (respond_wm_hscroll (wParam,lParam))
            return 0;
            break;
      case WM_VSCROLL:
            if (respond_wm_vscroll (wParam,lParam))
            return 0;
            break;
      case WM_QUERYENDSESSION:
            if (respond_wm_queryendsession()) return 0;
            break;
      case WM_CLOSE:
            if (respond_wm_close()) return 0;
            break;
      case WM_DESTROY:
            if (respond_wm_destroy(hwnd)) return 0;
            break;
      }  /*  end switch  */
    return
    default_window_proc (hwindow,message,wParam,lParam);
    }
```

B.2.2 MDI frame window

The *tmdi_frame_window* class is a direct descendant of *twindow* that implements a basic MDI frame window. The frame window displays the menus, interacts with the user through menu commands, and dispatches user commands to the client window. The client window either responds directly to the command, or sends it along to the appropriate child window. UWL does not modify default client window behavior, and so does not incorporate a C++ class corresponding to the client window.

Listing B.2.2 contains the class declaration for *tmdi_frame_window*. The linked list structure *tmdi_type_list_struct* facilitates the handling of a number of different child window types with a single frame window class. This structure ties a menu command, *type_id*, to a window class, *the_class*. When the frame window receives a menu command, it first cycles through its linked list of child types to see if the command matches any of these type id's. If there is a match, the frame creates a new child window of that type. This linked list enables the handling of any number of child window types without having to create a new frame class for each application. The only time you have to derive a new frame class is when the application requires some action other than opening a child window (for example, when the frame window must handle dialog input from the user).

The frame window responds to the Windows WM_CREATE message with the function *respond_wm_create*, which creates the MDI client window. The frame window then optionally displays an "About" dialog box. Each of the applications included here use an "About" box.

User-selected menu commands go to the *respond_wm_command* member function. This is where the child window types are checked against the *tmdi_type_list_struct* linked list. A match initiates the creation of a MDI child window of the appropriate class. If there is no match, the frame continues checking for other common commands, including the commands that carry out pre-defined MDI behavior, such as tiling and cascading of child windows. Note that this basic MDI behavior is accomplished merely by sending the appropriate message to the client window. The command structure defined here is general enough to handle most MDI applications. Specific needs, such as a frame that communicates with the user through dialog boxes, can be accommodated through derived frame classes.

Listing B.2.2 Class declaration for *tmdi_frame_window*.

```
typedef struct tmdi_type_list_tag {
   UINT type_id;
   LPCSTR the_class;
   LPCSTR the_title;
   tmdi_type_list_tag *next;
   } tmdi_type_list_struct;

void free_mdi_type_list_struct (tmdi_type_list_struct
       *type_list);

LRESULT CALLBACK _export FrameWndProc (HWND hwnd, UINT
     message, WPARAM wParam,LPARAM lParam);

#define NO_ABOUT   0
#define SHOW_ABOUT 1

class tmdi_frame_window: public twindow {
   public:
   tmdi_frame_window (HINSTANCE hInstance,
       LRESULT CALLBACK window_proc,int window_extra,
       LPCSTR menu_name,
       LPCSTR title_name,
       LPCSTR class_name,LPCSTR icon_name,
       tmdi_type_list_struct *child_types,
       int init_show_about);
   HWND hwndClient;
   CLIENTCREATESTRUCT clientcreate ;
   LRESULT CALLBACK      lpfnEnum ;
   HWND                  hwndChild ;
   MDICREATESTRUCT      mdicreate ;
   tmdi_type_list_struct *mdi_children_types;
   UINT latest_command;
   HMENU frame_menu,frame_submenu;
   int show_about;

   virtual void set_mdicreate (LPCSTR the_class,LPCSTR
           the_title);
   virtual void set_global_ptr (void);
   virtual int respond_wm_create (HWND hwnd);
   virtual int respond_wm_command (WPARAM wParam,LPARAM
           lParam);
   virtual int respond_wm_queryendsession (void);
   virtual int respond_wm_close (void);
   virtual int respond_wm_destroy (HWND hwnd);
   virtual int respond_wm_about (void);
   virtual LRESULT CALLBACK default_window_proc (HWND
           hwnd,
     UINT message,WPARAM wParam,LPARAM lParam);
   void init_menu (HINSTANCE hinst,LPCSTR menu_rc_name,
       WPARAM window_submenu_pos);
   };
```

B.2.3 MDI windows

Listing B.2.3 shows the class declarations that define basic MDI window behavior. The base class *tmdi_window* redefines the *default_window_proc* member function to call the Windows function *DefMDIChildProc*, which defines default MDI behavior.

Windows keeps track of the active MDI child windows through a list of HWND identifiers. As child windows are created and destroyed, Windows adds or deletes HWND identifiers so that this list correctly reflects the current windows that are open in the frame window. UWL represents each MDI child window with a descendant of the *tmdi_child_window* class, so it needs to maintain a separate list of pointers to the active C++ MDI child window class objects. The purpose of the *tmdi_manager* class is to maintain this list and take care of routing Windows messages to the active child window.

The structure type *child_window_struct* ties a Windows HWND identifier to a pointer to a *tmdi_child_window* object. The *window_list* member of *tmdi_manager* maintains the list of active child windows. This is a pointer to an *object_list* class, a class for handling an array of object pointers. The class *tmdi_manager* has a virtual function *new_child_window* that creates a new *tmdi_child_window*. To create child windows of a specific type, you need to derive a descendant MDI manager class that overrides this virtual function with a version that creates the desired child window type. Normally, *new_child_window* and *set_global_ptr* are the only member functions that you need to override in descendant manager classes.

The *tmdi_manager* member function *handle_message* processes WM_CREATE and WM_DESTROY messages itself, so that it can keep its active window list updated. Messages that are relevant to the child windows, such as paint and mouse movement messages, are sent to the active child window. All other messages get default processing.

The member functions *init_menu* and *set_frame_menu* set up the menu and submenus for the child window, and their relationship to the frame window menu. These functions are called once in the *WinMain* function, just after window registration. The identifier *menu_rc_name* is the string name for the window's menu as it appears in the resource file. The parameter *window_submenu_pos* tells Windows where to place the list of open MDI child windows. The appearance of this list in the menu is a benefit you get for free from Windows MDI management.

The *tmdi_child_window* class is a base class for specific child window types. It encapsulates behavior common to all MDI child windows. The most significant behavior is that of switching the frame window menus whenever a new child window is activated. Member function *respond_wm_mdiactivate* accomplishes this, in response to a WM_MDIACTIVATE message. This function uses two macros: ACTIVATE_MDI_CHILD_WINDOW and MDI_SETMENU_MSGPARAMS. There are two versions of these macros, one for 16-bit Windows (such as Windows 3.1) and one for 32-bit Windows (such as Windows 95, 98 and NT). These macros allow the use of one set of source code that can be compiled for either 16- or 32-bit environments.

Listing B.2.3 Class declarations for MDI windows.

```
class tmdi_window: public twindow {
   public:
   // Base class for tmdi_manager and tmdi_child_window
   tmdi_window (HINSTANCE hInstance,LRESULT CALLBACK
      window_proc, int window_extra,LPCSTR menu_name,
      LPCSTR title_name,
      LPCSTR class_name,LPCSTR icon_name):
      twindow (hInstance, window_proc, window_extra,
         menu_name, title_name, class_name, icon_name)
         {};
      virtual LRESULT CALLBACK default_window_proc (HWND
      hwnd, UINT message,WPARAM wParam,LPARAM lParam);
   };

#define MAX_NO_OF_ACTIVE_WINDOWS 20

class tmdi_child_window;   // Complete declarations given
                           // below
class tmdi_frame_window;

typedef struct {
   HWND hwnd;
   tmdi_child_window *window;
   } child_window_struct;

class tmdi_manager: public tmdi_window {
   public:
   HWND hwndClient,hwndFrame;
   HMENU window_menu,window_submenu,frame_menu,
            frame_submenu;
   tmdi_frame_window *parent_frame;
   object_list *window_list;
   int active_index;
   tmdi_manager (HINSTANCE hInstance,
      tmdi_frame_window *parent,
      LRESULT CALLBACK window_proc,
      int window_extra,LPCSTR menu_name,
      LPCSTR title_name,
      LPCSTR class_name,LPCSTR icon_name);
   virtual int respond_wm_create (HWND hwnd);
   virtual int respond_wm_destroy (HWND hwnd);
   virtual HWND get_active_hwnd (void);
   virtual int add_child_window (HWND hwnd,
         child_window_struct *child);
   virtual child_window_struct *get_child_window
         (HWND hwnd,int *index);
   virtual LRESULT CALLBACK handle_message
         (HWND hwnd,UINT message,
                   WPARAM wParam,LPARAM lParam);
   void init_menu (HINSTANCE hinst,LPCSTR menu_rc_name,
         WPARAM window_submenu_pos);
   void set_frame_menu (HMENU the_frame_menu,
            HMENU the_frame_submenu);
   virtual ~tmdi_manager ();
   };
```

```
class tmdi_child_window: public tmdi_window {
    public:-
    tmdi_manager *manager;
    tmdi_child_window (HWND hwnd,
        tmdi_manager *the_manager,
        LPCSTR title_name);
    virtual int respond_wm_mdiactivate (HWND hwnd,
        WPARAM wParam,
            LPARAM lParam);
    virtual int respond_wm_queryendsession (void);
    virtual int respond_wm_close (void);
    };
```

B.2.4 Graph window

UWL includes the *tmdi_graph_window* as a MDI window class for handling basic X-Y graphing functionality. Listing B.2.4 shows two structures that hold most of the parameters that define the graph window. The structure *graph_setup_rec* contains information specified by the user that defines the appearance of the graph, such as axis labels and tic marks. The computed values in *graph_window_struct* define the relationship between the X-Y values and the window's pixels. All of the graph drawing functions use these structures as arguments. This is a step toward portability, since the underlying drawing functions can be changed to a different window system (such as X-Windows) without changing the application code that calls these functions.

Listing B.2.4 Structures used by the MDI graph window.

```
/* graph_setup_rec holds items usually specified by the
/* user. If you add fields to graph_setup_rec be sure to /* change
the constant GRAPH_SETUP_ITEMS.*/
typedef struct {
   float x_min,x_max,y_min,y_max;
   BOOL scale_window_from_data,use_nice_numbers;
   BOOL label_x_axis,label_y_axis,label_axes,show_title;
   char x_axis_label,y_axis_label;
   char hor_axis_label[GR_LABEL_LEN + 1],
       vert_axis_label[GR_LABEL_LEN + 1],
       graph_title [GR_TITLE_LEN + 1],
       print_header_1 [GR_HEADER_FOOTER_LEN+1],
       print_header_2 [GR_HEADER_FOOTER_LEN+1],
       print_footer [GR_HEADER_FOOTER_LEN+1];
   BOOL show_x_tic_marks,show_y_tic_marks,
       label_x_tic_marks,label_y_tic_marks;
   float x_tic_size,y_tic_size;
   BOOL show_x_max_min,show_y_max_min;
   int x_len,y_len,x_dec_places,y_dec_places;
   BOOL show_x_grid_lines,show_y_grid_lines;
   DWORD line_color,text_color,back_color;
   } graph_setup_rec;

/* graph_window_struct holds items that are computed as /*
specific for this window  */
typedef struct {
   HDC hDC;
   HWND HWindow;
   RECT rect,draw_rect,iter_rect;
   SIZE label_extent;
   float x_min,y_min,x_max,y_max,x_range,y_range;
   int logical_x_max,logical_y_max,start_col,end_col,
       title_row,
       start_row,end_row,
       x_min_col,x_max_col,y_min_row,y_max_row,
       no_of_rows,no_of_cols,
       iter_row_1,iter_row_2,
       iter_col,done_row,
       x_row,x_center_col,
       y_col,y_center_row,
       tic_cols,tic_rows,
       x_space,y_space;
   DWORD line_color,text_color,back_color;
   } graph_window_struct;
```

The *tmdi_graph_window* class, defined in Listing B.2.5, provides a window environment for graphical display, but it doesn't actually graph anything. Descendant application class windows will do that. The *tmdi_graph_window* class provides an interface to the user for obtaining values for the *graph_setup_rec* structure. It also captures whatever is in the window to a bitmap, so that the window can quickly be redisplayed in response to a Windows paint message (such as occurs when the window is resized or a previously covered portion is revealed), without recomputing the values that make up the graph. It also provides the capability to copy this bitmap to the Windows clipboard, so that the graph image can be imported to other Windows applications.

Listing B.2.5 Class declaration for *tmdi_graph_window*.

```
class tmdi_graph_window: public tmdi_child_window
{  public:
   HDC memory_dc;
   HBITMAP hbitmap;
   graph_window_struct gr;
   graph_setup_rec gr_setup;
   tlist_box_data gr_setup_data;
   tmdi_graph_window(HWND hwnd,tmdi_manager *the_manager,
      LPCSTR title_name);
   virtual int save_image_to_bitmap();
   virtual int OnCopyToClipboard ();
   virtual int respond_wm_paint();
   virtual int respond_wm_print ();
   virtual int respond_wm_create(HWND hwnd);
   virtual int respond_wm_graph_setup ();
   virtual int respond_wm_command (WPARAM wParam,LPARAM);
   virtual int respond_wm_destroy (HWND hwnd);
   virtual ~tmdi_graph_window ();
};
```

B.2.5 *WinMain* in a UWL application

Every Windows application has a *WinMain* function. *WinMain*, analogous to the *main* function in an ordinary C/C++ application, is the main function that runs the application. The primary work that *WinMain* does is to dispatch Windows messages to the application. Thus, every *WinMain* function contains a message loop as its main body of code. The primary work that you, the programmer, do in setting up a *WinMain* function for your application is to tell it where to send the messages that it passes along.

The steps for setting up a *WinMain* function for a UWL application are straightforward and common to all UWL applications. Listing B.2.6 shows the code for the *WinMain* function for the IMG System, the fractal image compression application included with the accompanying software. One of the distinguishing features of the UWL framework is the ease with which it accommodates multiple types of windows, each with a different functionality, within the same MDI application. The IMG System includes five different types of windows. Sections A.2.1 - A.2.5 show examples of these window types and discuss their functionality.

The following steps for setting up the *WinMain* function are common to all UWL MDI applications. These steps are highlighted in the code shown in Listing B.2.6.

   1. Define Windows class names for the frame and each type of child window. These are strings that Windows uses to identify the window types.
   2. Define the linked list for the MDI child window types. This is a linked list of pointers to structures of type *tmdi_type_list_struct*.
   3. Define an object for the frame window, and an object for the MDI manager for each child window type. These are pointers to the appropriate C++ class for each type. For IMG, there are five such child window classes:

tenc_window_manager, for managing basic fractal image encoding windows; *tself_org_enc_window_manager*, for managing fractal image encoding with self-organizing domain classification; *tdec_window_manager*, for managing windows that decode and display fractal encoded images; *tsub_window_manager*, for managing image subtraction windows; *tplt2d_window_manager*, for managing windows that display two-dimensional surface plots of images.

4. Fill the entries in the child type linked list. Create one entry for each type of child window. The *type_id* is the menu resource identifier for the menu item that will open this child window; *the_class* is the Windows class string defined above. Note that IMG actually has six entries in this linked list, since the decode window type has two different menu commands that correspond to it. The menu identifiers for IMG are: IMG_OPEN (for the basic encoding window), IMG_OPEN_RANGE and IMG_OPEN_BINARY_RANGE (the decode window, corresponding to the two types of range files), IMG_SELF_ORG_OPEN (fractal encoding with self-organizing domain classification), IMG_OPEN_PLOT (the plotting window), and IMG_OPEN_SUB (the subtraction window).

5. Instantiate the frame object and each child MDI manager object. Allocate each C++ pointer using the constructor for that class.

6. Register the frame window and each child window type, using the class's *register_window_class* member function. This takes care of the Windows registration that is necessary in any Windows application.

7. Initialize the menus for the frame and each child window type. Each UWL MDI window class has an *init_menu* member function. The MDI window manager classes also have a *set_frame_menu* function that associates the child window menu with the frame window.

8. Set up the Windows code. Load the accelerators, create and show the frame window, and implement the message loop. Some variation of this code is common to all Windows applications, whether UWL or otherwise.

9. Clean up when done. Delete the frame and MDI manager objects and free the linked list of child types. It's important to free up your memory allocations in a Windows application, since these allocations may live beyond the end of the application.

Listing B.2.6 The *WinMain* function for the IMG System. The steps involved in setting up a *WinMain* function for a typical UWL application are highlighted.

```
//  IMGMAIN.CPP  WinMain for IMG system: Fractal image
//               compression.

#include <stdlib.h>

#include "uwl.h"
#include "imgwin.h"
#include "decwin.h"
#include "encwin.h"
#include "soencwin.h"
#include "subwin.h"
#include "plt2dwin.h"

// For menu position constants:
#include "mdifmids.h"
#include "imgrids.h"

// Step 1: Define Windows class names for the frame
// and each type of child window.
char    szFrameClass [] = "IMGFrame" ;
char    szIMGSClass [] = "IMGChild";
char    IMG_title [] = "IMG Window";
char    szDECSClass [] = "DECChild";
char    DEC_title [] = "DEC Window";
char    szSUBSClass [] = "SUBChild";
char    SUB_title [] = "SUB Window";
char    szPLOTSClass [] = "PLOTChild";
char    PLOT_title [] = "PLOT Window";
char    szSELFORGSClass [] = "SELFORGChild";
char    SELF_ORG_title [] = "SELF ORG Window";

HINSTANCE hInst ;

int WINAPI WinMain (HINSTANCE hInstance,
        HINSTANCE hPrevInstance, LPSTR, int nCmdShow)
     {
     HACCEL    hAccel ;
     HWND      hwndFrame, hwndClient ;
     MSG       msg ;

// Step 2: Define the linked list for the MDI child
// window types.
     tmdi_type_list_struct *child_list,*child_type;

// Step 3: Define an object for the frame window, and an object
// for the MDI manager for each child window type.
     tmdi_frame_window *img_frame_window;
     tenc_window_manager *enc_manager;
     tself_org_enc_window_manager *self_org_enc_manager;
     tdec_window_manager *dec_manager;
```

```
      tsub_window_manager *sub_manager;
      tplt2d_window_manager *pIt2d_manager;
      int width,height;

// Step 4: Fill the entries in the child type linked list. Create
// one entry for each type of child window. The type_id is the
// menu resource id for the menu item that will open this child
// window; the_class is the Windows class string defined above.
      child_list = (tmdi_type_list_struct *)
         malloc((size_t)sizeof(tmdi_type_list_struct));
      child_type = child_list;
      child_type->type_id = IMG_OPEN;
      child_type->the_class = szIMGSClass;
      child_type->the_title = IMG_title;

      child_type->next = (tmdi_type_list_struct *)
         malloc((size_t)sizeof(tmdi_type_list_struct));
      child_type = child_type->next;
      child_type->type_id = IMG_OPEN_RANGE;
      child_type->the_class = szDECSClass;
      child_type->the_title = DEC_title;

      /* Commands IMG_OPEN_RANGE and IMG_OPEN_BINARY_RANGE
       correspond to the same window type. */

      child_type->next = (tmdi_type_list_struct *)
         malloc((size_t)sizeof(tmdi_type_list_struct));
      child_type = child_type->next;
      child_type->type_id = IMG_OPEN_BINARY_RANGE;
      child_type->the_class = szDECSClass;
      child_type->the_title = DEC_title;

      child_type->next = (tmdi_type_list_struct *)
         malloc((size_t)sizeof(tmdi_type_list_struct));
      child_type = child_type->next;
      child_type->type_id = IMG_OPEN_SUB;
      child_type->the_class = szSUBSClass;
      child_type->the_title = SUB_title;

      child_type->next = (tmdi_type_list_struct *)
         malloc((size_t)sizeof(tmdi_type_list_struct));
      child_type = child_type->next;
      child_type->type_id = IMG_OPEN_PLOT;
      child_type->the_class = szPLOTSClass;
      child_type->the_title = PLOT_title;

      child_type->next = (tmdi_type_list_struct *)
         malloc((size_t)sizeof(tmdi_type_list_struct));
      child_type = child_type->next;
      child_type->type_id = IMG_SELF_ORG_OPEN;
      child_type->the_class = szSELFORGSClass;
      child_type->the_title = SELF_ORG_title;

      child_type->next = NULL;
```

```
      hInst = hInstance ;
      gdlg_instance = hInstance;

// Step 5: Instantiate the frame object and each
// child MDI manager object.
      img_frame_window = new tmdi_frame_window (hInstance,
        (LRESULT CALLBACK)FrameWndProc,0,"",
        "IMG System",szFrameClass,"IFS_ICON",
        child_list,SHOW_ABOUT);
      enc_manager = new tenc_window_manager (hInstance,
            img_frame_window,0,szIMGSClass,"IFS_ICON");
      self_org_enc_manager = new tself_org_enc_window_manager
            (hInstance,img_frame_window,0,szSELFORGSClass,
            "IFS_ICON");
      dec_manager = new tdec_window_manager (hInstance,
            img_frame_window,0,szDECSClass,"IFS_ICON");
      sub_manager = new tsub_window_manager (hInstance,
            img_frame_window,0,szSUBSClass,"IFS_ICON",
            enc_manager,self_org_enc_manager,dec_manager);
      plt2d_manager = new tplt2d_window_manager
            (hInstance,img_frame_window,
            "IFS_ICON",szPLOTSClass,"IFS_ICON",enc_manager);

// Step 6: Register the frame window and each child
// window type, using the class's
// register_window_class member function.
      if (!hPrevInstance)
        {
        img_frame_window->register_window_class();
        enc_manager->register_window_class();
        self_org_enc_manager->register_window_class();
        dec_manager->register_window_class();
        sub_manager->register_window_class();
        plt2d_manager->register_window_class();
        }

// Step 7: Initialize the menus for the frame and
// each child window type.
      img_frame_window->init_menu (hInst,"MainMenu",
            INIT_MENU_POS);

      enc_manager->init_menu(hInst,"IMGMenu",
            IMG_MENU_CHILD_POS);
      enc_manager->set_frame_menu
            (img_frame_window->frame_menu,
            img_frame_window->frame_submenu);
      self_org_enc_manager->init_menu(hInst,"SLFORGMenu",
            SO_ENC_MENU_CHILD_POS);
      self_org_enc_manager->set_frame_menu
            (img_frame_window->frame_menu,
            img_frame_window->frame_submenu);
      dec_manager->init_menu(hInst,"DECMenu",
            DEC_MENU_CHILD_POS);
```

```
          dec_manager->set_frame_menu
                  (img_frame_window->frame_menu,
                  img_frame_window->frame_submenu);
          sub_manager->init_menu(hInst,"SUBMenu",
                  SUB_MENU_CHILD_POS);
          sub_manager->set_frame_menu
                  (img_frame_window->frame_menu,
                  img_frame_window->frame_submenu);
          plt2d_manager->init_menu(hInst,"PLOTMenu",
                  PLOT_MENU_CHILD_POS);
          plt2d_manager->set_frame_menu
                  (img_frame_window->frame_menu,
                  img_frame_window->frame_submenu);

// Step 8: Set up the Windows code. Load the
// accelerators, create and show the frame window,
// and implement the message loop. This is standard
// Windows code.
          // Load accelerator table

          hAccel = LoadAccelerators (hInst, "MdiAccel") ;

          // Create the frame window
          width = GetSystemMetrics (SM_CXSCREEN);
          height = GetSystemMetrics (SM_CYSCREEN);
          hwndFrame = CreateWindow (szFrameClass, "IMG System",
                            WS_OVERLAPPEDWINDOW |
                            WS_CLIPCHILDREN,
                            0, 0,
                            width, height,
                            NULL,img_frame_window->frame_menu,
                            hInstance, NULL) ;

          hwndClient = GetWindow (hwndFrame, GW_CHILD) ;

          ShowWindow (hwndFrame, nCmdShow) ;
          UpdateWindow (hwndFrame) ;

          // Enter the modified message loop

          while (GetMessage (&msg, NULL, 0, 0))
              {
              if ( !g_modeless_dialog ||
                  !IsDialogMessage
                          (g_modeless_dialog->hdialog,&msg))
              if (!TranslateMDISysAccel (hwndClient, &msg) &&
                  !TranslateAccelerator (hwndFrame, hAccel, &msg))
                  {
                  TranslateMessage (&msg) ;
                  DispatchMessage (&msg) ;
                  }
              }

// Step 9: Clean up when done. Delete the frame and
```

```
// MDI manager objects and free the linked list of
// child types.
    delete enc_manager;
    delete self_org_enc_manager;
    delete dec_manager;
    delete sub_manager;
    delete plt2d_manager;
    delete img_frame_window;
    free_mdi_type_list_struct (child_list);

    return msg.wParam ;
    }
```

B.2.6 UWL dialogs

In addition to providing basic MDI window functionality, UWL also provides a set of basic dialogs for obtaining input from the user. Fig. B.2.2 shows the class hierarchy for the UWL dialog classes. The *tnum_input_dialog* class collects numeric input from the user. The input data is edited to ensure that it is true numeric data, and there is an option to check to see that it is within specified max-min bounds. Fig. B.1.2 shows an example of a dialog produced by the *tbool_dialog* class, which solicits a yes/no choice from the user. The *tabout_dialog* class is the base class for application "About" dialogs.

Scrolling list boxes are implemented by *tlist_dialog*. Windows provides support for a list box control that displays, scrolls through, and selects from a list of character strings. The *tlist_dialog* class inserts this control into a dialog box. This class loads the list box with a list of strings and retrieves the index of the user-selected string when the dialog box is closed. The class *tdata_list_dialog* takes this one step further. Here, the list box displays strings that are associated with typed data objects that are members of the class *ttyped_data_obj*. When the user double-clicks on an item in the list, a dialog appropriate for editing that item appears. For example, if the item is a numeric data item, a numeric input dialog appears; if the item is a file name, the Windows file name dialog appears, and so on. In Appendix A, this type of list dialog was called a data object list dialog. An example is shown in Fig. A.2.3. From a programming point of view, the advantage of the data object list dialog is that new input data items can be added to the list without redesigning the dialog. There is no need to modify resource files or add additional control logic to the dialog class. Simply insert the appropriate typed data object into the list, and you automatically get a dialog for editing that object's value. For more details on this type of dialog, see (Welstead 1995). For a Java implementation of this idea, see (Welstead 1999).

The *tmodeless_dialog* class is the base class for modeless dialogs. The *exec_dialog* member function for this class calls the Windows API *CreateDialog* function, which creates a modeless dialog (as opposed to the *tdialog exec_dialog* member function, which calls the API function *DialogBox* to create a modal dialog). The application *WinMain* function needs to know when a modeless dialog is open so that it can route messages to it. The link to a particular modeless dialog is established through the global pointer *g_modeless_dialog*, which is set to the address of the currently open descendant of *tmodeless_dialog*, by that class's *exec_dialog* function. With this approach, only one modeless dialog can be open at any one time in a single application.

The *tprogress_bar_dlg* class is a *tmodeless_dialog* descendant that implements a progress bar for graphically conveying progress during the execution of a program task. The IMG system displays a progress bar during training of the self-organizing network. As previously mentioned, this is the only instance of a modeless dialog in the accompanying software.

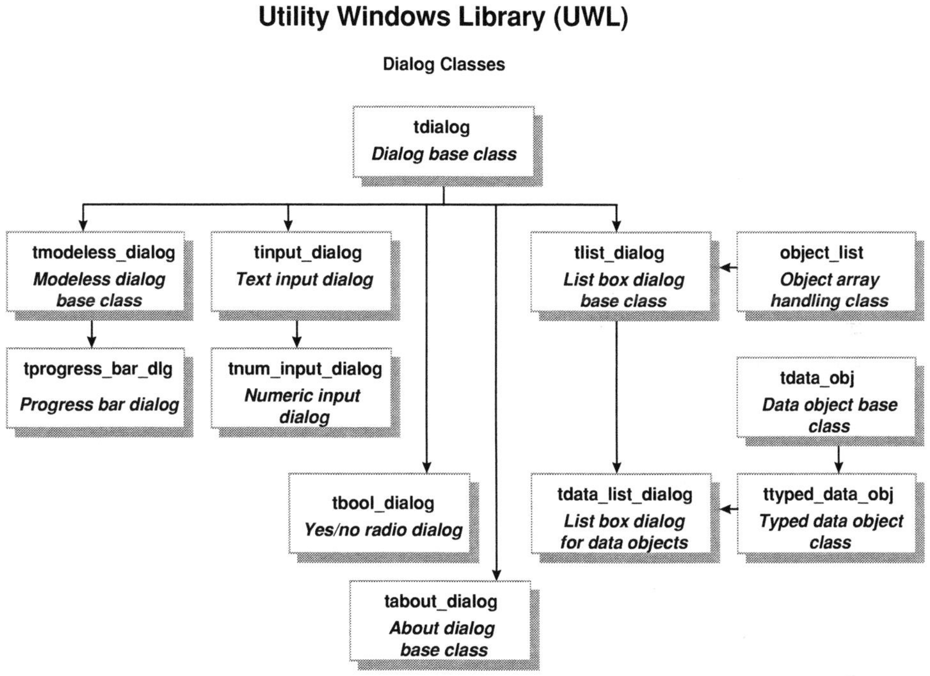

Utility Windows Library (UWL)

Dialog Classes

Fig. B.2.2 Class hierarchy for the dialog classes in UWL.

B.2.7 Building UWL

Source code files that make up the UWL are listed below. There are a few naming conventions. File names that start with a "u" involve some type of utility code. Code is defined as "utility" if it used by more than one system (thus, by definition, everything in UWL is "utility"). A "w" following the "u" indicates that this is a utility file that uses Windows-specific code. Most of the code in UWL is C++, although there are a few C files containing some all-purpose functions that were not appropriate to assign to any one C++ class. Header files (*.h) for these C/C++ files are shown in Listing B.2.6, as part of the header file UWL.h. Applications that use UWL should include the single header file UWL.h.

utobjlst.cpp: Contains the *object_list* class for handling arrays of objects.
uwabtdlg.cpp: Class definition for *tabout_dialog*.
uwcolors.c: Contains some basic C utilities for handling Windows RGB colors.

uwdatobj.cpp: Class definition for *ttyped_data_obj*.

uwdialgs.cpp: Contains a series of self-contained functions that instantiate, initialize, and execute various dialog classes. These functions obtain input from the user, then destroy the dialog object and return the input data to the calling program.

uwdlg.cpp: Class definitions for *tdialog*, *tinput_dialog*, *tnum_input_dialog*, and *tbool_dialog*.

uwgrnbrs.c: Contains C utility functions for producing "nice" numbers for graph axes.

uwgrset.c: Contains utility C functions for graphing and drawing.

uwgrsetp.cpp: Contains the functions *init_graph_setup*, for initializing the *graph_setup_rec* structure, and *graph_setup_to_collection*, which associates the elements of this structure with objects in an *object_list* array.

uwgrwin.cpp: Class definition for *tmdi_graph_window*.

uwmdichw.cpp: Class definitions for *tmdi_manager* and *tmdi_child_window*.

uwmdifrm.cpp: Class definition for *tmdi_frame_window*.

uwmdlsdg.cpp: Class definition for *tmodeless_dialog*.

uwprgbar.cpp: Class definition for *tprogress_bar_dlg*.

uwprtwin.c: C functions for printing a graphics window. These functions use the standard Windows printer dialog. However, the logic is set up to print black and white only. It is not suitable for printing grayscale images. To print grayscale, copy the image window to the clipboard and import it to an application with full printing capabilities.

uwwin.cpp: Class definition for *twindow*.

The application systems in the accompanying software link UWL as a static 32-bit Windows GUI library. Linking UWL as a static library means that the executable files for these applications are self-contained. You don't need to worry about porting additional library files when you move these applications from one machine to another. It is also possible to compile and link UWL as a DLL. If you choose this option, you need to copy the DLL file wherever the application is installed.

To build the UWL library, include all of the above C/C++ files in your project or Makefile. The target file type should be set to static 32-bit Windows GUI library. Define the constants WIN_32 and STRICT. STRICT is a Windows constant that ensures the code is compatible with Windows NT. WIN_32 is a UWL constant that ensures that correct macros will be selected for 32-bit Windows. While there are corresponding macros for 16-bit Windows (i.e., Windows 3.1), these macros have not been maintained, and no assurance can be made as to how the resulting code will run if these macros are used. Also, 32-bit code runs much faster than 16-bit code. If you are going to do image compression work, you should seriously consider upgrading to a 32-bit Windows system if you have not done so already. Finally, in your project or Makefile, you should indicate where the Windows and standard C "include" and "lib" directories are located.

B.3 WINDOWS PROGRAMMING REFERENCES

Petzold, C. 1992. *Programming Windows 3.1*, Microsoft Press.

Petzold, C. 1996. *Programming Windows 95*, Microsoft Press.

Welstead, S. 1995. "Data Object List Dialog for Windows", *C/C++ Users Journal*, Vol. 13, No. 9:23-41 (also appears as Chapter 8, pp. 115-139, in *Windows NT*

Programming in Practice, R&D Books, Miller Freeman, Inc., Lawrence, KS, 1997).

Welstead, S. 1996. "C++ Classes for MDI Windows Management", *C/C++ Users Journal*, Vol. 14, No. 11:41-50.

Welstead, S. 1999. "A Java Object List Dialog", *C/C++ Users Journal*, Vol. 17, No. 1:21-33.

Listing B.2.6 The header file UWL.H. C++ programs that use UWL should include this single file. C programs that use only the general purpose C functions in UWL should include only the header files for those functions (for example, uwgr.h or messages.h).

```
// File uwl.h  General UWL header. Application programs should
//            include this header when using UWL.

#ifndef UWL_H
#define UWL_H

#include "dlgids.h"
#include "grrscids.h"
#include "mdifmids.h"
#include "messages.h"
#include "utobjlst.h"
#include "uwabtdlg.h"
#include "uwcolors.h"
#include "uwdatobj.h"
#include "uwdialgs.h"
#include "uwdlg.h"
#include "uwgr.h"
#include "uwgrnbrs.h"
#include "uwgrwin.h"
#include "uwmdi.h"
#include "uwmdlsdg.h"
#include "uwprgbar.h"
#include "uwprtwin.h"
#include "uwwin.h"

#endif
```

Appendix C

ORGANIZATION OF THE ACCOMPANYING SOFTWARE SOURCE CODE

This appendix discusses the organization of the source code for the accompanying software.

C.1 IFS SYSTEM

C.1.1 IFS classes

Fig. C.1.1 shows the class hierarchy for the IFS system. The IFS system consists of three different types of MDI windows, each with their own MDI window managers and with supporting dialogs. There are also some utility C functions.

The first window type is the points window, implemented by the class *tpoints_window* and its MDI window manager classes *tnew_points_window_manager* and *topen_points_window_manager*. These two classes both manage points windows. The difference is that the "open" manager opens a previously saved points file, and so uses a file dialog to ask for the name of the points file before creating the new window. Fig. A.1.2 in Appendix A shows the points window and its two dialogs for editing the points. The *tpoints_window* is a descendant of *tmdi_graph_window* that displays an X-Y grid for locating points that will define the affine transformations. It also has the option of importing and displaying a bitmap image on that grid, so it uses a utility function for reading a bitmap file. Utility drawing functions are used for drawing the grid and displaying the points. The *tpoint_dialog* class implements a descendant of *tdialog* that edits the X and Y values of the point coordinate. It also has the option of deleting that point. The *tedit_points_dialog* class implements a list box dialog that displays a list of the points and allows them to be edited using the points dialog.

The next window type in IFS is the transformation window, implemented by *ttrf_window*. As was the case for the points window, there are two MDI manager classes, *topen_trf_window_manager*, which opens a previously saved transformation file, and *tnew_trf_window_manager*. In either case, the transformation window operates on a previously created points file, and so each of these managers uses a file dialog to obtain the points file name before creating the new transformation window. The transformation window draws the same grid as the points window, and also displays the points and their labels. It also has the capability of importing and displaying a bitmap image on the grid. The user creates a new affine transformation by designating two sets of three points. The first set of points is the domain of the transformation, and the second set is the range. As each set of three points are selected, the window draws lines to connect the points, with a triangle completing the designation of a set of three selected points. When the user completes the selection of the points, the *ttrf_pts_dialog* class presents a transformation points dialog for editing the point indexes and for selecting a color to associate with the transformation. The *tedit_trf_dialog* implements a list dialog that manages the list of

215

transformations. Each previously created transformation can be edited from this list with a transformation points dialog.

The transformation window provides a geometric description of the transformation. However, running the IFS requires that each transformation be represented in terms of its affine coefficients. The transformation window comput es these coefficients. When the user selects the "Create Coeff File…" option from the "File" menu, the *ttrf_window* class responds with its *OnCreateCoeff* member function, that, in turn, calls the external function *create_coeff_file*. This function computes the coefficients, using the approach outlined in Chapter 2. The computation includes a 3×3 matrix inversion that uses functions from the matrix utility library UTM, whose files are listed below.

Class Hierarchy for IFS System

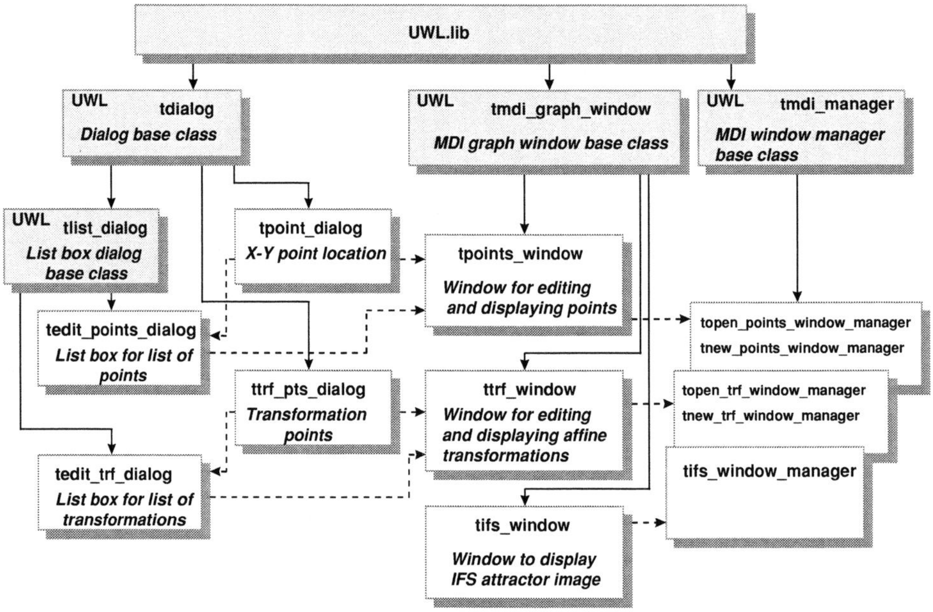

Fig. C.1.1 Class hierarchy for the IFS system. The solid lines indicate inheritance, and the dashed lines indicate that this class is used by another class.

The third and final window type is the IFS window, implemented by the *tifs_window* class. This is the window that actually displays the IFS attractor image. External functions *ifs_random_image_graph* and *ifs_deterministic_image_graph* graph the attractor image, using, respectively, the random and deterministic algorithms to produce the image iteratively, as discussed in Chapter 2. External functions are used here to keep the computational aspect of the code separate from the Windows-specific parts of the code. This makes for easier porting of the computational parts of the code to other non-Windows platforms. Note that the graphics calls here use the graphics structures of UWL, rather than Windows-specific arguments.

C.1.2 IFS code files

Here are the C/C++ files needed to build the IFS System:

ifsfiles.cpp: Functions for reading and writing points files and transformation files, and functions for creating (*create_coeff_file*) and reading affine coefficient files.

ifsmain.cpp: The *WinMain* function for the IFS System.

ifsproc.cpp: Functions for displaying IFS graphics, including *ifs_random_image_graph* and *ifs_deterministic_image_graph*.

ifswin.cpp: Contains the *tifs_window* class for displaying the IFS attractor image in a MDI graph window, and the MDI manager class *tifs_window_manager*.

ifswprcs.c: Windows graphic procedures for drawing grid lines and points in a MDI graph window.

ptdialg.cpp: Contains the *tpoint_dialog* and *tedit_points_dialog* classes.

ptswin.cpp: Contains the *tpoints_window* class for creating sets of points and displaying them on a grid, and also contains the MDI manager classes *tnew_points_window_manager* and *topen_points_window_manager*.

readbmp.cpp: Contains the function *read_BMP_file* for reading bitmap files, used by *tpoints_window* and *ttrf_window* to import bitmap images.

readln.c: Contains *readln*, a general-purpose function for reading data lines from a file.

trfptsdg.cpp: Contains *ttrf_points_dialog* and *tedit_trf_dialog* classes.

trfwin.cpp: Contains the *ttrf_window* class for creating sets of transformations and displaying them on a grid, and also contains the MDI manager classes *tnew_trf_window_manager* and *topen_trf_window_manager*.

utofile.c: Contains general-purpose utility functions for opening and closing text and binary files.

wkeys.c: Contains some general-purpose utilities for handling Windows keyboard messages.

In addition, you will need the corresponding header files that are included with these files, and you will also need the following resource files that are included in **ifsapp.rc:**

ifsmenu.rc: Menus for the frame window and child windows.

ptdialg.rc: The points dialog resource.

UWL\dlg.rc: The resource file for all of the dialogs in UWL (located in the UWL directory).

trfpts.rc: The transformation points dialog resource.

abifsdg.rc: The "About IFS" dialog resource, including **fern.bmp**.

fern.bmp: Bitmap of the fern image, used in the "About IFS" dialog.

fern.ico: Fern icon (appears in upper left corner of the windows).

To build the IFS application, you should include in your project or Makefile the C/C++ code files listed here, along with the resource file **ifsapp.rc**. In addition, you will need to link in the libraries **UWL32.lib** and **UTM32.lib**. Fig. C.1.2 shows the files needed to build **IFS32.exe**.

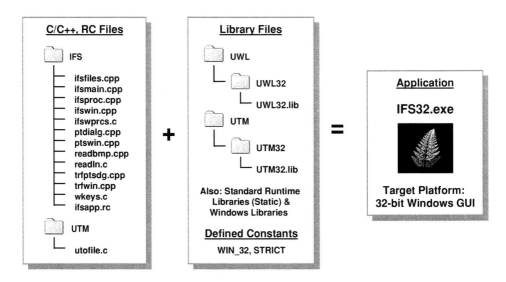

Fig. C.1.2 Building the IFS application. Your project or Makefile should include the C/C++, RC and library files shown here, and also define the constants WIN_32 and STRICT. The target platform for the libraries and application executable is 32-bit Windows GUI.

C.1.3 UTM Library

The Utility Matrix (UTM) library is a small collection of files that perform matrix and vector computations and manipulations. This library does not include any Windows-specific code, so it should be portable to other platforms. It is compiled as a 32-bit library that will be linked with a 32-bit Windows GUI application. The code files are listed here:

utintmat.c: Code to allocate and free integer matrices.
utmatinv.c: Matrix inversion using Gauss-Jordan elimination with partial (row) pivoting.
utmatrix.c: Code to allocate and free matrices (float).
utprod.c: Matrix-vector product and vector-vector dot (scalar) product.
utvect.c: Code to allocate and free vectors (integer and float).

C.2 IMG SYSTEM

C.2.1 IMG classes

Fig. C.2.1 shows the class hierarchy for the IMG system. The IMG system displays five types of MDI child windows. There are actually six MDI child window classes in IMG, since *timg_window* is the base class for the four classes that display images: *tenc_window*, *tdec_window*, *tsub_window*, and *tself_org_enc_window*. There is also a class for displaying the image as a two-dimensional surface plot, *tplt2d_window*.

The encoding and decoding computations are separated from the window classes by encapsulating them in their own C++ classes. *timage* is a simple class that defines an image object. The image pixels are contained in a two-dimensional array. *tfract_image* is a base class that handles the setup operations for manipulating domains and ranges that are common to both fractal encoding and decoding. The class *tfract_image* has three descendant classes. *tenc_image* implements the basic fractal encoding algorithm described in Chapter 3 and also the feature-extraction approach from Chapter 4. *tself_org_encode_image* implements the self-organizing neural network approach for encoding described in Chapter 4. Finally, *tdec_image* decodes fractal-compressed images. Each of these descendants of *tfract_image* uses a *timage* object to hold the image on which it operates.

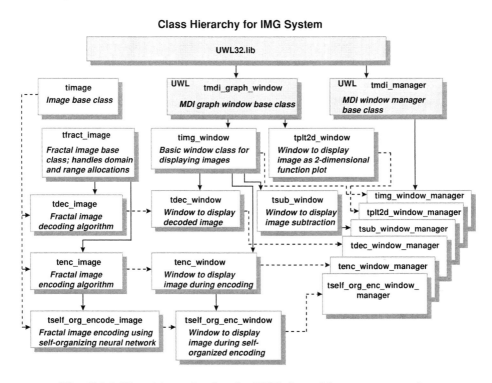

Fig. C.2.1 Class hierarchy for the IMG fractal image compression system. The solid lines indicate inheritance, and the dashed lines indicate that this class is used by another class.

C.2.2 IMG code files

Here are the C/C++ files needed to build the IMG System:

> **binrange.cpp:** Functions for reading and writing binary range files.
> **decimg.cpp:** Contains the *tdec_image* class for decoding fractal compressed images.
> **decwin.cpp:** Contains the *tdec_window* and *tdec_window_manager* classes for displaying an image during the decoding operation.

encimg.cpp: Contains the *tenc_image* class for encoding an image with the fractal encoding algorithm.

encwin.cpp: Contains the *tenc_window* and *tenc_window_manager* classes for displaying an image during the fractal encoding operation.

features.c: Functions for computing the features used during feature extraction.

frctimag.cpp: Contains *tfract_image*, the base class for manipulating domains and ranges.

image.cpp: Contains *timage*, the base class for holding an image.

imgmain.cpp: The *WinMain* function for the IMG system. The message loop is modified to accommodate messages for the modeless dialog that displays the progress bar during weights training for the self-organizing neural network.

imgproc.cpp: Miscellaneous procedures.

imgwin.cpp: Contains *timg_window* and *timg_window_manager* classes for displaying an image.

plot_2d.c: General purpose functions for plotting a two-dimensional surface in three-dimensional space.

plt2dset.cpp: Contains the function *plot_2d_setup_to_collection*, which associates the setup parameters used by the two-dimensional plotting code with an object list of *ttyped_data_obj* objects. This enables the updating of the parameter values through a data object list dialog.

plt2dwin.cpp: Contains *tplt2d_window* and *tplt2d_window_manager* classes for displaying a two-dimensional surface plot.

slforgw.cpp: Code for implementing the self-organizing neural network. Includes functions for reading, writing and training the network weights, as well as a function for using the trained network as a classifier.

soencimg.cpp: Contains the *tself_org_encode_image* class for using the self-organizing neural network with fractal image encoding.

soencwin.cpp: Contains the *tself_org_enc_window* and *tself_org_enc_window_manager* classes for displaying an image during fractal encoding using a self-organizing neural network.

subwin.cpp: Contains the *tsub_window* and *tsub_window_manager* classes for displaying the difference image obtained by subtracting one image from another.

utmatrix.c: Code to allocate and free matrices.

utofile.c: Contains general-purpose utility functions for opening and closing text and binary files.

utscan.c: Contains general-purpose utility functions for scanning a line of text.

utvect.c: Code to allocate and free vectors.

In addition, the following resource files are included in **imgapp.rc:**

abimgdg.rc: Resource for the "About IMG" dialog.

imgmenu.rc: The menu resources.

UWL\dlg.rc: The resource file for all of the dialogs in UWL.

bill.bmp: Bitmap file for the "cat" image used in the "About IMG" dialog.

IFS\fern.ico: The fern icon from the IFS system (used by some of the windows).

Building the IMG application is similar to building the IFS application. You should include in your project or Makefile the C/C++ code files listed here, along with the resource file **imgapp.rc**, and link in the **UWL32.lib** library. Since IMG only uses the allocation functions from **utmatrix.c** and **utvector.c**, it includes those files directly (alternatively, you could link the **UTM32.lib**, as was done for the IFS system). Fig. C.2.2 shows the files needed to build **IMG32.exe**.

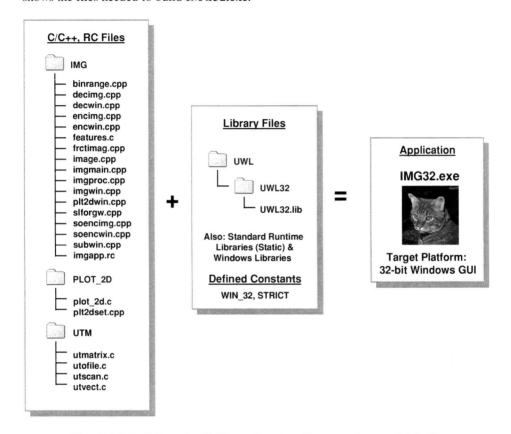

Fig. C.2.2 Building the IMG application. Your project or Makefile should include the C/C++, RC and library files shown here, and also define the constants WIN_32 and STRICT. The target platform for the libraries and application executable is 32-bit Windows GUI.

C.3 WAV SYSTEM

C.3.1 WAV classes

Fig. C.3.1 shows the class hierarchy for the WAV system. The WAV system displays seven types of MDI child windows. The *timg_window* class is the same base class for displaying images that is used by the IMG system. Here it is used for displaying the original image, so that it can be compared with the wavelet-compressed version via one of two types of subtraction window, also implemented by the same *tsub_window* class used by IMG. The *twavelet_window* class displays the wavelet-compressed image, using the simple decimation compression algorithm. The *twavelet_zerotree_window* and *tdecode_zerotree_window* classes handle zerotree encoding and decoding. The *twavelet_plot_window* class displays a plot of the wavelet function.

The WAV system provides three types of wavelets: Haar, Daubechies-4 and Daubechies-6 wavelets. The *twavelet* class is the base class for these wavelets. It includes the basic wavelet filter and its transpose, as well as the wavelet transform operator and its inverse. The three wavelet types used here differ from one another only in their coefficients, so *twavelet* provides for general coefficient values, while the derived classes *tHaar_wavelet*, *tDaub4_wavelet*, and *tDaub6_wavelet* implement specific values for these coefficients. The wavelet filter and transform code here is based on the public-domain wavelet code from W. Press, et al., *Numerical Recipes in C, 2nd ed*, Cambridge University Press, 1992 (note that most of the code in this reference is *not* public-domain, however the wavelet code has been placed in the public domain on their web site). The *twavelet_2d_array* class defines a wavelet transform and its inverse for application to two-dimensional arrays, such as images. This class simply applies the one-dimensional *twavelet* class transform to the columns and rows of the array, as discussed in Chapter 5. The *twave_dialog* class implements a simple dialog with three radio buttons for selecting from among the three wavelet types.

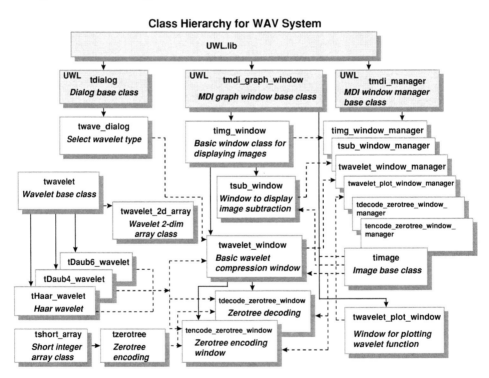

Fig. C.3.1 Class hierarchy for the WAV wavelet image compression system. The solid lines indicate inheritance, and the dashed lines indicate that this class is used by another class.

C.3.2 WAV code files

Here are the C/C++ files needed to build the WAV System:

uwplot.c: Contains the function *plot_xy*, a general X-Y plotting utility.

wavdzwin.cpp: Contains the *tdecode_zerotree_window* class, a descendant of *twavelet_window*, for decoding zerotree-encoded images.

wave_dlg.cpp: Contains the class *twave_dlg*, a radio-button dialog for selecting wavelet type.

wavelet.cpp: Contains all of the wavelet classes (*twavelet*, *tHaar_wavelet*, *tDaub4_wavelet*, *tDaub6_wavelet* and *twavelet_2d_array*).

waveproc.c: Contains the function *decimate_array*, used by *twavelet_2d_array* to remove all but the largest *x%* of the array values (this is really a general-purpose function that does not use any wavelet properties).

wavmain.cpp: The *WinMain* function for the WAV system.

wavplot.cpp: Contains the *twavelet_plot_window* and *twavelet_plot_window_manager* classes for displaying the wavelet function plot in a window.

wavwin.cpp: Contains the *twavelet_window* and *twavelet_window_manager* for displaying the wavelet-compressed image in a window.

wavzwin.cpp: Contains the *tencode_zerotree_window* class, a descendant of *twavelet_window*, for encoding images with the zerotree algorithm of Chapter 7.

zerotree.cpp: Contains the *tzerotree* class, a descendant of *tshort_array*, which includes member functions *mark_children* and *mark_parents* for implementing the zerotree encoding algorithm.

In addition, WAV shares the following files with IMG (discussed in the previous section):

IMG\image.cpp
IMG\imgproc.cpp
IMG\imgwin.cpp
IMG\subwin.cpp
UTM\utofile.c
UTM\utshort.cpp: Contains the *tshort_array* class.

In addition, the following resource files are included in **wavapp.rc:**

abwavdg.rc: Resource for the "About WAV" dialog.

wave_dlg.rc: Resource file for wavelet type radio-button dialog.

wavmenu.rc: The menu resources.

UWL\dlg.rc: The resource file for all of the dialogs in UWL.

daub4wav.bmp: Bitmap file for the Daubechies-4 wavelet plot image used in the "About WAV" dialog.

wavelet.ico: The wavelet function icon (used by some of the windows).

The WAV system also includes the **UTM32.lib** and **UWL32.lib** library files. Like IFS and IMG, WAV is a 32-bit Windows GUI application. Fig. C.3.2 shows the files and settings needed to build **WAV32.exe**.

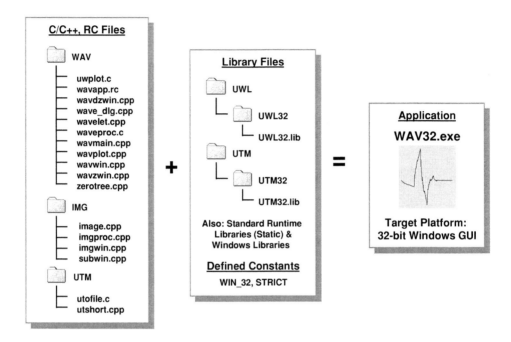

Fig. C.3.2 Building the WAV application. Your project or Makefile should include the C/C++, RC and library files shown here, and also define the constants WIN_32 and STRICT. The target platform for the libraries and application executable is 32-bit Windows GUI.

REFERENCES

Asgari, S., T.Q. Nguyen, and W.A. Sethares. 1997. "Wavelet-Based Fractal Transforms for Image Coding with No Search", *Proc. IEEE International Conf. on Image Processing*, (ICIP97).

Bani-Eqbal, B. 1995. "Speeding up Fractal Image Compression", *Proc. SPIE Still-Image Compression*, Vol. 2418.

Barnsley, M. 1993. *Fractals Everywhere*, 2nd ed., Boston: Academic Press.

Barnsley, M., and L. Hurd. 1993. *Fractal Image Compression*, Wellesley, MA: A.K.Peters, Ltd.

Barnsley, M., and A. Sloan. 1988. "A Better Way to Compress Images", *Byte*, January:215-223.

Barnsley, M., and A. Sloan. 1990. "Method and Apparatus for Image Compression by Iterated Function System", U.S. Patent #4,941,193.

Barnsley, M., and A. Sloan. 1991. "Method and Apparatus for Processing Digital Data", U.S. Patent #5,065,447.

Bogdan, A., and H. Meadows. 1992. "Kohonen neural network for image coding based on iteration transformation theory", *Proc. SPIE* 1766:425-436.

Burrus, C., Gopinath, R., and Guo, H. 1998. *Introduction to Wavelets and Wavelet Transforms*, Prentice-Hall, Upper Saddle River, New Jersey.

Chen, T., ed. 1998. "The Past, Present, and Future of Image and Multidimensional Signal Processing", *IEEE Signal Processing Magazine*, Vol. 15, No. 2, March:21-58.

Daubechies, I. 1988. "Orthonormal bases of compactly supported wavelets", *Comm. on Pure and Applied Math*, XLI:909-966.

Daubechies, I. 1992. *Ten Lectures on Wavelets*, SIAM, Philadelphia.

Davis, G. 1995. "Adaptive self-quantization of wavelet subtrees: A wavelet-based theory of fractal image compression", *Proc. of SPIE Conf. on Wavelet Applications in Signal and Image Processing III*, San Diego.

Davis, G. 1996. "Implicit Image Models in Fractal Image Compression", *Proc. of SPIE Conf. on Wavelet Applications in Signal and Image Processing IV*, Denver.

Davis, G. 1998. "A Wavelet-Based Analysis of Fractal Image Compression", *IEEE Trans. on Image Proc.*, Vol. 7, No. 2:141-154.

Davis, G., and A. Nosratinia. 1998. "Wavelet-based Image Coding: An Overview", preprint, to appear in *Applied and Computational Control, Signals, and Circuits*, Vol. 1, No. 1. (64 pages).

Digital Imaging Group 1999. "JPEG 2000 White Paper", available at the JPEG Web site, www.jpeg.org.

Fisher, Y., ed. 1995. *Fractal Image Compression*, New York:Springer-Verlag.

Gopinath, R., and C. Burrus. 1993. "A Tutorial Overview of Filter Banks, Wavelets and Interrelations", *Proc. ISCAS-93*.

Hamzaoui, R. 1995. "Codebook Clustering by Self-Organizing Maps for Fractal Image Compression", *Proc. NATO Advanced Study Institute Conf. on Fractal Image Encoding and Analysis, Trondheim, July, 1995*, Y. Fisher (ed.), New York:Springer-Verlag.

Hebert, D., and E. Soundararajan. 1998. "Fast Fractal Image Compression with Triangulation Wavelets", *Proc. of SPIE Conf. on Wavelet Applications in Signal and Image Processing VI*, San Diego.

Jacobs, E., R. Boss, and Y. Fisher. 1995. "Method of Encoding a Digital Image Using Iterated Image Transformations To Form an Eventually Contractive Map", U.S. Patent #5,416,856.

Jacquin, A. 1992. "Image Coding Based on a Fractal Theory of Iterated Contractive Image Transformations", *IEEE Trans. on Image Proc.* Vol. 1, No. 1:18-30.

Kohonen, T. 1984. *Self Organization and Associative Memory*, 2nd ed., Berlin:Springer-Verlag.

Lewis, A., and G. Knowles. 1992. "Image Compression Using the 2-D Wavelet Transform", *IEEE Trans. on Image Proc.*, Vol. 1, No. 2:244-250.

Lu, N. 1997. *Fractal Imaging*, San Diego:Academic Press.

Mandal, M., S. Panchanathan and T. Aboulnasr. 1996. "Choice of Wavelets for Image Compression", *Lecture Notes in Computer Science*, Vol. 1133:239-249, Springer-Verlag.

Mandelbrot, B. 1983. *The Fractal Geometry of Nature*, New York:W. H. Freeman and Company.

McGregor, D., R.J. Fryer, W.P. Cockshott and P. Murray. 1994. "Fast Fractal Transform Method for Data Compression", *University of Strathclyde Research Report/94/156*[IKBS-17-94].

Peitgen, H., and D. Saupe, eds. 1988. *The Science of Fractal Images*, New York:Springer-Verlag.

Polidori, E., and J. Dugelay. 1995. "Zooming Using Iterated Function Systems", *Proc. of NATO Advanced Study Institute Conf. on Fractal Image Encoding and Analysis, Trondheim, Norway, July, 1995*, Y. Fisher (ed.), New York:Springer-Verlag.

Popescu, D., A. Dimca, and H. Yan. 1997. "A Nonlinear Model for Fractal Image Coding", *IEEE Trans. on Image Proc.*, Vol. 6, No. 3:373-382.

Press, W., S. Teukolsky, W. Vetterling, and B. Flannery. 1992. *Numerical Recipes in C*, 2nd ed., Cambridge University Press.

Ritter, H., T. Martinez and K. Schulten. 1992. *Neural Computation and Self-Organizing Maps*, Reading, MA: Addison-Wesley.

Ruhl, M., and H. Hartenstein. 1997. "Optimal Fractal Coding Is NP-hard", *Proc. DCC'97 Data Compression Conference*, IEEE Computer Society Press:261-270.

Said, A., and W. Pearlman. 1996. "A New Fast and Efficient Image Codec Based on Set Partitioning in Hierarchical Trees", *IEEE Trans. on Circuits and Systems for Video Technology*, Vol. 6, June:243-250.

Said, A., and W. Pearlman. 1996. "An Image Multiresolution Representation for Lossless and Lossy Compression", *IEEE Trans. on Image Proc.*, Vol. 5, No. 9:243-250.

Saupe, D. 1994. "Breaking the Time Complexity of Fractal Image Compression", *Tech. Report* 53, Institut fur Informatik.

Saupe, D. 1996. "The Futility of Square Isometries in Fractal Image Compression", *IEEE International Conference on Image Processing (ICIP'96)*, Lausanne.

Sayood, K. 1996. *Introduction to Data Compression*, San Francisco:Morgan Kaufmann Publishers, Inc.

Shapiro, J. 1993. "Embedded Image Coding Using Zerotrees of Wavelet Coefficients", *IEEE Trans. on Signal Proc.*, Vol. 41, No. 12:3445-3462.

Strang, G. 1989. "Wavelets and Dilation Equations: A Brief Introduction", *SIAM Review* 31:613-627.

Stollnitz, E., DeRose, T., Salesin, D. 1996. *Wavelets for Computer Graphics*, Morgan Kaufmann, San Francisco.

Villasenor, J., Belzer, B., and Liao, J. 1995. "Wavelet Filter Evaluation for Image Compression", *IEEE Trans. on Image Proc.*, Vol. 4, No. 8:1053-1060.

Welstead, S. 1997. "Self-Organizing Neural Network Domain Classification for Fractal Image Coding", *Proc. of IASTED International Conference on Artificial Intelligence and Soft Computing, July, 1997, Banff, Canada*, IASTED Press:248-251.

INDEX

affine transformation, 21
    on grayscale images, 44
algorithm
    basic fractal image encoding, 48
    deterministic,
        for computing IFS, 25
    fractal encoding, using feature
        extraction (FE), 73
    Kohonen, 82
    lossless, 3, 7
    lossy, 3
    quadtree partitioning, 53
    random, for computing IFS, 30
    training, for self-organizing neural
        network, 84
    zerotree encoding, 141-150
analysis, multiresolution, 101-104
arithmetic coding, 4, 5
    see also entropy coding, Huffman
        coding
attractor of an iterated function system,
    19, 20
    see also strange attractor
average pixel error, 58-59, 63, 80, 81,
    89, 90, 117, 127, 146, 148-149,
    158

basis
    dual, 130
    orthogonal, 102
beta, 72
binary range file format, 61
biorthogonality, 130
biorthogonal wavelets, 130
bit planes, 142
Bolzano-Weierstrass Theorem, 15
bounded set, 15
brightness, 44

Cauchy sequence, 14
"Chaos Game", 25
closed set, 14
closure, 15
CMT. *see* contraction mapping theorem
    (CMT)

CMYK (cyan, magenta, yellow, black),
    2, 8
    see also color images
codebook, 6
coding
    arithmetic, 4, 5
    entropy, 4, 155
    Huffman, 4, 5
    linear predictive, 7
Collage Theorem, 19-21, 47, 69
    bound, 69
    for grayscale images, 47
color images, 2
    CMYK, 2, 8
    color map, 6
    palette, 6
    RGB, 2, 6-7, 8
    YIQ, 8, 9
complete metric space, 14
compact set, 15
compact support, 125
compression. *see* image compression,
    video compression
compression ratio, 7, 11, 50, 65, 82,
    117, 131, 132, 149-151, 154,
    155-163
contraction mapping, 16
    on grayscale images, 45
    theorem, 18, 45, 47
contraction mapping theorem
    (CMT), 18
    on grayscale images, 45
contractivity factor, 17, 45
contrast, 44
converge, 14

data modeling, 5
Daubechies wavelets, 124-126
    image compression with, 126
DCT. *see* discrete cosine transform
decimation, 6
decoding
    a fractal encoded image, 57
    a zerotree encoded image, 143
digital watermarking, 8
dilation equation, 123

dimension
    Euclidean, 12
    fractal, 35-37
    non-integer, 12, 36
    vector space, 103
discrete cosine transform (DCT), 3, 7, 8
distance function, 13, 14
domain cells, 50
    classification, 81
dual basis, 130
dynamical system, 30

encoding. *see* fractal image encoding,
    wavelet zerotree encoding
entropy, 4-5
entropy coding, 4, 155
    see also arithmetic coding,
    Huffman coding
error
    analysis, 69
    image, 59, 95
    measurement, 58-59, 146, 149, 154
    threshold, 51, 52, 57, 59, 60, 80
    tolerance, 49, 52, 53, 56, 74, 75,
        76, 77, 87, 89, 90, 156-157,
        159, 161
    see also average pixel error, peak
        signal-to-noise ratio (PSNR)
Euclidean dimension, 12

feature extraction, 71-80
filter
    highpass, 113, 120
    lowpass, 113, 119
    quadrature mirror, 120
fixed point, 18
Fourier transform, 3
fractal, 12
    dimension, 35-37
    zoom, 65-66
fractal image encoding, 48-50
    is N-P hard, 91
    operator representation, 66-69
    speeding up, 71-91

gradient, 72
grayscale images, 43
    affine transformations on, 44

contraction mapping theorem for,
    45
Collage Theorem for, 47

Haar wavelets, 105
Hausdorff
    metric, 16
    metric space, 16, 18
highpass filter, 113, 120
Huffman coding, 4, 5
    see also arithmetic coding, entropy
        coding
hue, 8
hybrid approaches, 150-153

IFS. *see* iterated function system (IFS)
image compression, 1, 3-4, 6-9, 11, 38,
    47, 94-95, 101, 109, 113, 124,
    160, 163-164
    error measurement in, 58-59, 146,
        149, 154
    fractal, 18, 38, 44, 56, 65, 71, 78,
        126, 152
    hybrid, 150
    problem, 3-4
    wavelet, 93, 95, 117, 119, 126,
        127, 130, 131
information, 4
inner product, 102
    space, 102
in-phase, 8
inverse wavelet transform, 109-111, 122
iterated function system (IFS), 11-42
    definition, 19
    deterministic algorithm for
        computing, 25
    implementation, 22
    random algorithm for computing,
        30
    see also partitioned iterated
        function system (PIFS)
iterates, 17

JPEG (Joint Photographic Experts
    Group), 2, 3, 7, 163-164
    JPEG 2000, 8, 163-164
    see also MPEG

Kohonen self-organizing feature map, 82

limit, 14
limit point, 14
linear predictive coding, 7
lossless algorithm, 3, 7
lossy algorithm, 3
lowpass filter, 113, 119
luminance, 8

mappings, 16
    contraction, 16
    contraction mapping theorem, 18, 45, 47
    domains to ranges, 54-56
metric
    Hausdorff, 16
    rms (root mean square), 43
metric space, 13-14
    complete, 14
    Hausdorff, 16, 18
MPEG (Moving Picture Experts Group), 7, 8, 163
    see also JPEG, video compression
multiresolution analysis, 101-104

neural network, self-organizing, 82-84
normalization, 104-105, 123
N-P hard, fractal image encoding is, 91

operator representation
    of fractal image encoding, 66-69
    of hybrid approach, 152
orbit of a dynamical system, 30
orthogonal basis, 103
orthogonal complement, 103
orthogonality, 102, 121, 123, 129
    see also biorthogonality, semiorthogonality

palette, 6
partitioned iterated function system (PIFS), 44
peak signal-to-noise ratio (PSNR), 58-59, 81, 89, 90, 118, 128, 146, 148, 149, 155-163
pixel error. *see* average pixel error

progressive transmission, 135, 164
PSNR. *see* peak signal-to-noise ratio

quadrature, 8
quadrature mirror filter, 120
quadtree partitioning, 48, 51-54
quantization, 4, 5-6
    decimation, 6
    scalar, 6
    vector, 6

range file format, 60
    binary, 61
rate distortion, 155
ratio, compression. *see* compression ratio
resolution, 96
resolution independence, 65
RGB (red, green, blue), 2, 6-8
    see also color images
robust transmission, 8, 64

saturation, 8
scalar quantization, 6
scaling function, 97, 123
self-organizing neural network, 82-84
self similarity, 11, 12
semiorthogonal wavelets, 130
semiorthogonality, 130
sequence, Cauchy, 14
set
    bounded, 15
    closed, 14
    compact, 15
Sierpinski triangle, 35
skewness, 72
somatotopic map, 82
source, 4
    image as, 5, 164
space
    inner product, 102
    metric, 13-14, 16, 18
    vector, 102-104
standard deviation, 72
standards, 8, 163
strange attractors, 11
support of a function, 98
    compact, 125

theorems
    Bolzano-Weierstrass, 15
    Collage, 19-21, 47, 69
    contraction mapping, 18, 45, 47
trajectory of a dynamical system, 30
transform
    discrete cosine, 3, 7, 8
    Fourier, 3
    inverse wavelet, 109-111, 122
    two-dimensional wavelet, 111-117
    wavelet, 93, 95, 96, 106-109, 122
transformations, 16
    affine, 21, 44
transmission
    progressive, 135, 164
    robust, 8, 64
triangle inequality, 13

vector quantization, 6
vector space, 102-104
vector space dimension, 103
video compression, 7

watermarking, digital, 8
wavelets, 99-101, 123
    biorthogonal, 130
    Daubechies, 124-126
    Haar, 105
    semiorthogonal, 130
wavelet image compression, 93, 115,
        126, 131-150
    Daubechies, 126
    compared with fractal image
        compression, 156-164
wavelet transform, 93, 95, 96,
    106-109, 122
    in two dimensions, 111-117
    inverse, 109-111, 122
wavelet zerotree encoding, 141

YIQ, 8, 9
    see also color images

zerotrees, 133-150
    wavelet encoding algorithm, 141

Stephen Welstead is a senior scientist at COLSA Corporation in Huntsville, Alabama, and an adjunct associate professor of mathematics at the University of Alabama in Huntsville, where he developed and taught a graduate-level course on fractal geometry. He received the Ph.D. degree in applied mathematics from Purdue University. He is the author of *Neural Network and Fuzzy Logic Applications in C/C++*, as well as a number of papers and presentations on neural networks, fractal image encoding, chaos and dynamical systems, and signal processing. He has presented several short courses and tutorials on fractal and wavelet image compression, as well as neural networks and fuzzy logic. He has also written several articles on Windows programming techniques. He is a member of the Society of Photo-Optical Instrumentation Engineers (SPIE), the Institute of Electrical and Electronics Engineers (IEEE), and the Society of Industrial and Applied Mathematics (SIAM). When he is not in front of a computer, Dr. Welstead can be found training for upcoming running races or riding his mountain bike.

Note about software

The files accompanying this Tutorial Text can be found at

http://www.spie.org/bookstore/tt40/

They contain executable programs that allow the reader to build and run examples illustrating material in the book. These programs run on 32-bit PC Windows systems, such as Windows NT, Windows 95, or Windows 98. There are three programs: IFS32 builds iterated function systems; IMG32 compresses bitmap images using fractal methods; WAV32 compresses bitmap images using wavelet techniques. The files also contain sample data for running examples, as well as complete C/C++ source code. It is not necessary to compile this code in order to run the executable programs. The file "readme.txt" describes the contents of the files in more detail.